5/8/15

7.99

3TT

-14

Withdrawn

B, o

THE NOODLE MAKER
OF KALIMPONG

Gyalo Thondup (left) and his brother the Fourteenth Dalai Lama, 2011 in Kalimpong

THE NOODLE MAKER *of* KALIMPONG

THE DALAI LAMA'S BROTHER *and* HIS STRUGGLE *for* TIBET

GYALO THONDUP
Elder Brother of the Fourteenth Dalai Lama

and

ANNE F. THURSTON
Coauthor of *The Private Life of Chairman Mao*

PUBLICAFFAIRS
New York

Published in the United States by PublicAffairs™,
a Member of the Perseus Books Group
All rights reserved.

Printed in the United States of America.

PublicAffairs books are available at special discounts for bulk purchases
in the U.S. by corporations, institutions, and other organizations.
For more information, please contact the Special Markets Department
at the Perseus Books Group, 2300 Chestnut Street, Suite 200,
Philadelphia, PA 19103, call (800) 810–4145, ext. 5000,
or e-mail special.markets@perseusbooks.com.

Book Design by Cynthia Young

Library of Congress Cataloging-in-Publication Data
Rgya-lo-don-grub, Lha-sras, 1928–
The noodle maker of Kalimpong : the Dalai Lama's brother and his struggle
for Tibet / Gyalo Thondup, elder brother of the 14th Dalai Lama and Anne
F. Thurston, coauthor of The Private Life of Chairman Mao.—First edition.
pages cm
Includes bibliographical references and index.
ISBN 978-1-61039-289-1 (hardcover)—ISBN 978-1-61039-290-7 (ebook)
1. Rgya-lo-don-grub, Lha-sras, 1928–   2. Politicians—China—Tibet—
Biography.   3. Bstan-'dzin-rgya-mtsho, Dalai Lama XIV, 1935—Family.
4. Central Tibetan Administration-in-Exile (India)—Officials and
employees—Biography.   5. Tibet Autonomous Region (China)—Politics
and government.   6. Tibet Autonomous Region (China)—Biography.
7. Tibetans—India—Biography. 8. Kalimpong (India)—Biography.
I. Thurston, Anne F.   II. Title.
III. Title: Dalai Lama's brother and his struggle for Tibet.
DS785.R44 2015
951'.505092—dc23
[B]
2014046680

FIRST EDITION
10 9 8 7 6 5 4 3 2 1

To His Holiness the Fourteenth Dalai Lama.

For the people of Tibet,

to those who have fought for our freedom,

and in memory of those who sacrificed their lives for the cause.

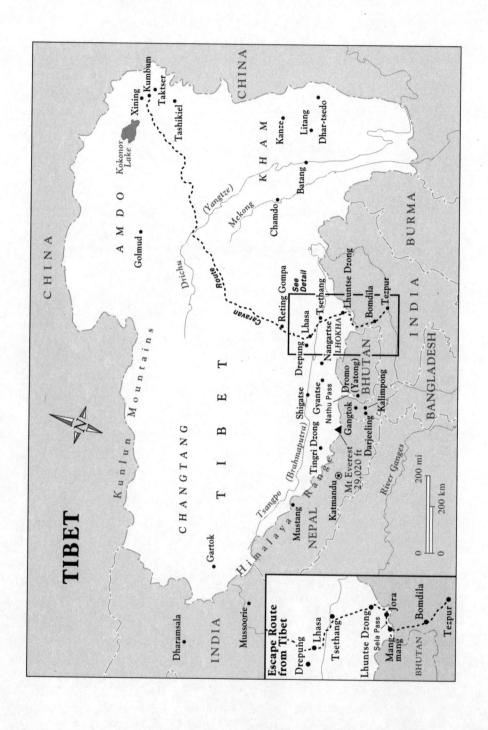

TIBET

CHINA

CHINA

Kunlun Mountains

Kokonor Lake

Xining •
• Kumbum
• Taktser
• Tashikiel

A M D O

Golmud •

Drichu

(Yangtze)

K H A M

Kanze •
Litang •
• Dhar-tsedo

Mekong

Chando •
• Batang

C H A N G T A N G

T I B E T

Gartok •

Caravan Route

Reting Gompa •

See Detail

Lhuntse Dzong •
• Tezpur
• Bomdila

B U R M A

Lhasa •
Drepung •
Tsethang •
Nangartse •
LHOKHA

I N D I A

(Brahmaputra) Shigatse
Gyantse •
Tingri Dzong •
Nathu Pass ▲

Dromo (Yatong) •
Gangtok •
• Kalimpong

BHUTAN

BANGLADESH

Tsangpo

Himalaya Range

Mustang •

NEPAL

Katmandu ✴

Mt Everest 29,020 ft

Darjeeling •

River Ganges

200 mi

200 km

0
0

I N D I A

Dharamsala •

Mussoorie •

N

Escape Route from Tibet

Drepung •
Lhasa •
Tsethang •
Lhuntse Dzong •
Sela Pass •
Mangmang •
Jora •
Bomdila •
Tezpur •

BHUTAN

TABLE OF CONTENTS

INTRODUCTION

Writing *The Noodle Maker of Kalimpong*

The Fourteenth Dalai Lama and his brother Gyalo Thondup could scarcely be more different. But the ties that bind them are unbreakable. They are two sides of the same struggle for the survival of Tibet. In the politics of modern Tibet, only the Dalai Lama himself has been more important than Gyalo Thondup.

The Dalai Lama is the spiritual leader of Tibetan Buddhists and of Buddhist believers everywhere. He has won the respect, admiration, and even adulation of a worldwide audience. "My message is always the same," writes the Dalai Lama, "to cultivate and practice love, tenderness, compassion and tolerance."

Gyalo Thondup sees himself as an obedient, selfless, and loyal servant to the Dalai Lama and Tibet. But his work has been conducted in secret, out of the limelight, in the nitty-gritty of international politics and the violence of a clandestine war of resistance.

Of the five male siblings who lived to adulthood, Gyalo Thondup alone did not become a monk. Instead, from the time the family moved to Lhasa in 1939, just after his brother Lhamo Thondup had been annointed the Fourteenth Dalai Lama, he was groomed to serve his brother on matters of state. Reting Regent, who had been chosen to serve as head of state until the young Dalai Lama reached majority, considered relations with China to be of such immense importance and Tibetans' knowledge of their giant neighbor so weak that Gyalo Thondup was sent to study in China. President Chiang Kai-shek was to become his sponsor.

When Chiang Kai-shek and his Nationalist Party lost the long civil war to Mao Zedong and the Chinese Communist Party, China's long latent threat to Tibet quickly turned real. The Tibetan government was forced under duress to sign the Seventeen Point Agreement ceding sovereignty to the recently established government of mainland China. As parts of Tibet rose up in resistance against their new rulers, Gyalo Thondup, then in exile in India, became the secret interlocutor between the CIA and the underground freedom movement in Tibet. His efforts helped keep the resistance movement alive. When the Dalai Lama was forced to flee his homeland in March 1959, Gyalo Thondup was at the border just inside India to greet him, having obtained from Prime Minister Jawaharlal Nehru a grant of political asylum for his brother and everyone who had accompanied him in flight.

With the Dalai Lama safely in India, Gyalo Thondup became a leading figure within the new Tibetan government-in-exile, serving as the major spokesman for Tibet to the Indian government and most of the outside world, including the United States and the United Nations. A rarity among Tibetans, Gyalo Thondup is fluent in Tibetan, Chinese, and English, allowing him to communicate directly with many of the world's most powerful leaders. In 1979, after the death of Mao Zedong and the ascension to power of Deng Xiaoping, it was to Gyalo Thondup that the new Chinese leader turned to re-establish contact with the Dalai Lama and the Tibetans in exile. For more than two decades, Gyalo Thondup shuttled between India and China trying without success to negotiate an agreement that would allow the Dalai Lama to return to his homeland.

For years, people close to Gyalo Thondup have encouraged him to write his memoirs, and for years he has promised that he would. Representatives of the Chinese Communist government even offered to send him to an island resort with a team of journalists to help put the story together. Gyalo Thondup called upon his friend

Elsie Walker instead, hoping she could find someone, an American perhaps, to help him write.

Elsie Walker's friendship with the Dalai Lama traces back for decades, and so, too, does her friendship with several members of his family, including Gyalo Thondup. Elsie had been instrumental in arranging the Dalai Lama's first meeting with an American president, her cousin George H. W. Bush, and later made the introductions that led to the ongoing friendship between His Holiness and the second President Bush. She had worked inside Tibet for years, cooperating with local officials on grassroots development projects. Elsie turned to me in the hope that I might help. She had read *The Private Life of Chairman Mao* that I wrote with Mao's longtime personal physician, Li Zhisui, and knew that I had experience interviewing.

When Elsie Walker broached the possibility of my working with Gyalo Thondup, I was fascinated. But I demurred. I was too busy. I was not a Tibet specialist. I am a student of modern and contemporary China. Elsie saw my China background as a plus. China looms so large in the life of contemporary Tibet that understanding what is happening in Tibet requires an understanding of China, too.

We found another China specialist, a young journalist who had once been a student of mine, to write the memoirs. But when the possibility of retaliation from the Chinese government proved too daunting, he had to pull out of the project. By then, even after 35 years of visiting China, living there for a number of them, being devoted to understanding China and promoting better cooperation between our two countries, and writing several books, the Chinese government had refused my request for a visa. China had been my life's work and my passion, and suddenly I was no longer allowed to go. But I could not stop writing. Gyalo Thondup gave me a new story to tell.

I have a longtime interest in Tibet. My files date from 1984 and the *New York Times* book review of John Avedon's *In Exile from the Land of Snows*. Avedon's book was my first serious introduction to Tibet and left a powerful impression. A visit to Tibet in 1985, just as it was opening to foreigners, further piqued my interest.

In the fall of 1987, I was living in Beijing, working with an organization that arranged academic study tours to China and Tibet, when riots broke out in Lhasa. We had a group of some 30 people in Lhasa at the time. I still have my notes, handwritten in pencil on yellow lined paper, of my telephone conversations with the group leader there, describing what was happening on the streets—the small protest that began on September 27 when several monks from the Drepung monastery were arrested after carrying the banned Tibetan flag and shouting slogans in support of the Dalai Lama and the independence of Tibet, and the much larger demonstration with many more arrests that took place on October 1, when the crowd set fire to the police station in order to allow the prisoners to escape. Soon someone sent me John Ackerly's photograph of one of the monks who had led his escape, the badly burned right arm held high, his hand in a fist, his left arm draped in a traditional white *khata* scarf.[1] The reports of the protests that I had received in near real time in Beijing complemented others I read later, including the congressional testimony of Indiana University professor Elliot Sperling[2] and reports by Robbie Barnett, who was making his first visit to Tibet when the riots began.[3] Barnett went on to become a professor at Columbia University and one of the country's leading specialists on contemporary Tibet.

Jeremy Bernstein's 1987 *New Yorker* article best captured my own thoughts about Tibet at the time. "There is something profoundly moving about the Tibetan way of life," he wrote, "about its religious essence. One feels instinctively that if this civilization were crushed and replaced by something that was yet another imitation of ourselves the world would be poorer for it."[4] I did not want to see Tibetan culture crushed or for the world to become poorer for it.

After my book *Enemies of the People*[5] was published, several American specialists of Tibet encouraged me to undertake a similar endeavor with Tibetans. They promised to find interpreters and offered to help make the arrangements. *Enemies* was based largely on interviews with Chinese who had been victims of Mao's Great Proletarian Cultural Revolution. I had cited Avedon's *In Exile from the Land of Snows* for its description of what he labeled the "cultural genocide" that had taken place in Tibet under Mao. The opportunity to expand my skills to include the story of Tibet was enticing. But the political situation did not permit it. Interviewing Tibetans in Tibet about what they may have suffered under Maoist rule was too politically sensitive.

My interest in Tibet was rekindled in the winter of 2002–2003 with my first visit to Qinghai. Qinghai was so distinctly different and the people so disarmingly outgoing that the place almost swept me off my feet. Qinghai includes a large part of the traditional Tibetan province of Amdo, and its population, particularly in more rural areas, is still largely Tibetan. The Fourteenth Dalai Lama and five of his siblings, including Gyalo Thondup, were born there. I began spending as much time as possible in Qinghai.

Gyalo Thondup and I spent many months together during the course of this project, briefly in Washington, DC, sometimes in Hong Kong, once in New Delhi, and mostly at his hilltop compound in Kalimpong, India, where he has lived in relative obscurity since 1999, running the noodle factory that he and his wife, Diki Dolkar, established nearly forty years ago. I had never been to India, and suddenly there I was with Elsie Walker, arriving exhausted at the New Delhi airport in the middle of the night, soon to be off to Kalimpong.

The heavily trafficked route from the Bagdogra airport to Kalimpong has become familiar, but the journey is always intense, a multi-sensory sociological smorgasbord of that part of West Bengal. The journey begins outside Siliguri on a hot, arid plain along a long, flat road lined with countless open-air stalls and jammed with cows, dogs, goats, carts, overfilled buses, motorcycles, bicycles, slow-moving cars, and throngs of colorful humanity. "Honk horn" the sign on the rear of the larger vehicles reads, and the sound of honking is constant, exuberant and conversational rather than angry.

The air grows cooler as the road begins to climb, and we pass through a tropical jungle dotted by waterfalls, shrines to the Hindu goddess Kali, and more open-air roadside stalls, progressing upwards through an endless series of switchback curves where rockslides are frequent and the road is in a never-ending process of repair. The trip can take anywhere from two-and-a-half to five or more hours depending on the state of the roads. Monkeys gather in families along the street observing the traffic and alert to the likelihood of edible treats proffered by passing travelers.

The road from the Teesta River to the heart of Kalimpong is named according to the number of miles from the river, and this last part of the journey always seems the longest—a combination of anticipation and the numerous switchback curves that slow the climb to a crawl. The center of Kalimpong is at 10-Mile Road. The streets are hilly, narrow, full of potholes, and lined with listless sleeping dogs. The town is crowded with shoppers during the day, with the number of women who still dress in saris giving color to otherwise drab surroundings. The countless tiny open air shops are crammed to overflowing with almost every imaginable commodity—medicines (both Western and homeopathic), saris, blue jeans, t-shirts, electronics, pastries, Tibetan antiques, Lux soap, carpets, imported British biscuits, magazines and comic books, tailors, silversmiths and shops selling nothing but gold. Restaurants serve Chinese, Nepali, and Indian food as well as Italian pizza. There is even a Café de Paris, owned and run by a young Nepalese woman and her French husband. The wife speaks excellent English with a strong French accent, and the cheerful young waiter is deaf and mute. The couple met when they were both working with an NGO serving the handicapped.

The foreign spies who once gave the town its unseemly reputation have disappeared, and so have the colorful Tibetan traders with their dangling earrings, long swords, and yaks and mules loaded with salt and wool. Traces of history can be still found at the Himalayan Hotel, once the home of David Macdonald, a leading officer in the Younghusband expedition to Lhasa in 1904, who helped the Thirteenth Dalai Lama escape to India in advance of the Chinese army in 1910, and later served as a British trade official in Tibet for some twenty years. The hotel is still owned and run by David Macdonald's grandson and his wife Nilam (though now, regrettably, the property is up for sale), and has played host to some of the world's great explorers and Tibetophiles, including the indomitable French explorer Alexandra David-Néel, Prince Peter of Denmark and Greece, Heinrich Harrer of *Seven Years in Tibet*, British diplomat and scholar of Tibet Sir Charles Bell, and numerous teams of mountain climbers off to conquer Mount Everest. Richard Gere was a more recent guest, renting the entire eight-room main building. I stay in room number five where, I am assured, Richard Gere once slept. David, my Roman Catholic Nepali waiter, is proud of the picture of himself at age fifteen standing next to the Hollywood star who is also a long-time friend and disciple of the Dalai Lama. David hopes that his son, now the same age as he was when he met Richard Gere, can someday study in the United States.

The violence of Kalimpong's Gorkha rebellion, described so chillingly in Kiran Desai's acclaimed novel, *The Inheritance of Loss*, has subsided, but descendants of immigrants from Nepal continue to demand a separate state. In the summer of 2013, shortly before one of my planned visits to Kalimpong, the rebels organized a non-violent strike that closed shops and kept the entire population at home. Periodically, the strike was lifted to allow residents to stock up on provisions and for vehicles to move in and out. Gyalo Thondup escaped to New Delhi during one of those brief openings, and we met there instead.[6]

GYALO THONDUP'S COMPOUND is just up a hill off 8-Mile Road, two miles down from the center of town. The compound is enclosed by a coral colored stucco wall broken by two turquoise wooden gates, the first giving access to trucks coming in and out of the noodle factory, the other opening on to the living compound. A discrete plaque at the entrance identifies the place as Taktser House, named after the family's village in Amdo.

The gate to the living compound opens to a broad sweep of deep green lawn bordered ahead by tropical jungle and on either side by four substantial buildings, the most impressive of which is the three-level family home, which was constructed from a blue-print bought in San Francisco for one hundred dollars during Gyalo Thondup's first visit to the United States in 1951 and features numerous large plate glass windows looking out over the grounds. The four buildings are all made of the same coral colored stucco, dark corrugated iron roofs, and wooden windows and shutters trimmed in turquoise.

Down a hill from the main house, just at the edge of the jungle, is a small cemetery where the ashes of Gyalo Thondup's mother Diki Tsering, who died in 1981, his daughter Yangzom Doma, who was killed in an automobile accident in 1983, and his wife Diki Dolkar, who died 1986, are buried. A tall Tibetan prayer flag stands next to a white incense-burning stupa, much like the one on the family property in Taktser village, at one edge of the lawn. The stupa is lit on special occasions such as Losar, the Tibetan New Year. It is then, too, that a long rope with fluttering Tibetan prayer flags in blue, white, green, red, and yellow is hung across the lawn from the roof of the family home to the roof of the guest quarters. The stupa is also lit, together with butter lamps, in times of particular need such as when noodle sales are down, to convey prayers to the family's mountain god in Amdo. The mountain god's powers are believed to extend to persuading people as far away as West Bengal and Bhutan to purchase more noodles.

Within the compound, Gyalo Thondup has solved the perennial problems of electricity and water faced by most people in Kalimpong with a generator that assures electricity even during the daily outages and a 100,000 gallon water tank that sits underneath the noodle factory and cost more than the main house to build. Internet connections are less reliable than electricity, but the Changia brothers who run the busy computer shop in town (and also book airline tickets) are geniuses at finding ways to get online. Their grandfather arrived in Kalimpong in 1936 with only five rupees in his pocket. He rose from service as a porter to worker in a fabric merchant's shop, to owning a fabric shop himself. The fabric shop is still in business, and the computer shop, which opened in 2000, is one of the most successful in town. Everyone knows the Changias.

Safety within the living compound is provided by two aging Tibetan mastiffs who sleep in their wooden doghouses by day and are set loose in the yard at night. Two lively mutts guard the noodle factory on the other side of the fence. Every family in Kalimpong seems to have a watchdog, and every watchdog for as far as the ear can hear can be relied upon to bark its protective warnings well into the night. Only once in the forty-five years since the land was purchased did an intruder actually make it on to the Takster House grounds. The dogs were asleep in their kennels at the time and awakened only when the would-be thief was discovered by the staff.

The compound is rarely quiet. The crows announce themselves around dawn, their rhythmic cawing soon turning to cacophony as the daily fight over what remains of the dogs' evening meal begins. Simultaneous with the cawing of the crows is the loud sound of skittering across the corrugated iron roofs—small rodents who are only heard and fortunately never seen. During the monsoon season, the clattering of the heaviest rains on the roofs is so deafeningly that even people sitting at the same table cannot make their voices heard.

The St. Philomena Catholic girls school just across the street provides many of the daytime sounds, of lessons being recited in unison, voices raised in song, shouts from the playground, and cheers for the team during school competitions. Rarely does a day go by without the sound of children singing "happy birthday" wafting through the open windows.

THE NOODLE FACTORY stands at the far end of the compound, closest to 8-Mile Road and looks out over the Teesta valley to row upon row of mountains, behind one of which is Darjeeling and beyond the last of which is Mount Kanchenjunga. The two cows are pastured within the factory grounds, too. They have outlived their usefulness as providers of milk, but the cows will be allowed to live out their natural lives. Gyalo Thondup and his small staff respect the Buddhist prohibition against taking the life of any sentient being. I have watched flies being caught in a jar to be released to freedom in the jungle and once witnessed several staff members tediously moving tens of earthworms from the concrete driveway where they had appeared after a heavy rainstorm to a spot of safety just outside the wooden entrance gate. Minutes later, another staff member, uninformed of the rescue, inadvertently drove over the worms, apparently crushing them all.

Gyalo Thondup may be suspected of a less rigorous adherence to the prohibition against taking the life of any sentient being than his staff. One afternoon while staying at the compound, I was startled by a loud noise that was unmistakably gunfire. Running outside, I saw my host pointing a rifle in the direction of the jungle. A large family of monkeys was invading his papaya trees, which were then laden with fruit. Gyalo Thondup was firing into the air to scare the monkeys away.

The monkeys did not stay scared for long. In the more than four years that I visited Taktser House, the monkeys have always succeeded in claiming most of the oranges and papayas that grow on the property. The staff has conceded defeat. The fruits on Gyalo Thondup's table now come almost exclusively from the local market. Gyalo Thondup can still claim that he has used his rifle with intent to kill only once, as a young boy, in defense of his pet rabbits who were being attacked by crows.

EVERYTHING ABOUT the Kalimpong noodle factory is antiquated. Nothing is automated. The building is made of wood, and the made-in-Calcutta equipment is old fashioned and often in need of repair. Some fifteen workers staff the factory, arriving a bit after nine in the morning, breaking at noon to go home for lunch, returning around one and ending the day around four. Tasks are allocated by gender, with the men mixing the dough, running it through the flattening machines, cutting the flattened dough into noodles, and hanging the cut noodles to dry. The women weigh, bundle, and package the noodles in a large room with plywood tables, concrete floors, and a couple of generally unlit light bulbs overhead. A *khata*-draped photograph of the Dalai Lama, perched atop a red calendar with the Chinese character for "prosperity," smiles down on them as they work. The factory is manned twenty-four hours a day. The drying of the noodles requires constant heat, and the fire must be stoked through the night. Jhangchu Dorjee, the factory foreman, oversees this task.

The workers are paid the equivalent of between two to two-and-a-half-dollars a day, and the women earn less than the men. For those with a similar level of education, between seven to nine years of schooling, the pay is about average for the area, though no one doubts that the pay is low and the workers are poor. The cost of daily necessities such as rice, cooking oil, and vegetables is high, and inflation cuts into wages. Some leave the factory for building and road construction work, where the pay is higher. But the hours of construction work are longer, the work is harder, and the time getting to and from the work site can be lengthy. Most of the workers in the Taktser House factory live no more than a five minute walk away, and Gyalo Thondup gives them the flexibility to work when they want or stay at home without pay if they like. Rarely is anyone fired.

Some of his staff have been with Gyalo Thondup for decades. Gyalpo was in his mid teens when he was hired and has worked on the compound for twenty-six years. His father fled from Tibet sometime in the 1970s, leaving his wife behind and carrying Gyalpo and his little sister in baskets slung from a bamboo shoulder pole. When his father remarried and his stepmother kicked him out, Gyalpo knocked on the gate of Takster House in search of a job. Today, he oversees the operations of just about everything that happens inside the compound, from shopping and cooking and upkeep of the property to delivering noodles to vendors, seeing that the factory is running as it should, and negotiating payments to repairmen. For this, he receives some 9,000 rupees, about 120 US dollars, a month, free food, and free, but decidedly modest, housing just outside the property gates. Gyalo Thondup pays for the education of Gyalpo's two children, for medical care when he or his family members are ill, and generous yearly bonuses.

The Dalai Lama first visited Taktser House in May 1974, well before he had attained the international stature that now requires a large staff and twenty Indian security soldiers when he travels. He stayed for several days, blessing the property, planting a tree in the front yard, and giving the main house its name—Lhundrob Gartsel, which roughly translates as "abiding success and happiness." A special multicolored wooden throne for the Dalai Lama was constructed for the occasion, and Gyalo Thondup's wife Diki Dolkar supervised the hundreds of townspeople who came to the compound to receive the Dalai Lama's blessing from his seat on the throne.

His later visit in 2011 was shorter—a quiet family affair with a lunch of chicken curry and rice prepared by Gyalo Thondup's staff and Tibetan *momos* (dumplings) made by the Dalai Lama's. The whole town of Kalimpong and hundreds more people from nearby areas seemed to turn out to welcome him, too many for the Dalai Lama to give his personal blessing, and thousands attended the teaching he gave in the Tharpa Choling Monastery. The Dalai Lama's throne still sits in the room designated as his, ready for his next visit.

GYALO THONDUP AND I approached our work from different points of view. Gyalo Thondup regards his story as truth and writes to set the record straight. I, on the other hand, take *Rashomon*, Akira Kurosawa's masterpiece on the unknowability of truth, as my starting point.[7] *Rashomon* is the story of the apparent rape of a woman and the murder of her samurai husband as told from the perspective of four different people who were party to the acts. Its message is that we each see and experience even the apparently most obvious and uncontested events in our own unique and different ways. Each of the witnesses to the apparent murder and rape provides a radically different description and interpretation.

Nowhere has the truth of *Rashomon* been stronger than in the story of Tibet as told by official China on the one hand and by most Tibetans on the other. Those two narratives are so different as to be almost hopelessly irreconcilable. But the corollary to the truth that all of life is *Rashomon* is that everyone has the right to his or her own story. It is a right in which I believe strongly, because I am convinced that the right to one's own story is fundamental to personal sanity and peace of mind, to human understanding, and ultimately to world peace. It is a right that the Chinese government has attempted to withhold from most Tibetans since the People's Liberation Army marched into Chamdo in October 1950.

Gyalo Thondup's story is unique, and it is important because of his preeminent role in Tibetan politics and in how the plight of Tibet has been portrayed to the international community, most importantly to India, China, the United States, and the United Nations. His story differs radically from the official Chinese version of Tibetan history. It differs, too, though less sharply, from versions of Tibet as recounted by some of his fellow Tibetans, including, in some details, even his brother the Dalai Lama.

My obligation to Gyalo Thondup has been to serve as the vehicle through which his personal history can be told as fully and as well as possible. I have read widely and deeply about Tibet during my time with Gyalo Thondup. The *Rashomon* phenomenon pervades the histories of modern Tibet, and I have often confronted Gyalo Thondup with alternative versions of his story. At other times, I have pressed when the evidence he has presented does not seem to warrant the conclusions he has drawn. Gyalo Thondup's viewpoint nonetheless prevails even when I would not personally have drawn the same conclusions. This, thus, is not *Rashomon.* It is not an attempt to tell the same story from different points of view nor an effort to weigh different versions of the same event. It is the story of Gyalo Thondup's own life as he experienced it and wants to have it told. His right to tell his own story in his own way remains paramount.

I have learned much from working with Gyalo Thondup. First, the United States is surely culpable for some of what went wrong for Tibetans in the early years under communist rule when the CIA lent its limited support to the underground resistance. The CIA's support to the Tibetan freedom fighters is an early instance of American involvement in complex situations we do not understand and over which we have little influence, making promises we cannot fulfill, raising hopes and expectations that cannot be met, and leaving the people we meant to help in utter disarray. It is yet another example of what Chalmers Johnson labels American hubris.[8]

I have also learned that political rule by incarnation is an almost certain guarantee of bad government. The interim between the death of one dalai lama and the coming to majority of the next almost inevitably provokes bitter, often violent, struggles between forces contending for power. Remarkably few dalai lamas in recent centuries have lived into majority. The power struggles that occured during the years that the Fourteenth Dalai Lama was growing up, before assuming the temporal reins of power, were also filled with intrigue, fighting, and even murder, bringing Tibet to near civil war. Surely one of the Fourteenth Dalai Lama's greatest contributions to the Tibetan people is to separate the theocratic from the political, insisting on the introduction of a new democratic form of government of which he is not a part. It is an innovation that he intends to last.

The assertion that political rule by incarnation will inevitably bring bad governance does not lead to the conclusion that China's attempt to govern Tibet has been better. In fact it has arguably been far worse. We have no good figures for the number of deaths that must have occurred in Tibet as a result of Chinese rule—deaths that would not have occurred had Tibetans themselves been in control, but we do know that the number as a percentage of population has been very high. The absolute figures in China, with its huge population, are much higher, of course. In October 1950, when Chinese troops were marching on the Tibetan outpost of Chamdo, villages throughout most of China were in the midst of a tumultuous land reform. Millions were labeled landlords and deprived of their land. The process was often violent, as Communist Party cadres roused local villagers, friends, neighbors, and even relatives in verbal and sometimes violent struggle against the so-called landlords, tearing communities that had lived together for centuries apart. Many have tried to calculate the human costs of this violence, but accurate records from the time simply do not exist. A number of serious efforts, however, suggest that as many as one and a half to two million Chinese may have been killed between 1947 and 1952.[9]

In 1959, when the people of Lhasa revolted against Chinese rule and the Dalai Lama was forced to escape, China was in the early stages of what was to become the worst famine in its long famine-filled history. Somewhere between thirty-five and forty-three million people died before it was over.

The Chinese revolution was violent, bloody, and long lasting, and the violence was often perpetrated not by the military, the police or party cadres but by ordinary people at the instigation of the party. Mao's evil genius was his ability to rouse the Chinese people to turn violently against each other. His was a politics of hate. The love, tenderness, compassion, and tolerance that are the Dalai Lama's unchanging message were anathema to Mao.

And to a large extent they still are. Upon telling a Chinese scholar from the China Tibetology Research Center in Beijing that I was writing a book with the Dalai Lama's elder brother, he informed me that the Chinese government considers anyone who is a friend of the Dalai Lama or his family to be an enemy of China. When I inquired as to why, he said because the government assumes that such a friend would share the Dalai Lama's values. The assumption itself is false, of course. And if it were logic of the Dalai Lama's values of love, tenderness, compassion, and tolerance would require treating even the enemy with compassion. Writing of his own spiritual struggle to come to grips with what China was doing in Tibet, the Dalai Lama writes, "Early in the morning, as I sat in prayer in my room..., I concentrated hard on developing compassion for all sentient beings. I reminded myself constantly of the Buddha's teaching that our enemy is in a sense our greatest teacher. And if this was sometimes hard to do, I never really doubted that it was so."[10]

ALL THE DISCUSSIONS of sovereignty and suzerainty, human rights and international justice aside, the fundamental differences between China and Tibet remain ethical and moral. In this regard, as Gyalo Thondup himself points out, for all the Tibetans have lost, the moral victory is theirs. Can any of us doubt that if the Chinese leadership were to embrace the Dalai Lama's values of love, tenderness, compassion, and tolerance that China and the world would be a better place? In a world where soft power is increasingly important, the Dalai Lama is among the world's most powerful men. We all have much to learn from him.

Anne Thurston
Himalayan Hotel,
Kalimpong, India
December 2014

PREFACE

More than sixty years have passed since I fled my native Tibet. I am an old man now. My home is in India, in the Himalayan hill town of Kalimpong. Taktser House is what I call my hilltop compound, in honor of the village where I was born and where my ancestors lived for centuries. Local people have lately begun referring to it as the Dalai Lama's house after my brother's recent visit here.

From my tree-filled garden just off 8-Mile Road, I look out over Sikkim, Nepal, and Bhutan. On a clear day, I can see the snow-capped peak of Mount Kanchenjunga. At 28,146 feet, it is the third tallest mountain on earth. Tibet is there, too, just behind the mountain, invisible except in memory. I earn my modest living from the noodles we make in the old-fashioned factory that sits at the edge of my property. I am known here as the noodle maker of Kalimpong.

My days begin in darkness, around four o'clock in the morning. I prepare a cup of coffee and make an offering to Palden Lhamo, the protective deity of Tibet and my family, the deity who has kept me safe over all these years. I sit in the predawn stillness waiting for the sun to rise and for the mountains to appear out of the darkness and for the crows to begin to caw. My mind is flooded with memories. Pictures of people and places and events of my past appear as if in life, some still strong and alive, others dim and fading. I see the village where I was born, the neighborhood where we lived, the faces

of our relatives and friends, the rivers, the mountains, the streets, my
mother carrying water on her back.

I remember the day of the local fair when my little brother was
born. I see the strange man with the turquoise earring who visited
our house when he was still a toddler. The months on horseback
traveling with my family across the Tibetan plateau from the Kumbum monastery in Amdo to the Tibetan capital of Lhasa are still
fresh in my mind. Just inside the border of Central Tibet, the official
announcement was made. My little brother Lhamo Thondup was
the fourteenth reincarnation of the Dalai Lama.

Our lives were changed forever. One day we were an ordinary
farm family in Amdo, and then we became the family of the Dalai
Lama, living in a huge fifty-room house looking up at the Potala
Palace where my little brother lived in the highest room atop the
tallest building in Tibet, cared for by a retinue of dedicated lamas
and monks. My own life changed, too. I was to be groomed to serve
as my brother's advisor, particularly in matters of state.

From those heights of joy, I could never have imagined the ca-
tastrophes to come. In 1950, the Chinese Communists attacked
Chamdo, the capital of Kham in eastern Tibet, and we were forced
to sign their Seventeen Point Agreement. Months later, the Chinese
People's Liberation Army marched into Lhasa. Tibet was declared
part of the Chinese "motherland."

I can still see Chinese General Zhang Jingwu, yelling loudly and
pounding his fist on the table, accusing Tibet's two prime ministers
of being tools of the American imperialists and threatening to have
them killed. In 1952, as the noose around my neck grew tighter and
popular anger against the Chinese grew, I fled on horseback to India.
From there, I tried to bring the plight of my country to international attention. I appealed to the United Nations. I wrote letters to
the American president asking for recognition and support.

As the situation in Tibet deteriorated and the underground resistance against the Chinese grew stronger, the American CIA came
to me with offers of help. They were willing to provide training and
weapons. They asked me to put them in contact with leaders of the

underground resistance. I came to lead a double life—one with a public persona, the other unknown to all but a handful of people.

The tragedy of Tibet only worsened after the Dalai Lama's escape to India in 1959. Tibet became one big prison camp, a living hell. The whole country—Central Tibet, Amdo, and Kham—was plunged into a reign of terror. The situation continued for almost twenty years. The Chinese government and the Tibetan government in exile had not a word of contact. Then, in 1979, Deng Xiaoping, newly returned to power, invited me to meet him in Beijing. I spent years going back and forth, meeting with China's top leaders, trying to start a real conversation about the problem of Tibet, trying to persuade the Chinese leaders that what the Tibetan people want is simply their legitimate rights, trying to convince them to meet the Dalai Lama to negotiate the terms of his return to Tibet. The talks went in circles with no result.

Tibet today is still a troubled place. In recent years, monks and nuns and ordinary people have begun to protest by setting themselves on fire. Travel from one part of Tibet to another is restricted, and the Chinese government refuses to grant Tibetans passports. Tibetans in exile are not allowed to visit their families inside Tibet. The pain goes on.

But there are reasons to hope. His Holiness the Dalai Lama has recently stepped down from his positions of temporal power. A new, younger generation has assumed the responsibilities that people of my generation once held. The Tibetan government in exile now has a democratically elected, young, intelligent, well-educated prime minister. I hope that he and his colleagues can bring a new approach to our old problems. I hope they can learn from our mistakes.

I write this book as a true history of Tibet, beginning from the time His Holiness the Fourteenth Dalai Lama was discovered. I tell the story as his elder brother who once sat in the inner circle, who served as his political advisor and his interlocutor with the world outside. It is a painful book to write, a bitter story to tell. Everyone will be offended—Tibetans, Chinese, Indians, Americans, the CIA. We Tibetans have so often been betrayed. People will not be happy to have those stories told. I, too, have come under criticism, sometimes for the choices I made, sometimes for mistakes I never committed. I want this book to set the record straight. Without this history, the new generation now taking the stage will not be able to reverse the mistakes of the past.

In the early morning hours with my eyes closed waiting for the sun to come up, I remember the people who died, the monasteries that were destroyed, the scriptures that were burned, the families sent to prison camps, the possessions that were robbed. And my soul is filled with agony. I still see the faces of those innocent, decent, able-bodied young men who met their deaths fighting for the freedom of Tibet. They are no longer here. I try to give names to their faces, but my memory has begun to fade. I write in memory of them.

1

Taktser Village and
Kumbum Monastery

We Tibetans have never been good at recording our history.
Most of our writings are sacred Buddhist texts. Other writings consist largely of extravagant tributes to the dalai lamas and the Buddhist saints, and they are filled with fantasy—visions and dreams, gods and demons, and feats of supernatural strength. The problem is even more acute at the local level, the history of ordinary Tibetan people. Ordinary Tibetans were illiterate. Only the monks in their monasteries could read and write. Both of my parents were illiterate.

My father, Choekyong Tsering, is the source of just about everything I know about my ancestral past. His knowledge was based not on written records but on stories passed down by word of mouth from one generation to the next. I know from him that my ancestors were descendants of soldiers in Songtsen Gampo's army. Songtsen Gampo ruled Tibet from 608 to 650 and is regarded as the greatest of our kings. His reign is considered our golden age. Songtsen Gampo was also a Buddhist, the first of Tibet's religious kings and, together with his Chinese wife, the Tang dynasty (618–907) Princess Wencheng, and his Nepalese wife, Princess Bhrikuti, is credited with having introduced Buddhism to the people of Tibet. Today, we still regard Songtsen Gampo as the incarnation of Chenrezig, the Bodhisattva of Compassion. Princess Wencheng is seen as an incarnation of Chenrezig's female consort, the goddess Tara. The two statues of Buddha that the princesses presented to their husband upon their marriage still sit in the Jokhang Temple and remain the most revered and sacred objects in all of Tibetan Buddhism. The statues are among the few objects of reverence that have not been destroyed under Communist rule.

The several kings who followed Songtsen Gampo were also incarnations of Chenrezig, and Buddhism became the state religion. But the golden age was not to last. In the centuries that followed, Tibet was frequently at war, usually with China and often with Mongolia. The Tibetan army was often victorious in battle, and in 763 even briefly captured the Chinese capital of Chang'an, near where the contemporary city of Xi'an now stands, forcing the Tang emperor to flee. But periods of peace were few. In later centuries, the Mongols invaded and by 1252 their influence over Tibet was strong.[1] But Tibet was never formally incorporated as part of Mongolia's Yuan dynasty, and the Mongols never ruled us directly. Close relations between Mongolia and Tibet, both political and religious, continued even after the collapse of the Yuan. The Buddhist lamas of Mongolia had a particularly strong influence on the lamas of Tibet. Indeed, the title of Dalai Lama, meaning "ocean of wisdom," was first conferred on Tibetan leader Sonam Gyatso in 1578 by the Mongolian Altan Khan.

As my father told the story, our ancestors were originally nomads, living in tents, herding yaks, and roaming freely across the grasslands. Gradually, they turned to farming and settled finally in the small village of Taktser, meaning "roaring tiger," located in the Amdo region of eastern Tibet. The village sits just at the edge of Tibet at a juncture of several cultures—Mongolian, Chinese, Uighur, Tibetan, and Hui, with each culture speaking its own distinct language. Much later, as more Chinese moved into the area and we began to intermix, we began speaking a mixture of Tibetan and Qinghai Chinese. The noisy tigers for which the village was named had long disappeared by the time my father came along.

In the beginning, my ancestors prospered in Taktser, but they suffered a devastating blow after 1644 when the Manchus conquered China and declared the establishment of the Qing dynasty. The Manchus set out to impress the Chinese by conquering the barbarian Tibetans. During the reign of the Yongzheng emperor (1678–1735), they sent some one hundred thousand troops under the command of the Manchu General Nangkinyo to conquer Amdo. The general led a bloody campaign of destruction and slaughter, and we Tibetans were too weak to resist. Thousands of people were killed, our animals were butchered, and our houses were burned to the ground. In one particularly egregious act, the Manchu troops were in such a hurry that they did not have time to chop off their victims' heads and buried several thousand people alive. In 1710, during the reign of the Kangxi emperor, a large part of my native Amdo had been incorporated into the Manchu empire as part of the region known as Qinghai.

Manchu control, like that of the Mongols, never reached our villages. The Manchus used a strategy of divide and rule, buying off the Tibetan chieftains and lamas with extravagant gifts, money, and high-sounding titles. The chieftains and lamas, in turn, served as the interlocutors between the people and the Manchus, thus keeping the local people in check and maintaining what was often an uneasy peace. When the emperor's ministers complained of the high cost of paying so many chieftains and lamas, the emperor retorted by noting that paying the barbarians was far less costly than keeping the thirty to forty thousand Manchu troops that would otherwise be necessary to maintain the peace. Still, outbursts of violence, even of outright rebellion, were frequent. Amdo was often unsettled.

Sometime in the declining years of Manchu rule, in the last quarter of the nineteenth century, not long before my father was born, another rebellion brought turmoil to Amdo. Manchu troops burned down every house in Taktser village, driving the entire population to seek refuge in caves in the surrounding hills. The Manchu's attempts to smoke them out with burning chili were unsuccessful, but my grandparents lost everything in the attacks. For years thereafter they lived in a cave, subsisting in grinding poverty.

Even through poverty and turmoil, Tibetan Buddhism continued to thrive. Several Manchu emperors, including Kangxi (1654–1722),[2] the greatest of them all, were Tibetan Buddhists. The Manchu court was a major supporter of Kumbum, Amdo's leading monastery and one of the six great monasteries of Tibet. Kumbum was located some twenty-five miles and seven hours by horseback from my family's village and was central to my family's life.

Founded in 1582, Kumbum was built on the spot where Tsongkhapa (1357–1419), one of the most important and revered figures in all of Tibetan history, was born. A wise scholar of Buddhism, and respected as a man of virtue, discipline, and integrity, Tsongkhapa is remembered as a great spiritual leader and teacher. Most importantly, he was the founder of the Gelugpa school of Buddhism, the Yellow Hat sect that was soon to produce the first Dalai Lama, from whom all subsequent dalai lamas have come. The chief abbot of Kumbum, Arjia Rinpoche, is the reincarnation of Tsongkhapa's father. Over time, Kumbum became a place of great monastic learning, the seat of tremendous wealth, and an institution with considerable political clout. Kumbum's magnificent architecture, with its red and white edifices and its golden roofs, is renowned throughout Tibet. Its most revered and famous building, the Great Hall of Golden Tiles, has a spectacular gold roof and a huge golden statue of Tsongkhapa. The eight stupas that still stand at the entrance to the monastery serve as reminders that even lamas were not exempt from the Manchu sword. The stupas were constructed in memory of eight reincarnated lamas beheaded by the Manchu troops.

My family visited Kumbum often on pilgrimages. We supported it financially and turned to its lamas for guidance and help. We relied on Kumbum's monks to propitiate the gods, drive away evil, protect us from harm, cure disease, bless the young, mourn the dead, and provide economic help in times of distress. Ordinary Tibetans in all of Amdo consider the monastery their own. But my family's relationship with Kumbum was particularly deep. Sometime in the 1860s, my paternal grandmother's older brother, my great uncle, was recognized as the reincarnation of the Taktser lama, one of the thirty or so reincarnated lamas who were part of Kumbum's tradition. He was taken from his family as a small child to be raised and educated by the monks of Kumbum.

During the turmoil of the Manchu decline, however, my great uncle left Kumbum for Mongolia, where the vast majority of the people were still fervent followers of the Gelugpa sect. Kumbum's ties to Mongolia traced back through centuries, and several of its leading abbots had been Mongolian. My great uncle spent several decades in Mongolia during the last decades of the nineteenth century and developed quite a devoted following there. His disciples showered him with money and presents of land, horses, and camels, making him a wealthy man. When he finally returned to Kumbum, at the beginning of the twentieth century, he was said to have owned ten thousand camels.

Such wealth was not unusual for a reincarnated lama. Monasteries have always been economic as well as religious institutions. Reincarnated lamas were often extremely wealthy. That wealth had accumulated over many reincarnations—ten, fifteen, or even twenty generations. Reincarnated lamas in Tibetan monasteries are divided into separate administrative households called *labrangs*, each of which are independent economic entities administered by trusted senior managers and their staff, all of whom are monks. In addition to receiving generous contributions from religious believers (and virtually all Tibetans are Buddhist believers, often fervently so), the wealthiest labrangs, including those in Kumbum, also owned numerous estates with vast tracts of agricultural land from which they could derive a sizeable income. Labrangs also served as informal banks, providing loans for the lama's followers, and the most prosperous of the labrangs were also engaged in business. Some of the wealthiest Tibetan trading companies were based in monasteries. Thus, the greatest wealth in Tibet lay not, as in Europe, with the aristocracy, but with the labrangs of the leading lamas in the country's major monasteries. The wealth of the richest members of the Tibetan nobility might be measured in the millions, but the wealth of the richest labrangs and monasteries was counted in the billions.

A labrang's wealth supported the activities of the monastery, both providing for the ordinary monks and supporting the many elaborate religious ceremonies that take place each year. Funds were generally distributed to monks during the Tibetan New Year according to rank. At the time my great uncle was alive, during the Chinese reign of Yuan Shikai, Kumbum had around three thousand monks, and the average monk would probably receive a few thousand silver dollars a year. Higher lamas, like the Taktser lama, would receive several times what an ordinary monk might get, in addition to the profit from his labrang. The largest monasteries, including Kumbum, have additional affiliated branches in smaller monasteries that also require attention and support. Shartsong monastery near my family's home, for instance, was affiliated with Kumbum under the domain of the Taktser Lama's labrang.

Families of lamas from wealthy labrangs also stood to benefit from their wealth. After my great uncle's return to Kumbum from Mongolia's Ulan Bator, my grandparents became special beneficiaries of my grandmother's brother's new wealth. Taktser Rinpoche bought back all of the forty-five acres of family land that had been lost with the earlier rebellion. My grandparents were able to build a new Chinese-style home that was large and spacious, with three courtyards surrounded by one-story buildings.

It was after his return to Kumbum from Mongolia that my great uncle came to know the Thirteenth Dalai Lama, Thubten Gyatso. The Great Thirteenth, as he came to be known, spent two extended periods at the Kumbum monastery. In 1904, when the British military expedition led by Sir Francis Younghusband fought its way into Lhasa and demanded the right to trade, the Thirteenth Dalai Lama fled first to Mongolia and then, in 1906, took refuge in Kumbum. He returned again in 1909, after he had visited Beijing and was en route back to Lhasa.

The Thirteenth Dalai Lama was not entirely popular with the monks of Kumbum. The young Dalai Lama had been a forward-thinking reformer almost from the time he assumed the throne in 1895 at the age of nineteen. His reforms began in the monasteries, where discipline had often become lax. Many monks had taken to drinking, smoking, and gambling. Some were ignoring their vows of celibacy. Some were charging usurious rates on the loans they made to their followers.

Kumbum was one of the monasteries that had fallen into moral decay, and during his two stays there the Thirteenth Dalai Lama set out to reform it, insisting on enforcing strict monastic discipline, expelling particularly wayward monks and punishing many others. While many of Kumbum's monks bridled at the reforms, my great uncle supported the strict new regime and thus won the Dalai Lama's respect. When the Thirteenth Dalai Lama left Kumbum to return to Lhasa in 1909, my great uncle, Taktser Rinpoche, left Kumbum, too. My great uncle's support for the Dalai Lama's reforms had made him unpopular with his fellow monks.

In contrast to the monks, the lay people of Amdo, including members of my own family, were thrilled that the Dalai Lama had taken refuge in Kumbum. During both of his stays, the Thirteenth Dalai Lama held public teachings for audiences that numbered in the thousands, bestowing his blessings on all who came to listen.[3] My father was still a small child when the Thirteenth Dalai Lama passed through our village en route to the nearby Shartsong monastery sometime during his first stay in Kumbum. When the Dalai Lama's entourage stopped to cook lunch just on the outskirts of Taktser, my grandmother carried my six-year-old father on her back to give him a glimpse of the Dalai Lama and to allow him to receive his blessing. When the entourage departed, my grandmother scooped up the ashes from the Dalai Lama's cooking fire and carried them home, burying some in the household courtyard and the rest in the family graveyard. Even ashes from the Dalai Lama's fire were considered sacred.

When my parents wed in 1917, Taktser Rinpoche had returned to Kumbum again. Their marriage, like all Tibetan marriages then, was arranged by their two families, and the wedding took place, with Taktser Rinpoche's blessing, when they were still quite young. My father was just seventeen years old when they married, and my mother was one year younger.

Taktser Rinpoche died only a year or two after my parents were wed. The search for his reincarnation began shortly after his death. The manager of his labrang organized the search. The labrang's estate passes economically and administratively from one incarnation to the next. During the lama's life, the chief administrator of the labrang is responsible for day-to-day operations and management. In death, the administrator, together with his most trusted staff, becomes responsible for identifying the new incarnation. One of my uncles on my father's side, my father's elder brother, was a monk in Kumbum and an assistant to the senior manager of the Taktser labrang, and thus became a member of the search team. Together, the senior manager, my uncle, and a team of close disciples scoured the Amdo region for little boys who might be candidates for my great uncle's reincarnation. Just as the reach of Kumbum monastery extended to the six different districts of Amdo, so any male child within those districts who had been born within a certain period after the lama's death could potentially be identified as the new incarnation. They were guided by omens and hints the lama had given before his death about who his reincarnation might be and where he might be found.

The final choice of such high-ranking incarnations rests with the Dalai Lama himself. After the search team has collected a list of names, and whittled the list to a select number of candidates, the search team must travel to Lhasa to present the Dalai Lama with the list and be informed of his choice.

My mother had given birth to her first child, my older sister Tsering Dolma, in 1920, not long after the Taktser Lama's death. My grandmother had been bitterly disappointed. She had hoped that my mother's first child would be a boy and could be put on the list of possible reincarnations. She wanted her grandson to be chosen as the new Taktser Lama, replacing her elder brother. When she learned that the new child was a girl, she was so distressed that she cried every day and refused to eat. Not long afterward, she became ill and died.

My grandmother died too early. She could not have imagined what happened when the list of possible new candidates was drawn up and my uncle and the senior manager traveled to Lhasa to present the list to the Dalai Lama for his consideration.

After traveling two or three months on horseback from Amdo to Lhasa, the senior manager and my uncle met with the Dalai Lama to seek his blessing, inform him of the my great uncle's death, and present him with the list of names of possible reincarnations. The Thirteenth Dalai Lama was saddened to learn of Taktser Rinpoche's passing. But he said that the new Taktser Rinpoche was not on the list. In fact, the new incarnation had yet to be born. The Dalai Lama instructed them to return home and come back later with a fresh list of names.

When the two men returned more than a year later with a new list of candidates, the Dalai Lama again said that the new Taktser Rinpoche was not on it. The reincarnation had still not been born. The manager who had been leading the search team cried when he heard this news. He was growing old and had already made two long trips to Lhasa and still the new incarnation of my great uncle had yet to be found. The Dalai Lama told him not to be sad. They were to come back again later with yet another list.

The elderly manager became ill on the trip back to Kumbum. He died shortly after the two men reached home. In keeping with custom, my paternal uncle then assumed the position of senior manager of the Taktser labrang. Responsibility for collecting another list of names for the new Taktser lama, his uncle, fell to him.

In the meantime, in 1922, my mother had given birth to her second child, my older brother, Thubten Jigme Norbu. Among the names on my uncle's new list was that of my family's new baby son.

Arriving in Lhasa carrying the third list of possible reincarnations, my uncle went first to the Jokhang, the holiest of Tibetan Buddhist temples. There he lit a butter lamp before the sacred statue of the Buddha Sakyamuni, the one that had been given to King Songtsen

Gampo by Chinese Princess Wencheng on the occasion of their marriage in 641. When the lamp toppled, spilling melted butter on my uncle's ornate brocade jacket, he interpreted the accident as an auspicious sign. Rather than cleaning the jacket or throwing it away, he packed it carefully to be taken back to Kumbum.

The Thirteenth Dalai Lama said nothing after studying the young boys' names. Instead, he gave the search party a sealed envelope containing a set of written instructions. He ordered them not to open the envelope until they reached the Kumbum monastery. Once they arrived, the abbot was to assemble the families of all the children on the list. Only then was the letter to be opened and read.

My parents were in the audience when the abbot of Kumbum opened the letter. The abbot announced that my brother Thubten Jigme Norbu was the reincarnation of his great uncle, the Taktser lama.

The selection of incarnate lamas is a mysterious process, full of strange spiritual connections. The Dalai Lama could not have known of my grandmother's wish for her grandson to become the next Taktser lama or that my mother had recently given birth to a son. No one could have known that my brother, Thubten Jigme Norbu, would be selected to be the new Taktser lama.

And it had never occurred to my grandmother that the reincarnation had yet to be born. If she had waited a few more years to die, she would have seen her grandson taken first to Shartsong and then to the Kumbum monastery to become the new Taktser Lama. She would have been so happy.

2

My Family

I never met my great uncle. He died some ten years before my birth. But I know him vividly through the legacy he left. The villagers of Taktser remembered my great uncle's visits as occasions for the community to come together for festivals of dancing, singing, eating, and drinking—and for the ten— or sometimes twenty—ounce silver ingots he often distributed to everyone who came. I still have a fifty-ounce ingot he once gave my aunt. The generosity showered upon my grandparents by Taktser Rinpoche after his return transformed their lives. Their decades of poverty came to an end. My parents inherited the house and the land. It was there that my siblings and I were born. It was Taktser Rinpoche who made our new lives possible.

Our village of fourteen families was nestled in the mountains about five thousand feet above sea level. Our house was one of the best in the village, with three separate courtyards. The compound was completely enclosed, entered through a big, multicolored, carved wooden gate that opened onto the first large courtyard that was edged by rectangular buildings. The main building was made of rammed, whitewashed clay with a flat roof accessible by ladder from the courtyard below. We often grew flowers on the roof, and from it we could look out across the mountains and valleys. The kitchen was just on the right after entering. It was the liveliest room of the house because it contained both the stove where my mother cooked and the *kang* where we ate our meals and spent much of the day, especially during the winter. Our kang was a raised rammed earth platform covered with rugs and pillows and short-legged tables where our food was served. It was warmed by burning wood underneath, fed through a door on the outside wall. The heated kang kept us warm during Amdo's long, cold winters.

Looking straight ahead from the entrance gate, horizontally, was my parent's room and the altar room where they prayed every morning. To the left, perpendicular to my parent's room, was a guest room and a storeroom. The rooms were connected to each other inside, and some also had doors out to the courtyard. An overhang ran the perimeter of the buildings, providing shelter in the rain or snow. The second courtyard had rooms for the servants and was where our animals were kept. Beyond that, the third courtyard was a storage area for dried food and horse feed.

On the land my great uncle had purchased we grew wheat, broad beans, soybeans, barley, oats, and the huge potatoes that grow so well in the fine red soil of that part of Amdo. The harvest was the most anticipated time of the year, because its success or failure determined how well we would eat in the months ahead. Our harvests were generally good. We never wanted for food. But farmers for miles around lived in fear of the hailstorms for which that part of Qinghai was famous. A big hailstorm could destroy an entire crop in a matter of a few quick minutes.

We called my mother Amala. She was an excellent cook, famous in our area for her delicious breads and pastries. Her breads were always my favorite food. We ate a traditional Tibetan breakfast of roasted barley, called *tsampa*, which we grew ourselves and had ground by a Chinese family in a nearby village. We ate it mixed with tea or butter. For lunch and dinner we ate my mother's homemade noodles, usually served in a broth with a few fresh vegetables. We rarely ate meat, but when we did, we ate mostly lamb—fresh and roasted in the fall after the yearly slaughters, salted and dried the rest of the time. We ate a lot of potatoes, too, cooking them in the ash from the fire that fed the kang, then salting them and eating them whole.

My mother moved into my father's household at the time of their marriage, as was the Tibetan custom. The family had no servants at the time, and my grandmother worked her new daughter-in-law hard. My mother's work began long before sunrise. She was responsible for fetching water from a stream a kilometer away and carrying it home in a huge canister on her back. Water was in short supply, and she had to make the trip several times a day. Often, she had already made four or five trips before the sun was up. My grandmother was a rigid and hot-tempered woman. Once, when my grandparents had to testify in court, my grandmother got so angry with the magistrate that she jumped out of her seat and slapped him on the face. She often beat my mother if she had not finished fetching the day's water early enough. My grandfather, in contrast, was thoroughly sweet-tempered, incapable of uttering, or even thinking, an angry word. He would comfort my mother after my grandmother beat her, urging her not to be sad. My mother, too, was a gentle woman and kind to everyone, including the Chinese beggars who sometimes fled west in the face of famine and came to our house to beg. My mother never failed to give them food.

As the family's economic lot improved with the return of my great uncle, my parents were able to employ three servants, a married Chinese couple and their son, thus taking some of the burden from my mother. The husband tended the animals and cleaned the stables. The wife helped my mother cook and tend the fields. And the son was our shepherd. We had over fifty sheep, a few yaks, and several *dzomo*—milking yaks that are a mix between a yak and a cow. We were still ordinary peasants, but we lived quite well. By the time I was born, we were among the most prosperous families in the village.

But it was still a primitive existence. Life expectancy was short. There were no doctors or hospitals. Sudden, unexplained death was a constant, pervasive threat. There was no electricity in my village, and I never saw a candle. Our home was lit with mustard oil lamps. Straw and yak dung served as cooking fuel. We had no clocks or watches to tell the time and no calendars to know what day it was or record the passage of the seasons. We relied on the sun, the moon, the stars, and the weather, as well as the numerous monastic festivals, to mark the passing year. My mother made all of our clothes, stitching them by hand. She was a good seamstress and crafted beautiful handmade embroidery, too. We had no running water, and the concept of a toilet, or even a latrine, did not exist. The courtyard where our animals were penned served as our open-air toilet, and we simply covered our waste with dirt. There was no such thing as bathing either, unless an occasional summer dip in the nearby river could be considered a bath. We had no concept of sanitation or cleanliness or soap. When some of the local monks saw their first bar of soap, they thought it was something to eat. We were so backward that we had no idea of a modern world beyond.

While I was still a young boy, the Chinese opened a school in the valley below our village, and I became the first member of my family to attend. It was several kilometers away, a two-hour walk each way, and I went there every day with six or seven other young boys from the village. The trek could become dangerous in the rain, when the bridgeless creek at the bottom of the hill would suddenly swell and the waters flowed so fast that they could wash a little boy like me away. My mother often came running after me in a rainstorm to make sure I was safe. Sometimes on nice days my companions and I never got to school. We played hooky in the hills instead. Even when we did go to school, we spent more time in play than study. By that time, many Tibetans who originally spoke only their native Amdo dialect had begun speaking the local Chinese dialect. Classes, such as they were, were taught in Qinghai Chinese. I did not learn much.

My earliest memories of childhood are of the series of misfortunes that struck my family when I was six years old. They began in early 1935 when my father became seriously ill. He lay in bed for months, unable get up, barely able to lift his head, and hardly eating at all. I watched as he slowly wasted away, turning into a skeleton, nothing but skin and bones, his cheeks sunken, his ribs sticking out. He looked like a ghost, and since I was afraid of ghosts, I tried to avoid him. Every day coming home from school, when I had to pass by his ground-floor window, I would put my head down low and bend over as far as I could, trying to sneak past without his seeing me. If he saw me, he might call me in for a visit. Everyone expected him to die.

The second disaster struck while he was still sick in bed. One of our servants was leading our horses to water at a nearby spring on the outskirts of the village when the horses suddenly broke free and bolted, galloping to the edge of a one-thousand-foot cliff. One by one, all five horses leapt over the cliff and down to their deaths. The horses of my native Amdo were huge and magnificent creatures, as strong and lively as tigers. They had been introduced centuries earlier from Arabia, where they had been used by the cavalry. Later, the Manchu army used them, too, and the imperial court continued to import them throughout the Qing dynasty. Horses like that had never leapt to such deaths before.

The horses were important to my father, a major source of my family's wealth. He made a good living buying and selling horses and was a natural veterinarian, too. He could diagnose an ailment just by putting his hands on a sick horse.

Then our mules began to die. One by one, all seven of them were struck with a mysterious disease. One by one, they died.

We saw the deaths of our animals as omens. Tibetans have two ways of interpreting misfortune. One is as retribution for sins committed in a previous life. The other is as a harbinger of good fortune yet to come. With my father so ill and the dramatic suicides of our horses, our neighbors were beginning to gossip. They wondered what terrible sins my parents had committed in their previous lives to bring the family such serious misfortune. So we tried to hide the deaths of our mules, fearful of what the neighbors would say. Ordinarily, we would have buried them in a vacant lot on the outskirts of the village, where everyone could see. Instead, we buried them secretly, within the walls of our family compound.

With so many portents of misfortune, my pregnant mother was terribly frightened. She feared for her unborn baby's life. She had reason to be frightened. There were three children in my family then. My sixteen-year-old sister, Tsering Dolma, was the eldest, born in 1920. My older brother, Norbu, had been born two years later. In the interim between Norbu's birth in 1922 and my own in late fall of 1929, my mother had lost three sons, one after the other, when they were still very young. My parents had been devastated.[1]

Religion was their only means of coping with these tragedies. Religion governed my parents' life. Propitiation of the evil spirits was the best hope for warding off disaster. Tragedy was explained and overcome through ritual and prayer. Every day, just after wakening and before they began their chores, my parents would visit the altar room adjacent to where they slept, lighting a small mustard oil lamp, burning some incense, and offering water to Palden Lhamo, the great protector of Tibet and of my family, and to the god of the great glacier mountain that overlooked our village. The altar room, with its Buddhist statues and colorful *thangkas,* was the most important in the house. Palden Lhamo and our mountain god were the deities who kept my family safe. Even today, these deities still determine my fate.

My mother blamed the deaths of her children on one of our local ghosts—the cat ghost that lived in a village some fifteen kilometers away. The cat ghost in our part of Amdo was said to be particularly powerful.[2] It was generous and helpful to members of its own human family, protecting them from harm, fighting on their behalf, and bringing them good. If the cat ghost was in good spirits, for instance, an extra chunk of meat might suddenly drop from nowhere into the family cooking pot. But the cat ghost could be nasty and vicious to outsiders. It was full of tricks, changing forms to suit the occasion. If it wanted sympathy, it might manifest itself as a small child. Sometimes it would enter into a local woman through a trance. My mother's discipline included warnings that if I did not finish my dinner quickly or if I disobeyed her orders, the cat ghost would punish me. I never saw the cat ghost. But my mother did, when she was caring for her dying children.

On the day that I was born, my father went immediately to the altar room, prostrating himself in thanks before Palden Lhamo, offering thanks to the Buddha, and making an oath that I would be a farmer, managing the family business, rather than a monk. My brother Norbu had been just a year old when he was identified as the reincarnation of the Taktser lama and was already living in the Kumbum monastery by the time I was born. Most Tibetan families in Amdo sent at least one son to the monastery to become a monk. But every family also needed at least one son to stay at home in order to take over the family business and care for their parents when they became old. That was my appointed role from the moment I was born. I was to be the only son of my family not to become a monk.

As an infant, when I became sick with a fever, my parents were afraid that this new son would also die. Only after being taken to a monastery to be treated by the lamas did my health return. Then my father invited the local Nechung oracle from the monastery in Gyatsang village to provide my family and me with his special protection. Nechung is the state oracle of Tibet, often called into service by the Dalai Lama when major decisions must be made. But he can speak through many different individuals in different parts of Tibet, monks and ordinary farmers alike, who are called into service as occasions arise. The Nechung oracle was a particularly respected source of advice in Amdo. When he visited my family's home and went into his trance, my father fell on his knees, clinging to the oracle's legs and sobbing. "What have I done wrong?" my father wanted to know. "I have never done anything bad in this life. Why has my life been full of such misfortune? I have lost three wonderful sons and now this son has been sick, too. Why am I suffering such punishment?" He asked the Nechung oracle to accept me as his adopted son, to protect me, to chain me to life and keep me free from harm.

The oracle agreed. I became his adopted son, and he promised to protect me. He told my father not to cry. "Don't feel so sad," he said.

"You are going to have many more sons in the future, and among them they will give you tremendous wealth. You will have so much money that it will flow to your house like a stream." From that time on, I was never sick. The oracle kept me safe.

When my parents had another son a few years after me, my father decided immediately that this son would be a monk. The little boy was originally called Rinzen Thondup. Lama Thubten from Shartsong monastery gave him his name. Lama Thubten gave all the children in my family their names, though months or even a year might pass between the interim of their birth and the rendering of the name. Shartsong is a small monastery with only four or five monks who spend most of their time in retreat, in silence and meditation. It is famous because the founder of the Kagyu sect, one of the four main schools of Tibetan Buddhism, came to meditate there some nine hundred years before. Lama Thubten, following the Shartsong tradition, spent most of his life as a hermit, only rarely coming out of retreat. It was during those rare forays out that local children were given their names.

Shartsong was a beautiful, peaceful place only two hours by horseback away from my home, and we visited it often in the summertime. Its grounds were filled with wild strawberries, gooseberries, and raspberries. My brother and I used to harvest huge baskets of the fruits, beating the bushes with a broom to shake the berries free and later feasting on the fruit.

Rinzen Thondup was a gentle little boy, always trying to protect me from the potential accidents of my natural obstreperousness, constantly running behind me warning me to be careful not to fall. Once, we both fell down together, off a horse my father had been leading, and Rinzen Thondup was unconscious for the better part of a day. My parents laid him on the kang, and my mother boiled dates in water as a way of learning his fate. If the dates congealed into a paste, she knew that he would recover. He did recover, waking up shouting that he was hungry and asking my mother to bring him some bread.

Rinzen Thondup's name was changed after that. He became Lobsang Samten instead. Tibetans often change their names after recovering from injury or illness. It is a way of tricking the spirits who were held responsible for the original misfortune.

Lobsang Samten went to the Kumbum monastery soon thereafter to begin his training for the monkhood. He was still so small that he needed help getting over the wooden barriers that stood across the thresholds of all the monastery's rooms, preventing evil spirits from entering. The monks had to grasp little Lobsang Samten's robe at the scruff of the neck to lift him across the threshold.

MY FATHER WAS STILL on his deathbed when my next baby brother was born. The date was the sixth day of the sixth month by the local Qinghai calendar; July 6, 1935, by the Western one. I remember it well. The sixth day of the sixth lunar month was the date of the annual fair in our area, and my elder sister, Tsering Dolma, and I were looking forward to going. We had awakened well before dawn and dressed in our best new clothes, ready to set out for the two-hour walk. The fair was about seven kilometers from my own village, and at least a dozen other villages participated. For adults, the fairs were a time to visit and do some trading. For children, they were a chance to see friends and neighbors, eat a few sweets, and have some fun. I had packed six hard-boiled eggs for the gambling game I would play with other boys my age. Two boys took turns tapping each other's egg. The boy who succeeded in cracking his competitor's egg was the winner, and his prize was the egg he had cracked. The game went on until all the eggs were cracked—or all the contestants grew tired and quit.

That day, just as Tsering Dolma and I were about to leave for the fair, my mother asked my sister to fetch the village midwife.[3] After conferring with the elderly woman, my mother told my sister that the new baby would be arriving that day, and she would need my sister's help. She could not go to the fair. Tsering Dolma was furious. She threw a tantrum, crying and screaming and pulling her hair. She was determined to go to the fair. But the old midwife insisted that she stay. I went without my sister, joining our neighbors instead.

My mother gave birth like an animal, in the stable that housed our horses and mules, delivering the baby on the dirt with no sanitary precautions at all. Our custom taught that women giving birth were unclean. Hardly any time was set aside for recovery, either. Shortly after cleaning herself and the baby, my mother would be back in the kitchen, boiling water, making tea, fueling the fire, and cooking the family meals. It is so sad and tragic to think back to those days, almost unimaginable how women had to live, how few rights they had. The rate of infant mortality was high, as my own mother's experience attests. Of the twelve babies my mother delivered during her lifetime, only seven survived to adulthood.[4]

But with the birth of this new baby boy, our family fortunes began to recover. As soon as my father heard that his wife had given birth, he shouted to the midwife, asking whether it was a boy or a girl. Told that he had a new son, he immediately rose from his sickbed, went to the altar room, bowed before the Buddha, and promised the god that this son, too, would be a monk. From that point on, my father's health began to improve. Within a month he was well, and soon he was back to his usual business of horse-trading.

I had been oblivious to the thunder and lightning the day my brother was born. Only later, when the day was recognized as having been particularly auspicious, did I learn that in Tibet, thunder and lightning mean flowers falling from heaven. Lama Thubten named my new brother Lhamo Thondup.

I DO NOT REMEMBER my little brother very well during the first two years of his life. My elder sister took care of him. My stronger memory is of the baby sister who was born about a year after my brother. I often looked after her. But she became ill when she was still an infant, and my parents feared for her life. As she grew sicker, they suggested that I might be able to save her. They thought that perhaps if we sacrificed another life in lieu of my sister's, the gods might see fit to spare her. My parents wanted me to sacrifice a

*Gyalo Thondupu, kneeling, with his parents and
baby brother Lhamo Thondup, Amdo 1935.*

rooster by chopping off its head. I was frightened at the thought of chopping off an animal's head, but I loved my sister dearly and often cried to see her so ill. Of course I would kill a chicken to save her. But perhaps my parents were joking. I never killed the chicken. My little sister continued to waste away. She died after several months, when I was around seven years old. So many children died in infancy then that we had no special ceremonies to mourn their passing. When elderly people in my village died, we had elaborate religious ceremonies, with monks coming to say prayers so the deceased could depart in peace. But so many infants died of high fevers and undiagnosed illnesses that their passing was never formally mourned. My parents buried my baby sister in the mountains without even a tablet to mark her grave. I did not go with them to bury her.

Only after my sister's death did I become more aware of my little brother.

3

The Search Team Arrives

I knew from the cut of his clothes and the dangling earring of turquoise and gold that the tall, strange-looking man on our roof was not from Amdo. The horses tethered outside and the voices coming from our kitchen told me that we had guests. They were pilgrims, my mother explained. They had just visited Kumbum and were en route to the Shartsong monastery. They had asked to stay the night.

We had no hotels in Amdo. Villagers were always hospitable to strangers, happy to house and feed anyone passing through. Since our house was among the best in the village, we often played host to travelers. We had nine or ten guests that day. Their leader was a young lama, and we naturally gave him the best of our rooms. His older servants stayed in the kitchen, helping my mother with the cooking and playing with my younger brother and me. Lhamo Thondup was a little two-year-old toddler then, just beginning to talk. He enjoyed the attention he was receiving and the sweets the guests were giving us to eat. The eldest servant in particular took a liking to Lhamo Thondup and often held him in his arms.

The pilgrims returned briefly after their visit to Shartsong and then were gone again, back to Kumbum monastery.

Only when the same guests returned a third time did we learn that they were not ordinary pilgrims. Apologizing for their earlier deception, they revealed themselves as the search team for the reincarnation of the Thirteenth Dalai Lama. The Great Thirteenth had died, or, as some would say, was called to the heavenly fields, nearly four years earlier, on December 17, 1933. My little brother Lhamo Thondup was one of the candidates to replace him. The elderly servant who had taken such a liking to him was not a servant after all. He was Kewtsang Rinpoche, a revered and learned lama from the Sera monastery in Lhasa and head of the search party. He was there on behalf of Reting Regent, the man responsible for overseeing the search, and he asked my parents' permission to perform a series of tests to help them determine whether my brother was indeed the Dalai Lama's reincarnation.

My older brother Norbu had already been declared the reincarnation of Taktser Rinpoche, and my parents knew something about the process of selecting a Dalai Lama. Of course they agreed to the search party's requests. The tests lasted several days, and both my mother and father were present when my brother was asked to choose from several similar looking paired objects, of which one in each pair had belonged to the previous Dalai Lama. If the young candidate consistently chooses the objects that had belonged to the previous Dalai Lama, the search party has strong evidence that the little boy is the reincarnation.[1]

Kewtsang Rinpoche said nothing to us about the results of the tests. He and the search party thanked my parents for the opportunity to test my brother, left them with presents of tea and Tibetan fabrics, and returned to the Kumbum monastery. We knew from Kewtsang Rinpoche that the team had spent months visiting dozens of families across the six districts of Amdo. We knew, too, that the search party had met the Ninth Panchen Lama in Jyekundo when they were en route to Amdo. The Panchen Lama had suggested that they meet a little boy from Lunba village not far from Taktser. When the Panchen Lama had met the little boy in Kumbum monastery some months before, the child had pulled on the Panchen Lama's rosary and asked for his blessing. Later we learned that Reting Rinpoche had sent search parties to all three Tibetan regions—Amdo, Kham, and Central Tibet. My parents were honored just to know that a son of theirs was among the many being considered.

A few days after the search party departed, some fifteen soldiers from the army of Qinghai's governor-general, Ma Bufang, suddenly arrived at our house. Ma Bufang was a Hui, a Muslim, from a powerful military family. In 1928, after Chiang Kai-shek became president of the Chinese Republic, Qinghai (Amdo) had been officially designated a province, and Ma had assumed the post of governor-general. Despite Ma's high-sounding official title, he was in reality a notorious warlord. His troops were nothing more than bandits with a reputation for plundering, burning, and raping young women. Ma's forces had conducted a particularly vicious campaign against Tibetans in Golok, robbing, looting, and terrorizing thousands of innocent people. He was widely hated in Qinghai—by Tibetans most of all.

Generally, though, Ma Bufang had no more control over the lowest reaches of society than the earlier Manchus or Mongols. Even when local Huis in a nearby village viciously stabbed to death the Chinese owner of the mill where my family had our barley ground, claiming that the Chinese owner's pigs had been eating the Muslims' vegetables, Ma Bufang's government did nothing to intervene. No attempt was ever made to bring the murderers to justice.

Only when Ma Bufang sent his soldiers to collect taxes, measuring our families' fields with strings and stakes and calculating the tax burden according to the size of the plots, were ordinary people usually reminded of the existence of the province's governor-general. My family had already had a terrifying encounter with Ma Bufang's army. Sometime before the visit of the search team, Ma's tax collecting soldiers had set themselves up in our house, using it as their base for making sure the local villagers were paying their taxes. We had no choice but to host them.

Relatively well-off families such as my own had no trouble paying taxes, but many of the poorer families in our area were so deeply in debt that they had no way to pay. They would run away and hide when the tax collectors came, and the soldiers would chase them down and drag them back. The soldiers set up a gallows-like contraption in one of our courtyards to punish those they had captured. They strung the would-be tax evaders upside down by their ankles and beat them mercilessly with bamboo sticks as the villagers gathered around screaming and begging them to stop. We were a small and close-knit village, all of us Tibetan Buddhists. Many of us were relatives, and we got along well, helping each other during harvests and holding prayer festivals together. As I joined my fellow villagers to witness the beatings, I was screaming and crying, alternately holding my hands over my eyes to shield them from the awful sight and peeking through the cracks in my fingers to see what was going on.

My family was terrified to see the soldiers again. They said they were a military escort from Governor-General Ma Bufang with orders to take my parents and little brother Lhamo Thondup to Xining, the capital of Qinghai province where Ma Bufang had his official headquarters. They ordered my parents to pack immediately. My parents had no time to think. What could it mean for an ordinary peasant family to be taken from their home by Ma Bufang's soldiers and brought to Xining? Were they being arrested? My mother, father, and little brother left with the troops. My older sister, Tsering Dolma, was already married by then, so I was left alone with the servants, crying every day. No one ever told us why my parents and little brother were taken away. Only later did I learn that when they arrived in Xining, my family had been put in the government guesthouse, where they were comfortable and well fed.

News of my parents' capture soon reached Kumbum, and Kewtsang Rinpoche, the head of the search party, rushed to Xining to meet with Ma Bufang. The governor-general wanted to know whether my little brother was the reincarnation of the Dalai Lama. Kewtsang Rinpoche explained that my brother was one of at least three candidates, the other two being from Kham and Central Tibet. The final decision would not be made until all three candidates could be assembled in Lhasa, in the Jokhang, before the statue of Sakyamuni. He pleaded with Ma Bufang to release my parents and brother and allow them to return home. But Ma was suspicious. He demanded to know the truth. Kewtsang Rinpoche insisted he was telling the truth. Ma Bufang was adamant that he would not release my family until Kewtsang Rinpoche disclosed whether my brother was going to be the new Dalai Lama. Kewtsang Rinpoche continued to insist that the search was still going on and the final choice had yet to be made.

Ma Bufang finally relented, not by allowing my family to return home but by permitting us to move to the Kumbum monastery. Relations between the monastery and Ma Bufang's government were strained. Kumbum's taxes were arbitrarily decided by Ma Bufang himself, and he often demanded luxurious gifts, such as horses, silk brocades, and carpets. In putting my family under the care of the Kumbum monks, Ma elicited a guarantee from them that neither my family nor Kewtsang Rinpoche and his search party would leave without his permission. And he demanded a payment of one hundred thousand silver dollars. Kewtsang Rinpoche borrowed the money from some traders in Xining, promising to return it when the search team was back in Lhasa. My parents and brother moved to Kumbum, and my father rushed home immediately to take me there, too.

Weeks passed and then months, and still we were at Kumbum. The search team needed to communicate with Reting Regent in Lhasa and could not trust that the contents of messages sent by telegraph, from Xining via India to Lhasa, could be kept secret from Ma Bufang. Trusted messengers had to be sent by horseback to Lhasa. The quickest one-way trip, riding at breakneck speed and changing horses every twenty-five miles, took at least twenty days. An ordinary caravan trip took three months or more. It could take a couple months at top speed to get a single message back and forth. Rumors were rife. Everyone was speculating about who the next Dalai Lama might be, and many agreed that my brother was the

Lhamo Thondup in Kumbum before
being chosen as the Fourteenth Dalai Lama

most likely choice. The Kumbum monks were often the source of such gossip. Ma Bufang must have had spies among them, because he heard the rumors, too.

Finally, Kewtsang Rinpoche decided that the time had come to take my family to Lhasa. The Tibetan government would pay for our journey, and Kewtsang Rinpoche would arrange the trip. But he still needed Ma Bufang's permission. The negotiations stretched on for several more months as Kewtsang Rinpoche continued to insist that the final decision on the Dalai Lama had not been made, and the next Dalai Lama would be chosen only when all the candidates were assembled in Lhasa. He told my family the same thing, and promised that if we went to Lhasa and Lhamo Thondup was not chosen, we would be generously compensated. Kewtsang Rinpoche was an amazingly able negotiator in the face of the shrewd and greedy Ma Bufang. Ma wanted money, and Kewtsang Rinpoche wanted to bring my family to Lhasa with minimal concessions to the warlord's demands.

In the end, Ma extracted another three hundred thousand silver dollars in return for letting my family and the search team travel to Lhasa, bringing Ma's total to four hundred thousand silver dollars. Again, the money was borrowed from traders who plied the caravan route from Xining to Tibet. Kewtsang Rinpoche got safe passage for us all and did not have to declare who the next Dalai Lama would be. Even so, Kewtsang Rinpoche had to leave a junior member of the search team behind as a hostage in Kumbum in case the Tibetan side reneged. And Ma Bufang sent a contingent of his own people—three officials and their bodyguards—to accompany us to Lhasa. We began the journey in July 1939. Almost two years had passed since the search team first visited my family's house. My brother was just turning four years old.

4

My Brother Is Recognized as the Fourteenth Dalai Lama

Word that the next Dalai Lama might be residing in Kumbum had spread well beyond the grounds of the monastery, and so had the news that his entourage was about to depart. Thousands came to Kumbum to send us off—lamas, monks, and ordinary Tibetans alike. Crowds lined the route as we left the monastery grounds. Making our way to Kokonor Lake, nomads from Amdo, Xinjiang, and Mongolia came to greet us with presents of butter, cheese, yogurt, and meat. Everyone wanted to pay homage to the child they hoped and believed would be the next Dalai Lama. Everyone wanted the little boy's blessing. My deepest memory of the journey is still the kindness and generosity of the thousands of ordinary Tibetan people who came to wish us well.

On the first day out, I sat with my mother in a *palanquin*—a small, enclosed carriage sitting on poles strapped across two horses—while my brothers, Lobsang Samten and Lhamo Thondup, rode in another. But most people were on horseback, and I wanted to ride horseback too. I had been on horses often, but always with my father, clinging to him from behind, accompanying him as he went about his work. Now he agreed to let me try riding on my own. I caught on quickly, riding monkey-style, sprawled flat on my stomach, clinging to the reins. I rode like a monkey all the way to Lhasa.

Our entourage was part of a huge caravan of traders. By the time the various groups were fully assembled, we had representatives from some 1,500 trading houses, upwards of 5,000 people, some 5,000 horses and yaks, and countless mules carrying their heavy loads. Trading was a major business for Tibetans, and for some a source of great wealth. Amdo horses and mules dominated the trade between Amdo and Lhasa, but trade in alcohol, vinegar, cloth, silk, and even porcelain was also substantial. The big caravans generally traveled twice a year, once in the summer and then again in winter. Traveling by caravan both provided protection against the bandits, for whom the traders were valuable prey, and insured that seasoned muleteers could guide the uninitiated traveler through the perils of crossing high mountain passes and fast flowing rivers on horseback.

Preparations for such a caravan were meticulous. We had to carry enough food and provisions to last us through the entire three-and-a-half-month journey. Our mules were laden with Tibetan staples of *tsampa,* hard rolls, dried meat, and flour, and my mother made certain we had some variety with tea, persimmons, and dates.[1] The caravan was divided into two large parties. One group carried most of the provisions and took the lead, using yaks to carry the heavy loads. This group was generally about ten days ahead, and would have a camp set up and be prepared to restock our supplies by the time the second group arrived. The second group carried only enough to feed us until we reached the next camp, with mostly horses and mules carrying the loads. We generally stayed several days at each new camp—resting, washing our clothes, and packing the next round of provisions. We followed the same route from Xining to Lhasa that traders and pilgrims had been crossing for centuries. The path was so wide and flat and well-worn that no one could get lost. We traveled mostly by dark, setting out after midnight and stopping by mid-morning. The sun was strong on the high plateau, and we thought the sunlight was bad for the animals' eyes. The nights were cool, and the horses were faster and friskier then. The summer weather was beautiful, with bright sunshine, no rain, and a cloudless deep blue sky. The stars were bright in the night and guided our way. When the moon was full, the whole night was filled with light. Lhasa was due west.

We unloaded our horses and mules and pitched our white cotton tents every morning when we arrived at a new site. Our horses and mules were kept in check by tying a long, strong rope around three of their legs, loose enough to allow them to walk but tight enough that they could not go very fast or far and would be close enough to find even in the dark before we set out. We slept on rugs spread on the ground. We had tea and tsampa in the morning when we arrived and my mother's homemade noodles with soup and sometimes a little dried meat as our evening meal. About once a week someone among us would kill a yak or a sheep and share the freshly killed meat with the neighbors. Muslims and Tibetans traveled together in these caravans, the Muslim men distinguishable by the white caps they wore on their heads. Tibetans dislike killing animals them-selves, and the Muslims could always be relied on to slaughter them for us without asking a fee.

The entire trip was like riding on horseback through a vast nature reserve. In Amdo, I had seen a few foxes or wolves occasionally but nothing like what we saw on the way to Lhasa. Wild animals and birds were everywhere. As we camped along the banks of Kokonor Lake, we saw thousands of red tufted cranes and wild geese. My brothers and I would chase the cranes, trying to catch them, but they were never frightened. They just ran away. Kokonor is Mongo-lian for what is known in Chinese as Qinghai Lake—the largest lake anywhere in China or Tibet and situated at an altitude of some ten thousand feet. A small Tibetan monastery sits on one of its islands, accessible only in winter when the whole lake freezes and thousands of Tibetans circumambulate the frozen lake gaining merit for their next life.

Later, when we passed through the vast grasslands of Chang-tang, the entire area was filled with antelopes, wild yaks, musk deer, gazelles, wild goats, sheep, and wild ass. Sometimes on the distant mountains we would see thousands of wild yaks, black dots on a background of green. Sometimes huge herds of wild ass would run alongside us, thousands at a time. None of the animals were ever afraid. Today, Changtang has become the victim of wanton poaching, and its once rich wildlife has been decimated.

When we came to the Tsaidam Basin, we traveled more than two months and hundreds of miles without seeing even one small village or a single human being who was not part of our caravan. Somewhere before we crossed the border into Central Tibet, Phala, a monk official from an aristocratic family who was already rising in the ranks of the Tibetan government, hosted a picnic for my brother Lobsang Samten and me. It was there at his small hilltop monastery that I had my first taste of delicious pineapple and discovered that food could be preserved in a can. Later Phala would become my brother's lord chamberlain and one of the most powerful men in Tibet.

An amazing contingent of one hundred Tibetan troops greeted us as we passed the Tangla ridge and crossed the border into Central Tibet. Their colorful uniforms, fur caps, and the rifles slung over their shoulders were a stark contrast to Ma Bufang's motley Qinghai troops. The army escorted us the rest of the way to Lhasa, and the nature of our journey changed. The personal attendants of the Thirteenth Dalai Lama had accompanied the army, and they immediately took over the care of my brother. They had brought the former Dalai Lama's accoutrements of travel—huge tents as big as houses, cooking equipment, food, and coracles made of yak or sheepskin to take us across the rivers ahead. It was mid-September by then. We were almost three months into our journey. In two more days we were in Nagchuka, some one hundred miles from Lhasa.

It was when we reached Nagchuka, just inside Central Tibet, that the General Assembly in Lhasa made the formal, official announcement. My little brother Lhamo Thondup from Taktser village in Amdo was the fourteenth reincarnation of the Dalai Lama. The announcement had been delayed until our entourage was safely across the Qinghai border inside Central Tibet and in the Tibetan army's hands. But Kewtsang Rinpoche had known all along that my brother was the final choice, that there would be no gathering of the other candidates in the Jokhang. My parents probably knew, too, though they never told me. Had Ma Bufang known that Lhamo Thondup was the new Dalai Lama, he probably would have demanded millions of silver dollars. Ma Bufang had been outsmarted. The small delegation he had sent to accompany us stayed with us all the way to Lhasa, and the leader of the group, Ma Sizhang, transliterated my name into Chinese: Jiale Dunzhu (嘉乐顿铢). But Ma Bufang's authority ended once we crossed the border into Central Tibet. The warlord would get no more silver dollars from us.

Reting Regent himself came to meet us in Nagchuka, welcoming us with gifts and elaborate ceremonies. The regent is the singularly most powerful person from the time one Dalai Lama passes and the next one reaches majority at the age of eighteen and formally comes to power. During the interregnum, the regent is charged with overseeing the search for the new Dalai Lama, supervising the young Dalai Lama's education, and leading the government. The Tibetan General Assembly had selected the leading rinpoche of Reting monastery to assume the role of regent in 1934, not long after the Thirteenth Dalai Lama's death. Reting Rinpoche was only twenty-three years old at the time, but the choice of him as regent had been a popular one, supported by the Kashag (the Tibetan cabinet), the General Assembly, the leading lamas of all the major monasteries, and ordinary Tibetans alike. His previous incarnation is said to have had a close relationship with the Thirteenth Dalai Lama. In 1904, when the Younghusband expedition began marching toward Lhasa, forcing the Dalai Lama to flee, he had sought refuge in the Reting monastery about a day's ride away.

As the ceremonies to celebrate the choice of the new Dalai Lama began in Nagchuka, suddenly everything was strange and new—the officials, secretaries, and monks; the processions going on for hours; the food; the tea; the incense; the drums; the horns; the cymbals; the huge masks; the colorful costumes; the dancing and dramatic reenactments. The ceremonies continued for days, and again the no-mads came to celebrate and receive the blessings of the new Dalai Lama. Everyone was overjoyed at the outcome of the search. Every day was like a magnificent fair. Something marvelous was happening during every waking hour.

From Nagchuka, we reached the Reting monastery, a small and beautiful edifice perched atop a hill under a forest of juniper and pine, with the Kyichu River flowing below and Lhasa just seventy miles away. The Reting labrang was one of the wealthiest, and Reting Regent, like my father, was an avid trader of horses. His stables housed dozens of the magnificent creatures. After we settled in Lhasa, the regent often invited my father to the elaborate picnics on his monastery grounds where his staff staged a variety of horse-riding competitions. My father visited him often. The caravans bringing Amdo horses back to Lhasa for my father always stopped at the Reting monastery, giving the regent his pick of the best.

Rigya, a small monastery only five kilometers outside of Lhasa, was our final stop. Thousands of people were already there, awaiting the arrival of the new Dalai Lama, living in a small city of white tents that dotted the fields in a series of concentric squares. Lamas and monks from the three great monasteries of Lhasa—Drepung, Sera, and Ganden[2]—came to greet us, together with monks and lamas from the fifty or sixty small monasteries in the surrounding area. Ordinary citizens from Lhasa came, too. From inside his tent, the new Dalai Lama received everyone who had come to greet him, accepting their presents and giving them his blessing.

It was from Rigya that I got my first glimpse of the Potala Palace. There it suddenly was, far in the distance, atop Red Hill, its red and white exteriors a startling contrast to the intensely blue Tibetan sky, so impressive, so beautiful and huge. King Songtsen Gampo, in whose army my ancestors served, is said to have meditated on the site. Earlier kings had built edifices on the hill but it was not until 1645, during the reign of the Great Fifth Dalai Lama, that construction of the palace as we know it today began. Building continued for years after the Great Fifth's death. Even today, I still wonder, in awe, how it could have

Potala Palace

been built. Beijing's Forbidden City pales in comparison. For us Tibetans, the Potala Palace is the symbol our country, the embodiment of our history, testimony to the inseparability of the Dalai Lama and Tibet. It was about to become my brother's new winter home.

From Rigya, the final leg of the journey began, with Reting Regent accompanying the new Dalai Lama. As we entered Lhasa on October 8, 1939, the streets were lined with thousands of people in strange and colorful costumes and amazingly elaborate headdresses, some in the traditional Tibetan style, some in the Mongolian style, and others in imitation of the Manchu imperial court. We went straight to the Jokhang, the great temple, where, more than a decade before, my uncle had toppled a butter lamp in front of the sacred statue of Sakyamuni and seen it as an omen of good fortune yet to come. All the high officials of Tibet were there, and again our days were filled with ceremonies, celebration, prayers, and visits to other temples and monasteries—Drepung, Sera, Ganden, and Ramoche.

Only after we arrived in Lhasa did Kewtsang Rinpoche tell my family how the choice of the Fourteenth Dalai Lama had been made and how well my little brother had performed. Before he died, the Thirteenth Dalai Lama had told Reting Rinpoche that his next incarnation would be found in eastern Tibet, meaning Amdo, where my family lived. After his appointment, Reting Regent, together with a contingent of high lamas and ranking representatives of the Tibetan government, sought further clues to the reincarnation's whereabouts in the sacred, clear blue waters of Lhamo Latso lake. Sitting at a height of seventeen thousand feet and located near the Chokhorgyal monastery some one hundred miles southeast of Lhasa, Lhamo Latso is said to be the home of Palden Lhamo, the protector deity of the Dalai Lama and Tibet. It holds spiritual powers capable of emanating visions and foretelling the future. Gazing into its deep blue waters can bring forth images that will guide the search party in its quest for a reincarnation. A visit to the lake is one of the necessary first steps in discovering the clues as to where the new Dalai Lama will be found.[3]

Reting Regent's visit to the lake brought forth at least four visions that were to guide the search. One was the Tibetan letter *ah,* which the regent concluded was the *ah* of Amdo in eastern Tibet and also, perhaps, the *ah* of the famous hermit Agama Repa, who had spent years meditating in Shartsong, the small monastery near my home that had already played so large a part in my family's life. Another was the letter *ka* for the Kumbum monastery. And he saw a vision of a village house with a stupa in the courtyard and a small white dog.[4]

It must have been in 1906, when the Thirteenth Dalai Lama passed through my family's village on his way to Shartsong and my father had caught a glimpse of him from my grandmother's shoulders and my grandmother had scooped up the ashes from his cooking fire, that the Thirteenth Dalai Lama had seen my family's house. When the search party sent Reting Regent a sketch of our house with the stupa in the courtyard, it conformed perfectly to the house the regent had seen in the vision in Lhamo Latso. And our family had a little white dog. It was my Lhasa apso. I was very fond of that dog.

Kewtsang Rinpoche also told us how pleasantly surprised the search party had been when my little brother correctly chose all the articles that had belonged to the previous Dalai Lama—his rosaries, drum, and walking stick. He had also known that the jacket Kewtsang Rinpoche was wearing was not his own. "Why are you wearing someone else's jacket?" Lhamo Thondup had asked. "That's mine." Indeed, the jacket had belonged to the Thirteenth Dalai Lama. Lhamo Thondup had also asked the search party why they had come so late, as though he had known they would be coming and had expected them earlier.

Our first days in Lhasa were consumed by ceremony. Every day the new Dalai Lama sat high on his throne as hundreds of people lined up for hours to receive his blessing and offer their *khatas*—the white scarves that symbolize the purity of intention. The leading lamas—Reting, Tsomoling, Kundeling, and Sakya—were there, together with all of the government officials and abbots and monks from monasteries for miles around. The honored guests— the Kashag ministers and Tibetan officials—looked on as ordinary citizens from Lhasa and far flung villages made their offerings and prostrated themselves before the new Dalai Lama. Several foreign representatives were in the audience, too, including Wu Zhongxin from China, Basil Gould representing Great Britain, and diplomats from Nepal and Bhutan. My family and I sat in a special spot adjacent to the Dalai Lama's throne. My little brother remained invariably poised, attentive, and calm throughout the endless ceremonies. He must already have begun receiving instructions from the lamas who were about to become his teachers.

Even after all these years, my memory of those days is still vivid. I was so happy. I was more than happy. I was thrilled. The whole trip had been fantastic, each part of the journey more exciting than the last. Never could a little eleven-year-old village boy like me have imagined the drama that had become my family's life. In one giant leap, all the calamities that had befallen us a few short years before had been transformed into almost miraculous good fortune. My family had reached all the way to heaven. Our lives had changed forever.

5

The Dalai Lama's New Life

With my brother ensconced in the Potala, my family was set up in a huge house just outside the palace gate, where we looked up at the palace and the Dalai Lama could look down on us. Reting Regent and the Dalai Lama's monk attendants made every effort to reduce the little boy's pain at being separated from his family. In the beginning, we continued to see my brother almost every day, and he could visit us whenever he liked. Our brother Lobsang Samten, two years older than the Dalai Lama, lived with him in the palace, thus allowing the Dalai Lama a playmate closer to his own age than the elderly monks who looked after him. The two boys were tutored together, and they studied, played, and sometimes fought together. My mother often joined them for Sunday lunch, bringing her home-made breads and pastries and staying afterward to visit.

My brother lived in the same rooms on the top floor of the eastern wing of the Potala as those occupied by most of the dalai lamas before him. His quarters included a bedroom, a private chapel, and several large anterooms, all decorated like temples, full of ornate Buddhist thangkas and art. Three personal attendants, whose offices and living quarters were in anterooms just outside his bedroom, looked after him.

*Dalai Lama's mother on roof of family house with
Potala Palace in background*

Reting Regent, the Dalai Lama's official representative and
the highest and most powerful official in the land, selected my
brother's staff. One, the master of the kitchen,[1] was in charge of
the Dalai Lama's general welfare, including his living quarters and
meals. The huge kitchen was in a separate building and had upwards of forty cooks, not just for the Dalai Lama but for members
of his staff and government officials as well. The second attendant,
the master of the robes,[2] was in charge of his wardrobe and dress.
On most days, the Dalai Lama wore the garb of an ordinary young
monk, but the numerous religious ceremonies over which he offici-
ated during the year each required a different and often ornate type
of dress. The third attendant, the master of the rituals,[3] oversaw
the Dalai Lama's religious studies and ceremonial rituals. Standing over the attendants was the chikyab kenpo, a sort of chief of
staff,[4] who was in charge of all the monk officials, the Dalai Lama's
staff, and the Dalai Lama's treasury. The staff also included the lord
chamberlain (doyer chenmo),[5] who had a more secular role and
was a bridge between Dalai Lama and the government. Together,

Dalai Lama on left, Lobsang Samten on right, surrounded by
Dalai Lama's personal attendants at the Potala Palace

these five men were responsible for the Dalai Lama's daily spiritual and secular activities and for his well-being and comfort. They were thus very close and devoted to my brother, sacrificing their own lives to bring the little boy up.

The chief of staff was particularly close to the Dalai Lama, and since he was the most senior and powerful, he was generally also the most elderly. Even the youngest chief of staff must have been at least sixty years old. Several of the elderly men died while the Dalai Lama was growing up and new ones came in.

Beyond the confines of my brother's living quarters were the palace's hundreds of rooms, chapels, and ceremonial halls, all filled with the priceless treasures of Tibet—some 698 murals, 10,000 statues and scrolls, priceless jade and silver, 3,000 images of the Buddha and other deities, and ancient sacred manuscripts written in ink of powdered gold, silver, and turquoise. The walls were hung with colorful thangkas depicting stories of the Lord Buddha, Tibet, Tibetan saints, and the life histories of the dalai lamas. The tombs of all the dalai lamas, beginning with the Fifth, were within the palace walls. The tomb of the Great Fifth alone stands over fifty feet tall, covered with 7,500 pounds of pure gold gilding and even more priceless jewels. Many of the Dalai Lama's leading officials and staff also lived in the palace, including the regent, the lord chamberlain, the chief of staff, the Dalai Lama's tutors and some 250 monks from Namgyal, the Dalai Lama's personal monastery. The offices of the Tibetan government were housed there, too.

For all its grandeur and awe, the Potala Palace was not an easy place for a little four-year-old boy to live. It was still primitive and rough. There was no electricity. The rooms were dimly lit by thousands of butter lamps, and the air was permeated with the smell of centuries of burning, often rancid, butter. The edible offerings left before the countless small altars scattered throughout the palace insured that the population of mice outnumbered that of the humans by the thousands. There was no heat. The only way to stay warm during the winter was to bundle up in layers of wool. I visited my brothers often, and together we explored the countless rooms, sliding down the slick wooden banisters that connected one floor to another. But I would have been frightened to live in a place like that. Had I been selected to become the Dalai Lama, I think I would have run away. I preferred my own room and living with my parents. At least we had a stove to keep us warm.

Our lives were very different. My brother, after all, was the new Dalai Lama and had to be groomed as such, following the same rigorous training and education of all the Dalai Lama's before him. Even as a young child, the Dalai Lama's regimen was strict. He was awakened at six in the morning, and began the day with prayer and meditation. His personal attendants brought him a breakfast of tea and tsampa with honey, which was eaten in his room. At the same time, in a large antechamber just beyond the Dalai Lama's private quarters, the regent, the lord chamberlain, and the four cabinet members also assembled for breakfast. Beyond them in another hall, another group of monk and lay officials was served. Everyone, regardless of rank, brought his own wooden bowl, carried in his robes. They ate seated on the floor on cushions before short, individual wooden tables. Breakfast began with three kinds of Tibetan tea, brought in from the kitchen and served by four or five monks. Following tea, everyone was given buttered rice topped with a small sweet fruit and yogurt. The last course was a piece of Tibetan bread, sweet and fried. Some 150 monks and officials took breakfast in these antechambers every day, after which the officials received their daily work instructions, and members of the Kashag met the Dalai Lama in his chambers to pay their respects and receive his blessing before dispersing to their offices.

My brother remained in his private quarters, his day intermixed with scheduled sessions of study and tutoring, play, meditation, memorization, meals, and tea. His meals were always simple—tea, broth, sometimes with a little meat, yogurt, and often bread that my mother had cooked. Sprinkled in with the tutoring and prayers and play were meetings with the lord chamberlain, who was responsible for initiating the Dalai Lama into the political realm and teaching him how to interact with officials and foreign dignitaries.

During the summer months, the Dalai Lama moved from the Potala to the Norbulingka (meaning "Jewel Park"), the eighteenth-century palace some four kilometers away. His departure from the Potala was always a grand occasion, with a procession of high-ranking officials, leading lamas, his bodyguards, and a contingent from the Tibetan army. My parents and I were part of the procession, too, riding on horseback alongside the Dalai Lama as he sat almost shielded from view inside his ornately painted sedan chair. Thousands of citizens would line the streets to catch a glimpse of the young Dalai Lama as the procession passed by. The entire Tibetan government moved into the Norbulingka together, re-creating within its grounds the same daily rituals and offices as in the Potala. Only the monks of the Namgyal monastery stayed behind.

We lived in the Norbulingka, too, just outside the yellow, inner wall that enclosed the Dalai Lama and his attendants. Surrounded by lush, green, flower-filled gardens with its own miniature zoo, the Norbulingka was more livable and less imposing than the Potala. The grounds provided plenty of opportunities for little boys to romp and play. Family visits were easier and more frequent there. My brother would sometimes bolt from his attendants and run unannounced to join us.

The most important aspect of the Dalai Lama's daily life was the religious instruction he received from the eminent and learned reincarnated lamas who served as his tutors. Their pupil was the reincarnation of Chenrezig, Bodhisattva of Compassion, and the tutors were responsible for insuring that he fulfilled that role. They were selected by Reting Regent and were expected to serve for life.[6] Taktra Rinpoche was his first tutor, but Ling Rinpoche soon became the senior tutor with Trijang Rinpoche as the junior one. Ling Rinpoche was the perfect teacher, so highly learned and respected that he was almost worshipped by everyone who knew him. He personally provided most of the Dalai Lama's religious instruction, and he remained devoted to the Dalai Lama until his death years later in India, with never even a whisper of controversy. Both the Trichang and Taktra Rinpoches, later and at different times, became contentious and controversial: Taktra for his involvement in political scandal while he was serving as regent, and Trichang for his role in a religious controversy related to the worship of the controversial deity named Shugden.

The Dalai Lama's education began with the basics of reading, writing, and penmanship and progressed to memorization of sacred texts and increasingly complex and rigorous subjects. Like all dalai lamas before him, he was required to master logic, Tibetan art and culture, Sanskrit, medicine, and all the complexities of Buddhist philosophy, including dialectics and the art of debating, upon which one's grasp of Buddhist philosophy is judged. The final, highest stage of the Dalai Lama's formal studies was the Geshe exam, requiring him to subject himself to rigorous questioning and debate by Tibet's finest monastic scholars from the three great monasteries of Sera, Drepung, and Ganden.

My respect for my brother's education grew over time. Without his strict religious training and the discipline he acquired through long periods of meditation, he could never have attained the depth of spirituality, compassion, and equanimity that I was to later see in him so powerfully. His sense of justice without revenge, of forgiveness for all, of compassion even for those who have done wrong, and his utter absence of hatred are qualities that can be acquired only after long years of study and meditation. They are the qualities that later made my brother the man of greatness that he was to become and who so many people everywhere revere.

6

My Family's New Life

My family was officially anointed into the aristocracy with my brother's ascension to the Dalai Lama's throne. Our original family name of Taktser was changed to Taklha. My father was given the title Yabshi Kung, reserved for the father of the Dalai Lama. He had no official government position, but his status as the Yabshi Kung was higher than that of government officials, so he attended the morning breakfasts with the ranking officials and was accorded great respect. As the years progressed and other members of the family saw the Dalai Lama less often, my father still saw him almost every day.

My mother became the Gyayum Chemo, the Great Mother, and her name was changed from Diki Tsering to Lhamotso. Almost overnight, she went from being an ordinary, illiterate peasant woman to become the Gyayum Chemo, responsible for entertaining the whole panoply of Tibetan officials, aristocrats, society ladies, and monks from the highest to the middle ranks.

Reting Regent did everything possible to ensure that our material life matched our newly exalted status as members of the nobility. When we first moved to Lhasa, everything we needed—our housing, food, clothes, brocades, and cash—was provided by the government, paid for from the government's treasury. Soon, Reting Regent arranged for us to be given five large estates: two near Lhasa, on the other side of the Kyichu River; two in southern Tibet, near the Indian border; and another given to us by the aristocratic Phala family, between Shigatse and Gyantze.

Traditionally, Tibet had three types of estates, one type owned by monasteries, another owned by members of the nobility, and the third owned by the government. The majority of estates were government-owned. Families working on the estates paid a yearly tax to the estate owner, in kind rather than in cash, and could be called upon to provide service to the owner and management of the estate. In the case of my family each of our estates was run by a senior manager and his staff, and our household servants, even those who worked in our home in Lhasa, also came from families on the estates. They were paid in kind, usually about sixty kilograms of tsampa a month and one new outfit of clothes a year. The household servants were provided with living quarters and daily meals from the common kitchen that served both the family and the household staff.

With the transfer of these estates, the Tibetan government no longer supported my family financially. Selling barley from the estates generally brought us the yearly equivalent of some 35,000 rupees, about $15,000 at the exchange rate then, and we received taxes and other income from the estates as well. My father continued to trade the same strong and lively horses that we had owned in Taktser. In Lhasa, though, he also had access to loans from the Dalai Lama's treasury and could trade on a much larger scale. The loans were generally between 15,000 and 20,000 rupees (about $8,000), and interest was about seven or eight percent a year, to be paid back in one or two years. Anyone could take out a loan so long as he had collateral to serve as a guarantee. Most borrowers deposited some of their family's jewelry until their loan was paid back.

Later, Reting Regent had a new three-story, fifty-room, Tibetan-style stone house constructed for us. The new house, like the previous one, was also adjacent to the Potala Palace. It was built to last for centuries and had several large courtyards, offices, storage areas, chapels, two huge kitchens, living quarters for both my family and

*Family and servants at Lhasa estate. The Great Mother is
holding the infant Jetsun Pema. Tsering Dolma and Gyalo Thondup
are standing behind their parents at the right.*

our dozen or so servants, and a banquet hall and meeting room that could accommodate upwards of forty people. We lived there, in Lhasa, rather than on our estates.

My favorite part of the house was the huge flat earthen roof where I grew flowers and vegetables and raised rabbits for a while. The rabbits were a gift from Reting Rinpoche and were doing fine until I returned home one day to find them being attacked by a flock of crows after I had opened their cages to let them run free. Two of the rabbits were already dead, and the crows had gouged out the eyes of several others. I quickly fetched a rifle and began shooting at the birds. I was astounded when hundreds of crows suddenly appeared from nowhere, hovering overhead and cawing noisily in complaint, protesting my attempts to kill their friends. Most of the crows survived, but all of the rabbits died.

People are sometimes surprised to discover that my family had guns. In those days, almost every Tibetan family owned guns and knew how to use them. Growing up, I was responsible for my family's collection, and I engaged in target practice at least once a week. We had some thirty weapons, including a few light machine guns. My failed attempt to kill the crows is the only time in my life that I have used a gun against sentient beings.

Thus, in Lhasa, my family came suddenly into considerable wealth. The wealth of most members of the Tibetan nobility, like reincarnated lamas and their labrangs, is usually accumulated over a period of centuries. Our wealth came quickly, thanks in large measure to the generosity and help of Reting Regent. But our wealth was not extravagant. We may have made more than other Tibetan nobility, but our new wealth came nowhere near that of the European aristocrats or Tibet's leading monastic labrangs. And despite our vast estates and huge house, our living conditions remained primitive and simple. We still had no electricity or running water.

My mother accepted her new role as the Great Mother with dignity and grace and learned to cope with all the complexities and complications of Lhasa high society and the Tibetan nobility. The Dalai Lama's birthday and Losar, the Tibetan lunar New Year, were holidays that required us to entertain most of Lhasa's high society, religious and lay alike. At New Year's, we would entertain nonstop for a week, hosting some fifty guests each day from ten in the morning on into the night. Morning tea and mahjong would be followed by an elaborate luncheon banquet. A walk through the gardens would end with another round of mahjong. The evening would conclude with an elaborate Chinese style banquet, in a somewhat pale imitation of what must have been served in the imperial court of Beijing. During our first few years in Lhasa, we relied on friends and neighbors to loan us the plates and dishes required for such formal entertaining. Not until 1946, when I first visited Beijing, was I able to buy the porcelain place settings worthy of such banquets. Many of the pieces I bought dated to the Kangxi and Qianlong periods and had been used on the Qing emperors' tables. I had the dishes and bowls meticulously wrapped in cotton and bamboo, packed in seven large wooden crates, and then shipped by truck from Beijing to Qinghai and from Qinghai to Lhasa

Two adults, standing, from left Phuntsog Tashi and his wife Tsering Dolma;
sitting, mother of Gyalo Thondup and Dalai Lama; children standing from left,
Tenzin Ngawang (son of Phuntsog Tashi and Tsering Dolma) Tenzin Choegyal
(youngest brother of Gyalo Thondup and the Dalai Lama), Khando Tsering
(daughter of Phuntsog Tashi and Tsering Dolma), Jetsun Pema,
younger sister of Gyalo Thondup and Dalai Lama.

by mule with one of the semiannual caravans. Only much later, when
I auctioned some of the tableware at Christie's, did I fully realize how
valuable the porcelain was. I had spent some $30,000 on 3,000 pieces
of porcelain; at Christie's, fifty pieces fetched a total of $50,000.

My mother's character never changed despite our new trappings
of aristocracy. During formal public ceremonies and the entertaining
she was required to do on special occasions, she wore the elaborate
brocades of the nobility. Otherwise, she continued to wear the simple Amdo-style *chuba* she had worn in Taktser village. She remained

a patient and kind-hearted woman, facing life serenely even in the most difficult of circumstances. She was a great lady and a wonderful mother to my sisters, my brothers, and me.

My father was criticized by many people in Lhasa both for being arrogant and for being too easily roused to anger. Some of those criticisms were deserved. He was an illiterate farmer who was suddenly thrust into an extraordinarily high position. As the Yabshi Kung, he was treated with such elaborate respect that perhaps he became spoiled. He dressed in the silk brocades worn by all high-ranking Tibetan officials and traveled with an entourage of five or six servants, attendants, and aides. One job of the retinue accompanying such high-ranking men is to clear the path for their master, and the accusations that my father's aides sometimes required people to dismount and step aside as he passed, that they sometimes hit horses or people who did not get out of the way fast enough, may well be true.

Sometimes my father abused his power, cursing people unnecessarily or charging higher-than-market prices in his business dealings. He was a notoriously hot-tempered man. The character trait seems to run in our family, passed perhaps through my grandmother's genes. Most members of my generation inherited it—my older brother Norbu, my sister Tsering Dolma, and me. Even the Dalai Lama has a temper that he had to learn to subdue. In fact, my native village, even all of Amdo, has a reputation for producing straight-talking, hot-tempered people. Maybe it is the effect of our mountain god. But five minutes after blowing up, our equanimity returns. Our anger has no lasting effect.

Ngabo Ngawang Jigme was the most famous object of my father's temper. Lhautara, a high-ranking monk official, and his deputy, Ngabo Ngawang Jigme, were in charge of the construction of our new house in Lhasa. My father heard rumors that Ngabo was siphoning off building materials to construct a house of his own. The rumor was almost certainly false. Ngabo had plenty of money to build his own house. But rumors and gossip were a staple of life in Lhasa, and my simple farmer father was susceptible to believing what he heard. I returned home one day to witness him chasing

Ngabo out of the house with a stick. My father's anger with Ngabo soon passed, and Ngabo became a good friend of the family. Later, Ngabo would play a singularly important role in Tibetan history. He was the governor of Chamdo when the Communists attacked.

My father, despite his temper, was not a bad man. He was deeply religious, often inviting the leading lamas of Lhasa to our home to share a meal, give us their blessings, and pray for us when we were sick. He was fond of me and treated me well. From the time I was a small child, he taught me to forgive and forget, to suppress my anger when wronged, to bear mistreatment with serenity, to remain silent even when abused. He knew that I would be rewarded later. His advice has served me well. My memories of my childhood with him are nothing but pleasant. I loved my parents.

7

My Life Changes

With my brother's installation as the Fourteenth Dalai Lama, my own role in the family changed, too. I was no longer to be groomed to take over the family business; I was to serve my brother instead. I entered Tarkhang, a private school where young boys from both aristocratic and ordinary families were educated for government service. The teaching was thoroughly traditional. There was no such thing as modern education in Lhasa. The Tibetan educational system was hopelessly backward. Several efforts had been made to introduce modern, British-style education, but all of them had failed, opposed by conservative monastic leaders who feared that educational reform could challenge Buddhism, the Tibetan way of life, and their own power.

Frank Ludlow, a British civil servant who had served with the Indian Educational Service and later (from 1942–1943) in his country's mission in Lhasa, was the first to try to introduce modern schools to Tibet. In 1923 he set up a school in Gyantse where students received a combination of both British- and Tibetan-style educations. The school was plagued with problems from the start. Ludlow was forced to close it some three years after it began.

In 1944 another effort was made to open a modern British-style school in Lhasa similar to Ludlow's in Gyantse. It had a British headmaster named Ronald Parker and classes were taught in both Tibetan and English. Many people were excited by the prospect of this new style of education, but the conservatives triumphed once again. The school was ordered closed only months after it opened.

Classes for the seventy students at Tarkhang began at six in the morning with everyone shouting religious texts aloud in unison. Then we turned to writing and grammar. We used wooden slabs spread with white dust to practice our writing, with a dry bamboo stick serving as a pen. Only after several months, when our writing skills were deemed sufficiently advanced, did we earn the right to use paper.

Even soccer, my favorite sport, was out of the question at Tarkhang. Leading officials in the Tibetan government had concluded that the ball so central to the game represented the head of the Lord Buddha, thus rendering kicking it scandalously sacrilegious. Our headmaster, Thubten Samphel, was more modern than most. He was a monk official who had been trained as a wireless operator in India, and he worked in the government treasury and ran the government's wireless station in addition to his responsibilities at school. But he still would not allow us to play soccer.

My schoolmates and I were great fans of the sport and took every opportunity to play surreptitiously. When we were finally caught, Thubten Samphel ordered that all twenty-two of us, two teams of eleven, be punished by twenty-five lashes with a bamboo pole on our bare behinds. The punishment took place outdoors, with four people holding each of us down, as we went one-by-one through a painful, five-minute, bloody ordeal with all of us crying and shouting at once. I was so angry that I ran home to my parents.

The Dalai Lama soon heard about the incident and came to the Norbulingka to inspect my wounds. He could not have been more than seven or eight years old at the time, but he shared my anger and wanted to order the principal to our house to receive his own punishment. My parents would have nothing to do with this. Thubten

Samphel, in their eyes, had every right to use corporal punishment on errant students. Punishing disobedient schoolboys by use of a bamboo stick was the norm back then. Later, when the headmaster came on his own to explain why he had ordered the beatings, my parents sided with him. They continued to hold Thubten Samphel in high esteem. The use of corporal punishment in the school continued. We never played soccer again. Only later did the game become both a popular and an acceptable sport.

The only way for a Tibetan to receive a modern education was to study abroad. As early as 1912, the reform-minded Thirteenth Dalai Lama had sent four young Tibetans to study in Rugby, England, in the belief that Tibet needed modern technology and that a mastery of English was a prerequisite for its introduction. He asked Lungshar, one his most able and trusted officials, to accompany them. Lungshar, like the students, learned English, traveled widely in Europe, and came face to face with Western democracy. He became convinced that Tibet needed major political reform, and upon his return, he became a powerful advocate for change and the leader of a new progressive faction within the government. Serving officially as the minister of finance and domestic affairs, he made tremendous contributions to the cause of reform during the Thirteenth Dalai Lama's reign, becoming one of Tibet's most important, respected, and popular officials.

By the early 1920s, a few aristocratic families, such as the Tarings and Tsarongs, also began sending their children to study abroad, usually at the British-run St. Joseph's North Point and Loreto Convent schools in the Indian Himalayan hill station of Darjeeling.[1] With their excellent English and proper British manners, these young aristocrats mingled easily with British officials in both India and Tibet. They were rewarded with special licenses to import goods from British-held India. The wealth of the Taring and Tsarong trading houses expanded considerably as a result, and these two influential families became part of an informal pro-British faction.

Lungshar and his political reforms did not fare so well. In 1934, after the death of the Thirteenth Dalai Lama and before my brother

had been identified as his reincarnation, Lungshar was accused of
plotting to overthrow the Tibetan government with the intention
of instituting a Communist system like the one that had come to
nearby Mongolia when it became a satellite of the Soviet Union
some ten years before. The charge was ridiculous, but Lungshar lost
his political battle and nearly his life. Lungshar and at least ten of
his supporters, including two of the Thirteenth Dalai Lama's trusted
personal attendants, were arrested. Lungshar was sentenced to life
imprisonment, and the officials overseeing his case decreed that his
eyes be gouged out. That was a rare and drastic punishment in Tibet.
Of the many reforms that the Thirteenth Dalai Lama had attempted
to introduce during his reign, one was a softening of the punishments to criminals. The death penalty was abolished except in ex-
traordinary cases, as were punishments meant to mutilate and maim
the convicted. Indeed, one of Buddhism's core tenets is the prohibition against bringing harm to any sentient being. But Lungshar's
punishment was administered nonetheless.

The punishment began by drugging Lungshar with alcohol and
herbal medicine to numb the pain. Then the knucklebones of a yak
were placed on each of the convicted man's temples and gradually
tightened by means of a leather strap wound around his head. The
method was meant to force the eyes to pop out, after which burning
oil would be poured into the empty sockets. But the method only
half succeeded. Only one eye popped out. The other had to be extracted by means of a knife.

Lungshar's bitter fate remains a tragic example of how vehe-
mently the conservative Tibetan elite opposed almost any effort at
modernization and reform. His punishment haunted me even as a
child. I worried that Reting Regent, who had been in charge of the
search for the Fourteenth Dalai Lama and was so generous to my
family, might have participated in such a cruel decision. Only much
later did I learn from Lungshar's son Lhalu that Reting had not been
part of the decision and had been distressed to learn of the verdict.[2]
Reting had just been appointed regent then, and the search for the
Fourteenth Dalai Lama had not yet begun. He did not want to be

associated with such drastic measures. He was a monk, after all, and could not condone anything so cruel and inhumane. The decision to expel Lungshar from office and to gouge out his eyes came from Trimon, the ultraconservative chief of the Kashag, who was Lungshar's leading opponent and saw his proposed reforms as a threat. Trimon wanted to wipe Lungshar out politically. But he wanted to keep him alive both to prolong his suffering and to guard against the dead man's ghost returning to haunt him. Reting and Trimon were enemies from the start.

NOT LONG AFTER MY STUDIES at Tarkhang began, Reting Regent suggested to my parents that I be sent to China to study. My uneducated peasant father could not have fully understood what studying in China might mean. But he readily agreed to the regent's suggestion.

The idea of a Tibetan being educated in China was novel. While a few aristocrats had studied in British schools, hardly any Tibetans had studied in China. China was almost completely unknown to Tibetans in Lhasa, and the Chinese were an unknown people. Only a handful of Tibetans in Lhasa spoke Chinese, my brother-in-law, Phuntsog Tashi Takla, among them. But he had learned his Chinese in Amdo.

Reting Regent's suggestion made sense. He had taken to heart the warnings of the Thirteenth Dalai Lama in his last will and testament predicting that if Tibet did not find a way to defend itself, what had happened in Mongolia when it became a puppet of the Soviets could happen in Tibet as well. In Mongolia, the practice of reincarnated lamas had been forbidden after the Soviet-backed government was established, and many religious practices had been brought to a halt. Monasteries had been looted, and their property had been confiscated.

Reting Regent had also taken seriously the Thirteenth Dalai Lama's admonition to maintain friendly relations with both India and China, the two great powers along the Tibetan border. Some people have argued that Reting Regent was too pro-China. But he was not pro-China; he was searching for a way to balance Britain and China, one against the other. The British influence had already expanded too far, he thought, with the door to trade forced open and the incorporation of the Tibetan territories of Ladakh, Sikkim, and Bhutan into the British Empire. Many Tibetans were suspicious of the British, believing they could not be trusted either to maintain Tibet's territorial integrity or to support us against outside intruders.

Reting Regent saw better ties with China as a way to balance the demands from Great Britain. When a Guomindang delegation headed by Huang Musong attended the funeral of the Thirteenth Dalai Lama and presented the Tibetan government with a new telegraph system, they were allowed to leave a couple of men behind to run the new machines. Later, Chiang Kai-shek sent another delegation, led by Wu Zhongxin, the head of China's Office of Mongolian and Tibetan Affairs, to attend the Dalai Lama's enthronement ceremony and present His Holiness with a *khata*. The telegraph officers were gone by then, but Reting and the Kashag permitted the Guomindang to open a small office in Lhasa that later became an informal Chinese mission, similar to the offices run by the British and the Nepalese. The Tibetan government, in turn, set up an Office of Tibet—first in the Nationalist's wartime capital of Chongqing and later in Nanjing. Both offices functioned essentially as consulates.

Reting was committed to the continuing independence of Tibet. He saw our growing ties with China as an essential balance against British India. This is why he wanted me to study in China. Reting knew that, for better or worse, China was going to have an influence on Tibet. I was being groomed to become an advisor to the Dalai Lama. If a member of the Dalai Lama's family, so clearly slated for government service, had a good understanding of China—its history, culture, politics, and language—surely he would be helpful in our interactions with the Chinese. Such knowledge and understanding, an ability to see China as the Chinese saw themselves, could be important for the Dalai Lama and his government as they managed relations with the two great countries.

I began studying Chinese with Reting Regent's Chinese interpreter, the Muslim Ma Baoxun.[3] After four years of studying, I spoke
broken Chinese and had a solid foundation in reading and writing.
By the fall of 1945, I was ready to depart for Nanjing.

Reting called me to his monastery shortly before I was to leave.
My father had been there often, enjoying the picnics, horse races,
and shooting practices he staged on the beautiful grounds, but this
was only my second visit. Drastic political changes had taken place
in Lhasa by then. Reting had resigned from his post as regent just
before the Tibetan lunar New Year of Losar, in February 1941. My
family had been astonished. Rumors had been circulating in Lhasa
about omens pointing to impending personal disaster, even death,
if Reting did not step down from his official position for a time of
meditation and prayer. Reting had taken those warnings to heart. I
still remember the meeting when Reting told us his plan. He assured
us that his resignation was only temporary. He would be back in
six months. He was searching for a suitable caretaker regent in the
meantime, a wise and spiritual lama who could assume temporary
control. He chose Taktra Rinpoche, the elderly and learned lama
who served as one of the Dalai Lama's tutors, to serve as a temporary
interim regent during Reting's retreat. Reting trusted Taktra. The
Dalai Lama's tutor was a spiritual monk with no interest in politics.
He was not the type of person to make a grab for power.

My parents had tried to persuade Reting Regent not to resign,
even temporarily. They hoped that even if he needed time for retreat,
he could remain as regent and continue to live in Lhasa. We had
expected him to remain as regent until my brother reached majority. When Reting insisted on resigning temporarily, we still expected
that when the six-month retreat was over, Taktra Rinpoche would
step down and Reting would resume his regency.

But the retreat that was to end after six months lasted almost four
years. Not until December 1944 did Reting emerge from his monastery and return to his residence in Lhasa to discuss the transfer of
power with Taktra. He entered Lhasa full of pageantry and fanfare
accompanied by a retinue of hundreds of richly dressed monks and

officials astride their splendid horses. My father accompanied the Kashag to the outskirts of Lhasa to welcome him. I was in the crowd lining the streets to witness his entry into the city.

But something went wrong with Reting's plan. Taktra Regent had become politically ambitious. When Reting met with Taktra to discuss the transition, Taktra refused to relinquish the post. Reting—and my family—were shocked.

I still do not understand why Reting resigned or why he believed the warnings about omens that he might die if he did not retreat into a long period of meditation. Perhaps he was tired of the job and wanted a break. Serving as regent and running the Tibetan government was a complicated, difficult business, and political tensions were high. The interregnums between the death of one dalai lama and the assumption of power by the next have often been filled with strife. Several dalai lamas never reached majority, dying during their childhood of illnesses often suspected but never proved to have been deliberately induced. Others died in suspicious circumstances not long after assuming power.[4] The deaths of the young dalai lamas were never officially recorded as murders. There could never be any real proof that what began as a stomachache was really slow death by poison. Many may have known of such crimes but none would have dared to raise a voice in protest. The protester's tongue could be cut out, his throat slit. Power struggles were an inherent part of the Tibetan political and ecclesiastical systems. Reting's regency was no exception.

During the three weeks I spent with Reting before my departure for China, we talked every day about the problem of Taktra, trying to understand why the plan to return the regency to Reting had failed, why such a simple and foolish old lama was still holding on to power. Reting was still angry and indignant. He felt badly betrayed. And he had not given up. He was still biding his time, pondering how to return to his post.

I suspect that the British were behind Taktra's refusal to step aside. Hugh Richardson, then chief of the British mission in Lhasa, was openly wary of the potentially growing influence of China over

Tibet. He wanted to ensure that Great Britain remained the dominant international player. He was one of the people who saw Reting as too pro-China, and Reting was, in any case, a difficult man to manipulate. I can imagine Richardson working behind the scenes at Lhasa's social gatherings, mingling with officials and collaborating with the aristocrats, subtly manipulating them to turn against Reting, convincing Taktra's managers to dismiss Reting's supporters and appoint younger, less qualified anti-Reting people instead. I even suspect that the British had encouraged the rumors about the omens predicting the regent's death if he did not resign. Taktra would never have spread such gossip on his own. He allowed himself and the managers around him to become tools of the pro-British aristocrats.

When the time came for me to take my leave and say good-bye to Reting Rinpoche, he asked me to deliver a message on his behalf to President Chiang Kai-shek upon my arrival in China. It was a verbal message. Reting wanted me to tell President Chiang that he hoped the president would support his efforts to return as regent and use his good offices to persuade Taktra to hand the regency back. I was just sixteen years old at the time and had no idea what Chiang Kai-shek's "good offices" might be or what effect they might have.

But I never delivered Reting's message to the Chinese president. Reting was dead before I could find the right opportunity, and so was my father. A power struggle was going on in Lhasa, and both my father and Reting were its victims. The Taktra faction, consisting of some twenty high-ranking conservative officials, was determined to remove all opposition and ultimately to depose my brother by claiming that he was not the legitimate reincarnation. They had their own candidate to replace him, a young lama, Detuk Rinpoche, who was about my brother's age and had been one of the three candidates to become the new Dalai Lama. They wanted to bring up their Dalai Lama under the tutelage of the forces behind Taktra. Both my father and Reting Rinpoche were standing in their way.

My father was the first of their victims. News of his death reached me shortly after I arrived in Nanjing. My father had been one of

Reting's strongest supporters. Reting had been extraordinarily generous to my family, and we were grateful for his kindnesses. It was clear that so long as my father was alive, his support for Reting Regent would continue, and he might help Reting find a way to resume his regency.

My father's death was never officially ruled a murder. The official verdict was that he had died of natural causes. But I and many others, including my mother, believe that he was poisoned with a rare herb called *langchen nyonpa*, "mad elephant" in English, that can only be found in the high snow mountains of Tibet. The poison shuts down the digestive system. Eating and drinking become impossible, and the victim gradually starves. My father became ill shortly after dinner during a visit to Ramagang, our family estate just south of Lhasa across the Kyichu River. We believe on good evidence that a junior manager in my family's household, acting on instructions from the Taktra government, administered the poison. The manager was not acting on his own. He was merely a tool in the larger plot.

It took forty-four days for my father to die. At first, he was still able to eat noodles or drink soup. Then he could not eat or drink at all. Tibet had no modern medicine then, no way to save his life. Later, my mother told me that as he was dying, my father cried out for me and told her that he regretted having let me go to China. I have often thought that had I been there with him and not in Nanjing, I could have taken him to India, where the doctors could have saved him. He was only forty-seven years old.

Reting Rinpoche was next in the line of attack. He had to be killed because he was refusing to give up his fight to return as regent. The official accusation against him was that someone on his staff had planted a homemade bomb meant to kill Taktra and that Reting himself was behind the plot. I do not know whether there really was a bomb or whether, if there was, Reting was associated with it. Even official reports admit that no bomb ever went off or ever reached Taktra. But this accusation was somehow treated as evidence of Reting's intent to kill.

Reting was arrested in April 1947. Two of the pro-British members of Taktra's faction, Surkhang and Lhalu, led some two hundred troops to Reting's monastery to bring him back to Lhasa. Reting had been warned in advance that the troops were on their way, but he refused the pleas of his bodyguards and followers to resist arrest or escape to Amdo. Reting wanted to face his accusers directly. He believed he had done nothing wrong. Reting was put in jail in the Potala Palace. He demanded a meeting of the General Assembly where he could meet Taktra Regent face to face and defend himself openly against the charges against him. But Taktra refused either to hold a meeting or to meet with Reting in person.

On May 8, 1947, three days after his imprisonment, Reting Rinpoche was dead. The official verdict declared it a death from natural causes, but no one believed that then and no one believes it today. Later, in India, one of Reting's personal attendants who had helped remove the corpse told me that his body was covered with wounds, so badly battered that it was nearly unrecognizable. Blood had obviously poured from his nose, ears, and mouth. Reting had been tortured. The attendant suspected that he had been poisoned, too.

The official proclamation following Reting's death accused him of having connections with the Guomindang government. I, Gyalo Thondup, was named as someone who had been close to Reting. They connected my going to China with him. Reting must have been tortured into confessing the whole story of our relationship, from his suggestion that I study in China to the message that he had asked me to deliver to Chiang Kai-shek requesting the Chinese president use his good offices to persuade Taktra to return the regency to him, the message I never delivered.

I was in China when my father and Reting regent died. I did not learn the full details of their deaths until after I left. My brother Norbu was the first to suggest that our father had been murdered, when he passed through Nanjing on his way back to Qinghai to bury our father's ashes in the family graveyard. My sister, who visited later, shared his concern. But neither of them had proof.

I HAD LEFT LHASA in November 1945, traveling by horseback to India accompanied by my brother-in-law Phuntsog Tashi Takla, a guide, and several attendants to help with the horses. There were no roads going east across the mountains that separated Tibet from China, and certainly no airport. Once in India, China could be reached by air or by sea. India was, at the time, the fastest way to eastern China. India was also the country where Buddhism began. I wanted to make pilgrimages to the holy sites—to Bodh Gaya, where the Buddha attained enlightenment, and Benares, along the Ganges, where the Buddha delivered his first sermon and thus the religion of Buddhism was born. Seventeen days after leaving Lhasa, I crossed the border into another world.

8

My Student Days in Nanjing

Everything about India was exciting and new—the language, the customs, the food, the clothes, the shape of the faces, the color of the skin, and the hair. Everyone was dressed in white. Calcutta was a modern city. The British administered it well. I had never imagined anything like it. The roads were paved, and the trains were fast. I had never stayed in a hotel, and suddenly I was staying in the five-star Grand Hotel. I wandered the streets, explored the parks, visited the British-run, British-owned department stores, and frequented the Metro Cinema. I watched a movie starring blonde-haired, blue-eyed Lana Turner, saw Charlie Chaplin's silent films, and became enamored of American Westerns. They reminded me of the Tibetan nomads. *Custer's Last Stand* was one of my favorites. I saw it many times. Later, I would associate Custer with the Chinese People's Liberation Army and their slaughter of the Tibetan resistance fighters.

The Indians and British had apparently never seen anyone like me, either. I was still wearing my chupa and a dangling earring of turquoise and gold. My hair had never been cut. It reached almost to my waist. Heads seemed to turn whenever I walked into the hotel lobby. I soon stopped wearing my earring and had my first haircut.

The female barber wondered whether I was a boy or a girl. Later, in China, I exchanged my Tibetan robes for Western-style clothes.

I left Calcutta for China in early April 1946 aboard an American C-46 transport plane flown by a Chinese pilot. I was accompanying the Tibetan government's official delegation being sent to the Chinese capital of Nanjing to congratulate President Chiang Kai-shek on his recent military victory against the Japanese. The headmaster of my school, Thubten Samphel, was one of the two men leading the delegation, and T. L. Shen, (Shen Tsung-lien), the new head of the Chinese representative office in Lhasa, was escorting them. Shen had been a secretary to President Chiang Kai-shek and was a devout Buddhist. He had great respect for the Tibetan religion and culture. Like Reting Regent, he favored closer ties between China and Tibet and believed that my education in China could help foster such ties. He arranged for me to be a special student in the Central University of Politics (*Zhengzhi Daxue* [政治大学]) in Nanjing. Chiang Kai-shek himself would be my sponsor.

Our route to Nanjing took us over the hump and across the Himalayan Mountains to Kunming, the same route the American military had used to get supplies to Chiang Kai-shek's army after the Japanese closed the Burma Road. The route was notoriously dangerous, with heavy winds, unpredictable changes in weather, and limited radio contact.

It was a bumpy flight. We flew between the mountains at an altitude of around ten thousand feet. The cabin was neither pressurized nor heated, so we were all wrapped in blankets as protection against the freezing cold. There were more than twenty Tibetans on board, including members of the victory delegation; Thubten Sangbo, the newly appointed director of the Office of Tibet in Nanjing; and the personal staff for both the officials and me. Our interpreter, Yeshi Targay, was a nephew of Thirteenth Dalai Lama's representative in Beijing and had lived in China for many years. He spoke perfect Chinese, with a Beijing accent. The older members of the delegation were visibly uncomfortable during the flight, but as a teenager and the youngest of the group, I could not contain my excitement.

Gyalo Thondup (center front) with long earring and uncut hair.
Brother-in-law Phuntsog Tashi Takla is on the left, Reting Regent's trade
representative is on the right. Taken in Kalimpong in 1945 en route to China.

I tried to take in everything at once, hopping from one window to another to see what I could see.

In Kunming, the weather was beautiful and mild in contrast to steamy Calcutta, and here everyone was wearing blue. We were whisked from the airport straight to the guesthouse of Yunnan's governor, the infamous warlord Long Yun (though, like the warlord Ma Bufang, his official title was not warlord but governor-general). The banquet was lavish, and the welcoming speeches were profuse. Kunming was visibly less modern than Calcutta, with only a few tall buildings. Parts of the city had been badly damaged during the war. Its legacy as an American supply base was evidenced by the many American servicemen we saw on the streets.

President Chiang Kai-shek and his wife were still in the wartime capital of Chongqing negotiating the peace when we arrived in Nanjing on April 7. The Chinese Communists had occupied large chunks of Manchuria when the Japanese troops withdrew at the end of the war, and the United States was brokering talks between the Nationalists and the Communists, trying to persuade them to negotiate. Zhou Enlai was the lead negotiator on the Communist side. This was the first I heard of the man who would later become China's premier and Mao Zedong's most faithful follower.

The governor of Jiangsu province and the mayor of Nanjing served as our interim hosts. They put us in a government guesthouse and welcomed us with a lavish banquet, introducing us to the situation at war's end and explaining how the Chinese Nationalist government was gradually resuming control over the city. Thousands of Japanese soldiers were still in Nanjing awaiting repatriation. The Chinese government had put them to work repairing roads and rebuilding the airport.

Nanjing had been China's national capital during the early years of the Ming dynasty and still had something of an old imperial flavor. The thick city walls, broad boulevards, and two- and three-story buildings were impressive. Summers in Nanjing were sweltering, but the weather in spring was beautiful. We visited Sun Yat-sen's hilltop memorial, paid calls on several local monasteries, took a side trip to

Shanghai, and climbed Putuoshan, one of China's four sacred Buddhist mountains. The monasteries and temples were in disrepair, but the monks were delighted to greet a delegation sent by His Holiness the Dalai Lama. Again I was thrilled. Everything in China was new and different, too. China and India were both so different from Tibet and each was so different from the other. China, though, was easier for me. I liked Nanjing from the start. I knew the language and liked the food. It was in Nanjing that I became a lifelong devotee of Chinese cuisine. Speaking Chinese allowed me to befriend people at all levels of Chinese society, from the president to shopkeepers and the ordinary man on the street. I got along well with everyone regardless of status. The Chinese people impressed me.

MY FIRST ENCOUNTER with President Chiang and his wife was at the lunch they hosted for our victory delegation shortly after their return to Nanjing in early May 1946. I was the youngest at the table and not even a member of the delegation, but my status as the brother of the Dalai Lama gave me a seat of honor. Over time, I came to know the Chinese president and his wife quite well, and they came to treat me as a son. I visited their home frequently and often dined with them on the weekends. They were unfailingly warm and gracious hosts, and I was always impressed by how well they treated their staff. They lived austerely. Dinner at the home of President and Madame Chiang was always simple, with only one or two dishes. Madame Chiang Kai-shek was a charming, strong-willed woman, always elegantly dressed. With her American education, she was an invaluable help to her husband, both in his dealings with the United States, where she traveled the country and lobbied Congress on behalf of China, and with other world leaders as well, including both Churchill and Stalin.

President Chiang was a generous sponsor. He went out of his way to make my stay in China a success. He paid all my expenses and gave me a monthly allowance that allowed me to live in style. His staff found me a comfortable three-bedroom house and provided me with a cook, servants, and a car with a driver—until I learned to

President and Madame Chiang Kai-shek host luncheon for Tibetan delegation.
Gyalo Thondup, with new haircut, is at the table on the far right,
President Chiang is third from right, followed by Madame Chiang.

drive myself and sent the chauffer away. He appointed the president
of the Central University of Politics, Dr. Gu Yuxiu, to supervise my
studies. Dr. Gu had studied in the United States and held a PhD
in engineering from MIT. He selected six faculty members—one
each in Chinese history, world history, geography, literature, arith-
metic, and music—to tutor me in private. I met my tutors every day,
morning and afternoon, in a classroom set aside especially for me.
And I often sat in on university lectures with the rest of the students,
becoming good friends with a number of them.

I never discussed politics with the Generalissimo and his wife.
We talked about my studies and the future of Tibet instead. His
view of Tibet was different from the story told later by the Communists. The Communists would argue that Tibet had been a part of
China since the Yuan dynasty and that they were merely liberating

us from the imperialists. Chiang Kai-shek never said that Tibet had ever been part of China. His view of Tibet grew out of Sun Yat-sen's three principles of the people—*minzhu* (democracy), *minsheng* (people's livelihood), and *minquan* (democratic rights)—as well as Sun's notion of bringing the five nationalities of China—the Han, the Hui, the Manchus, the Mongols, and Tibetans—together as equals under a single united republic. Sun believed that the incorporation of the five nationalities into a single republic should be voluntary, with the same rights and privileges for everyone.

Chiang was also willing for Tibet to remain independent. With the Dalai Lama running Tibet and me by his side, if Tibet still wanted independence without foreign exploitation, Chiang said, he would support it. Tibet was China's back door. The two countries would always have close ties. He trusted the Dalai Lama and me. In the meantime, President Chiang worried that Tibet could easily be exploited by other countries, including both Great Britain and India. He was suspicious that some members of the Tibetan nobility were already coming under the spell of the British.

The president urged me to take my study of Chinese history particularly seriously. He felt it would be useful when I returned to Tibet. So I explored the history of China from ancient times to the present—from the Xia and Zhou dynasties of antiquity to the fall of the Qing and the establishment of the new republic in the early twentieth century. The most important, indelible lesson I learned from those studies was that never in five thousand years had Tibet been a part of China. Nothing in Chinese history suggested that Tibet had ever been a part of China, and no Chinese historian had ever made that claim. Nothing that I have learned since has suggested otherwise.

My study of world history helped me to see my own country in a different light and inspired me to think about how to bring about reform. I was particularly inspired by President Lincoln's emancipation of the slaves during the American civil war, which led me to wonder about the condition on Tibet's estates. I never saw our estates as a form of serfdom or slavery, but I did realize that they needed major reform. I learned something about European history, too—Napoleon and the French revolution, Metternich and his dip-lomatic activities, Garibaldi and the red shirts of Italy, and the evolu-tion of the British parliamentary system. I was intrigued by the Meiji restoration in Japan and admired how the emperor had first resisted when Admiral Perry came knocking on his door, only later opening the country up to foreign trade, thus beginning a new era of mod-ernization and prosperity. I studied the First World War, the Russian revolution, the Second World War, and Gandhi and his nonviolent resistance movement in India.

I had known that Tibet was backward from the time I first set foot in India, and my studies in China only confirmed that judgment. As I compared the histories of so many different countries to the history of my own Tibet, I came to see that the Tibetan way of life was badly out of sync with the rest of the world. Our systems of government, land ownership, law, administration, agriculture, and education belonged to a time long past. Elsewhere, old political systems had collapsed and new forms of government had been established. But we Tibetans were still clinging to our useless traditions. We had no roads, no telephones, no newspapers. We had no contact with other peoples. We did not know what was happening outside our own land. There was no Gand-hian movement of nonviolent resistance. No one was talking about freedom of speech, freedom of movement, freedom of thought, or Sun Yat-sen's three principles of the people. In China, everyone was talking about equality, land reform, and the rights of the people.

I greatly admired the late Dr. Sun Yat-sen and his three principles of the people. These concepts were unheard of in Tibet. In Tibet, the Kashag gave orders. The people remained ignorant and obedient. I felt strongly that Tibet's survival depended on reform and modern-ization, a complete political change with a new, more democratic form of government. I wanted to see the hereditary rule of the Ti-betan aristocracy abolished, their estates liquidated, and I envisioned the introduction of a new civil service system with government offi-cials paid salaries rather than living off the proceeds of their estates. Our educational system needed radical restructuring, to include lay people as well as monks and to include the study of natural and

Gyalo Thondup with his jeep in Nanjing

social sciences, world history, and foreign languages. Without such change, I believed, Tibet could not survive.

But I was never really a serious student. I spent my weekends and holidays enjoying myself, taking my schoolmates to restaurants and teahouses and performances of Chinese opera. I lived extravagantly, regularly managing to spend all of my generous allowance. Perhaps if I had studied harder, I could have received a PhD and become a scholar and professor. Instead I see myself today as half-cooked and only partially educated. But if I had stayed in Tibet and not gone to study in China, I might well have become like so many other sons of the Tibetan nobility, living off the proceeds of my estates, becoming a dissolute, corrupt, and useless official. For the education

I did receive, I remain grateful first to President Chiang Kai-shek for believing that a wild Tibetan like me could be trained. And I am thankful to the professors who taught me. They were kind and selfless men, teaching a barbarian like me, and their teaching left a lasting impression. They taught me that with enough determination anything can be achieved. Never give up was their lesson. I cannot praise or thank them enough. Whatever little knowledge I have today is from the education I received from them.

I had never heard of communism before I went to China. I started learning about it not long after arriving in Nanjing. Eight years under the Japanese occupation had brought tremendous suffering to the Chinese people. Lives and families had been turned upside down, and many people were still living in grinding poverty. People had tremendous expectations for Chiang Kai-shek after the war. They hoped that the Guomindang could restore order, wipe out corruption, and bring new prosperity. They wanted an honest government. But many were disappointed.

People at the time were talking about the four great corrupt families—the Chiangs, the Chens, the Soongs, and the Kongs. I do not think that there were really four corrupt families. I thought there were only two. I knew President Chiang Kai-shek well. The president himself was never corrupt. Chiang Kai-shek had no money. He lived simply. His sons were poor. But many of Chiang's subordinates were corrupt, seizing land illegally, engaging in all sorts of illicit deals. I knew the Chen brothers, Chen Guofu and Chen Lifu, well, too. There were exceptionally well-educated and cultured men, and they also lived austerely. They were not corrupt, either. But the Soong family, Madame Chiang Kai-shek's relatives, were extremely wealthy. Everyone believed that they were corrupt. And the Kongs, the leading financial barons of China at the time, were also corrupt. Corruption was undoubtedly one of China's biggest problems.

By the beginning of 1947, people had begun demonstrating in the streets of Nanjing, rightists and leftists alike. Demobilized military officers gathered at the Sun Yat-sen memorial, crying because the Generalissimo had dissolved their units and they had no work or pay.

Wave after wave of students went on strike in support of the Communists. Left-wing Guomindang intellectuals openly criticized Chiang Kai-shek on the streets and in newspapers and magazines. Soong Qingling, the widow of Dr. Sun Yat-sen and sister of Madame Chiang Kai-shek, was the leader of one of the pro-Communist groups.

Some of my friends did not care which side won. They saw no great difference between the Communists and the Nationalists. What they wanted was peace. They were tired of conflict and war. Others, like the shoemaker who practiced his trade in front of my house, wanted a Communist victory, the sooner the better. He was fed up with Chiang Kai-shek's government and believed that the Communists were going to liberate him.

The Communists' slogans and the propaganda about liberation eventually won the hearts of the Chinese people. For all the bloodshed of the civil war, Mao Zedong finally defeated the Nationalists not through force of arms but through psychological warfare. He promised to wipe out corruption, to give land to the landless and wages and work to the poor. China would prosper. People like the shoemaker in front of my house believed his propaganda. Even some American intellectuals, such as Owen Lattimore and John King Fairbank, and government officials, such as US ambassador to China John Leighton Stuart and George Marshall, believed that he was only an agrarian reformer.

The civil war progressed rapidly. By late 1948, the Communist army was just north of the Yangtze River that ran through Nanjing. The army was closing in fast. There was no doubt that the Communists would win. The Guomindang was losing all the battles.

President Chiang remained kind to me until the end. But finally, he knew that the time had come for him to leave Nanjing and for me to return to Tibet. He left so quickly that we had no opportunity to say good-bye, but even at such a difficult time, he still gave instructions to his subordinates to make sure that I had sufficient funds to return home.

Chiang Kai-shek resigned the presidency in January 1949, returning first to his native village in Zhejiang and then fleeing the mainland for Taiwan. I left Nanjing in March. The city was in chaos. Roads were jammed with families on foot and every variety of vehicle with wheels. Trains were filled to overflowing, with people hanging out the windows and piled on the roofs. Inflation was rampant. Everyone was fleeing the Communists.

I fled with my new Chinese wife, Zhu Dan. We had met in 1946 and been married two years later in a ceremony at Shanghai's Grand International Hotel. I had been introduced to Zhu Dan by her brother, a naval officer, who had been part of a group sent by the Nationalist government for military training in London. Nanjing had many government officials and military officers then, and I was often invited to their social gatherings, which is where I met my wife's brother. Eventually, he invited me to a large gathering at his home, where I met his parents and two sisters. Zhu Dan and I began doing things together, sightseeing and traveling, and finally I proposed. Many Tibetans had hoped that I would marry a Tibetan woman, or a princess from Bhutan or Sikkim. But I married for love. Zhu Dan's family was from Suzhou, which is known throughout China for its beautiful women. She had spent the years after the Japanese invasion at Southwest University in Yunnan and returned to Nanjing to graduate from Jilin University with a degree in social work. She was older than I and was already an administrator in the Baptist hospital, working with children and refugees still suffering the aftereffects of the Japanese war. Many of them still did not have enough to eat.

Zhu Dan's father, Zhu Shigui, had been a leading general in the Guomindang army and had close ties to the Communists, too. He had attended Jiangwutang Military Academy in Yunnan, where his roommate was Zhu De, who joined with Mao Zedong in 1927 to form the Chinese Communist army. Zhang Guotao, one of the founders of the Chinese Communist Party who later split with Mao, was also a student then, and he and my father-in-law had been friends. Earlier in the civil war that was then reaching its denouement, Zhu De and Zhu Shigui had faced each other on opposite

Gyalo Thondup and Zhu Dan on their wedding day

sides in battle. My father-in-law had enough troops and weapons to wipe Zhu De's forces out, and he received an order to exterminate them. But he did not have the heart to destroy his old friend. He let Zhu De and his army escape instead.

My wife and I were lucky to get airline tickets from Shanghai to Hong Kong. We reached the British colony in April just as Nanjing fell to the Communists. I had arrived in China with no official travel documents. Now, both my wife and I were traveling on Chinese passports issued by the Guomindang government. By May, we were in India. The Communists took over the ancient capital of Beijing that month and made it the seat of their new government.

9

Stranded in India

I was wary about returning home. I knew little of what was happening there. The Chinese media carried no news about the situation in Tibet. The people of China were almost as ignorant of Tibet as Tibetans were of China. What little I learned came mostly from Thubten Sangbo and his assistants in the Office of Tibet and from the Guomindang's own Office of Mongolian and Tibetan Affairs. The news was often disturbing. The power struggle between the forces loyal to Reting and the forces keeping Taktra in power continued. Officials appointed by Reting were still being purged. Something was badly amiss.

The Tibetan government had tried to get me to return to Lhasa almost from the time I arrived in China. The first effort came when Thubten Samphel, my former headmaster and one of the leaders of the victory delegation, delivered the news that my father had died. The message had come by telegraph in the name of Taktra Regent and the Kashag. Thubten Samphel had been instructed to ask me to return home. My mother would not be able to manage without me, the message said, and upon my return, I would be given both my father's title of Yabshi Kung and his honorary position in the

government. The offer of a high position was meant as an entice-
ment, but the request was really an order.

Thubten Samphel did not agree with Taktra Regent's instructions. He took me aside after officially delivering the message and
asked me to meet him privately in his guestroom. His obligation as
a Tibetan official required him to convey the regent's instructions
ordering me to return, he told me. But his personal opinion was
that I should stay and continue my studies. He also warned me to be
careful. "The Tibetan government is suspicious of you," he said.

I agreed with Thubten Samphel. I was shocked and saddened to
learn of my father's sudden death, but I saw no reason to leave. I had
been sent to China to study and could not return until I had completed my work. But I did not understand why the Tibetan government should be suspicious of me.

The second effort to lure me back came after Reting Rinpoche's
death. T. L. Shen, the Chinese diplomat who had accompanied the
victory delegation to Nanjing, had officially informed me of Reting's passing. My first thought then was that I should tell President
Chiang about the message Reting had given me requesting him to
use his good offices to convince Taktra Regent to return power to
Reting. I regretted not having told him earlier. But not long after
my first meeting with the president, I had set out with the victory
delegation on a two-month tour of Beijing and eastern China. Then
I was busy with my studies. My meetings with President Chiang up
to that point were always with other people, and I wanted to deliver
the message to him alone. But T. L. Shen advised me against telling
him. It was already too late, he said, and too much had changed. He
was afraid that if I told President Chiang and word got out, my family might face "complications." Both my mother and the Dalai Lama
might suffer, he said.

Later I grew suspicions of T. L. Shen. He was siding too strongly
with Taktra Regent and had suddenly gotten very rich and been pro-
moted to become mayor of Shanghai without any obvious qualifica-
tions. I thought perhaps he had been bribed.

The request that I return to Lhasa following Reting Regent's death was sent to Thubten Sangbo, the monk official who headed the Office of Tibet in Nanjing. I used to stop by his office on weekends to chat with him and his staff. One Saturday morning I paid an unscheduled visit. The ground floor office was empty. Thubten Sangbo and his staff were upstairs playing mahjong. A cable was sitting open on the desk downstairs, and I could not resist the urge to read it. It was a missive from Taktra Regent and the Kashag, instructing Thubten Sangbo to persuade me to return home. The regent said that my presence in China was harmful to the Tibetan government and asked Thubten Sangbo to use whatever influence he could and whatever funds were required to get me to return.

I folded the cable, put it in my pocket, and went upstairs. The mahjong players professed happiness at seeing me and said they had planned to pay me a visit. I apologized for interrupting and encouraged them to continue their game. But they sent the interpreter away and closed the door. The conversation turned serious. They told me that the Kashag and the regent were worried about my prolonged stay in China. The civil war in China was spreading and the situation was getting dangerous, they said. The Kashag officials were worried about my safety. Besides, my mother was getting old and needed my help. I should return, they insisted. They told me that the government was willing to pay whatever was necessary for me to go back.

They were embarrassed when I confronted them with the cable alleging that my presence in China was harming the Tibetan government. They insisted that the government's intentions were good. I instructed them to convey a message on my behalf saying that I was not returning and, moreover, that my presence in China was not harming the government of Tibet. They need not worry about my presence here, I said. I would return when I finished my studies. Instead of worrying about me, they should unite and work sincerely for the people of Tibet. If they did not want to send that request or listen to my suggestion, then they could tell the Kashag and regent to go to hell. My language was crude.

Tsepon W. D. Shakabpa, Taktra's chief advisor on foreign affairs, akin to a secretary of state, was the next to try to get me back. Shakabpa was one of the most powerful noblemen in the Tibetan government, a longtime foe of Reting Regent, part of the small inner circle surrounding Taktra Regent, and no doubt one of the leaders behind the plot to kill my father and Reting.

Shakabpa had arrived in Nanjing in early 1948 as head of a trade delegation that had already visited India and would be traveling to the United States and Great Britain as well. The trade delegation was the first of its kind and the first time Tibetans had traveled on their own passports. For many, the fact that both Great Britain and the United States had issued the delegation visas stamped in Tibetan passports was proof that the two leading countries in the West viewed Tibet as an independent country.

Shakabpa's request that I return to Tibet took the form of an invitation to join his trade delegation. I would return to Tibet together with them after visiting the United States and Great Britain. My refusal of Shakabpa's offer was considerably more diplomatic than my response to Thubten Sangbo.

In the end, it was the civil war in China rather than the Tibetan government's orders that forced me to leave. But I did not know what to expect upon my return to Tibet. I wanted to talk to my mother before returning home. In my three years in China, we had never been able to speak. There was no phone connection between Nanjing and Lhasa. We wrote occasional letters, but they took months to arrive and passed through so many hands on the way that she would not dare say anything she would not want others to know. Aside from the news I had received when my brother and sister visited, I knew only the barest outlines of what was happening with my family.

Kalimpong was to be the jumping off point for our return. The Himalayan hill station was just at the end of one of the caravan routes from Tibet and was a lively, colorful place filled with Tibetan traders, Indian merchants, and thousands of yaks and mules that transported goods back and forth. There were no phone lines in Kalimpong, but Sikkim's capital of Gangtok was only fifty kilometers away and had a radiophone that could reach Hugh Richardson, the former British consul, who had stayed on in Lhasa as the Indian consul after India's independence in 1947. Harishwar Dayal, the Indian political officer in Gangtok, made arrangements with Richardson for my mother and me to speak.

The connection was terrible; I could barely understand what my mother was saying. But I knew that something was wrong. We talked about my mother's health and about how the Dalai Lama and my other brothers and sisters were doing. My mother asked about my wife and wondered where we were staying. But she said nothing about my return and never asked when I would be coming home. She wanted me to wait in Kalimpong. My uncle, her younger brother, would be arriving soon with an urgent message.

The message was shocking. My mother did not want me to go home. If you do return, she warned, the life of the Dalai Lama could be in danger.

It was then, from my uncle, that I learned the full story of how my father and Reting Regent were murdered. And finally I understood why the Tibetan government had tried so hard to get me back. They wanted to get rid of me, too, because they thought that I might try to avenge my father's death. They were afraid that if they did not depose my brother as the Dalai Lama, he might, after reaching majority, try to bring justice against those who had killed both his father and Reting. I think they were afraid that if they deposed the Dalai Lama without getting rid of me first, I might later return and attempt to avenge the death of my father and the deposing of my brother. By staying abroad, I may have provided them with just the right amount of fear to prevent them from carrying out their plans.

No words can describe how cruel and barbaric those power struggles were or what kind of people were ruling Tibet. There was no law, no justice. Even in Kalimpong, I continued to hear about new arrests and murders and more confiscations of property. People close to Reting and my family were still being rounded up. I felt powerless. The situation seemed hopeless. I could not go back in those circumstances. I was stranded in India.

10

Becoming an Intermediary

We moved to Calcutta, renting a small flat at 5 Robinson Road near Park Street in the diplomatic quarter. My wife was pregnant with our first child, and the medical facilities were better in Calcutta. We depended almost completely on my mother's financial help. Without her, we could barely have paid our rent of 250 rupees a month.

I soon became a conduit for messages to Tibet. The governments of India, Great Britain, and the United States all wanted to know how Tibet was going to respond to the impending establishment of a new Communist government in Beijing. Everyone had advice. Everyone wanted to help. But Tibet had no official representative in India, and no Indians had direct contact with government officials in Tibet. As the brother of the Dalai Lama, if I could get messages through, at least they had a chance of reaching the highest levels.

The Indians were the first to approach me. Harishwar Dayal, the Indian political officer in Sikkim, must have reported my presence in India to his superior. Soon Jawaharlal Nehru, who had become India's first prime minister in August 1947 when India acquired its independence, invited my wife and me for a week-long stay at the elegant, colonial-style Imperial Hotel in New Delhi.

He hosted a dinner in my honor that included his daughter Indira Gandhi and Sardar K. M. Panikkar, Nehru's senior foreign affairs advisor who was soon to become India's first ambassador to China. S. N. Sinha, who had already spent time in China and was about to become India's representative in Lhasa, joined my wife to serve as an interpreter. My wife spoke fluent English.

Mr. Nehru was a democratic, humane, and cultured man. He believed in the rule of law. He was tolerant and willing to listen to criticism. Later I would contrast Nehru's openness to the ruthlessness of China's Mao Zedong. During Mao's so-called Hundred Flowers Campaign of 1956, the party chairman used pretty words to entice his country's intellectuals to speak out honestly in criticism and then, when they did finally speak out, he turned viciously against them, sentencing hundreds of thousands to decades in prison or labor reform camps. Mao could not stand even the slightest glimmer of criticism.

Nehru seemed genuinely sympathetic to Tibet and knew something of its history, but I was the first Tibetan he had ever actually met. The dinner was an opportunity for him to understand what kind of person I was. He wanted to hear my views on the Chinese civil war, the Chinese Communist Party, and the current situation in Tibet. He wondered about my future plans and encouraged me to consider enrolling in the Indian Military Academy in Dehra Dun, where I could receive both military training and a good education in government administration. He offered to help with the arrangements.

My meeting with Prime Minister Nehru had been reported in the New Delhi newspapers, so my presence in the city was already publicly known. Loy Henderson, the American ambassador to India, invited me to lunch that same week and asked me to convey a message to the Tibetan government on his behalf. He wanted Tibet to send two officials to meet secretly with the American consul general in Calcutta pursuant to an official meeting with Ambassador Henderson himself in New Delhi. Henderson, too, was concerned about what the Communist takeover in China would mean for Tibet. He wanted the Tibetan government to know that the United States was willing to help in every possible way.

Ambassador Panikkar soon called on me with a message from the prime minister. Nehru wanted me to serve as an intermediary between him and the government of Tibet. I was still the only Tibetan he had ever met. Nehru was suspicious of the Communists. They had yet to give any overt sign of attacking Tibet, but he urged the Tibetan government to prepare for the possibility nonetheless. He thought the Tibetans would be foolish not to begin mobilizing their military, even if in the end no attack occurred. And he wanted the Tibetan government to know that India was willing to help with arms and military aid.

Nehru wanted me to transmit his messages through my own channels rather than relying on the channel that went through Hugh Richardson, still India's official representative in Lhasa. I had met Richardson in Calcutta not long before, during one of his holidays. He had nothing but praise for Tibet and its government. No other country had such a unique and wonderful system, he told me. Nothing about it should be changed. Having been convinced from the moment I first arrived in India that nothing but massive reform could save Tibet, and knowing something of the political turmoil then tearing my country apart, I was appalled by Richardson's views. I saw him as a British agent attempting to manipulate the ignorant officials of Tibet. I was happy to serve as the Indian prime minister's intermediary, allowing Nehru to avoid relying on Richardson to get his messages through.

Tibet had no official representation in India, but Thubten Sangbo, the monk official who had headed the Office of Tibet in Nanjing and to whom I had been so rude when he tried to persuade me to return home, had set up a telegraph station in Kalimpong and was able to communicate directly with Lhasa through the same code he had used in Nanjing. He was happy to convey my messages directly to Lhasa. Over the next several months, I often made the six-hour train trip from Calcutta to Kalimpong, delivering secret messages from Nehru, the United States, and China for Thubten Sangbo to pass on to the Kashag and Taktra.

One of those messages was a letter from my father-in-law, Zhu Shigui, sent from Hong Kong. His former military academy roommate, Zhu De, had just been appointed the minister of defense in China's new Communist government. Zhu De had contacted my father-in-law, inviting the Tibetan government to send a delegation to Beijing to discuss relations with the new government there. He sent assurances that Tibet's status under the Guomindang would not be changed under the Communists. The new government had no intention of altering either the position of the Dalai Lama or the position of Tibet, he said. Up to this point, Tibet had had no direct contact with the Chinese Communists. I was now an intermediary for the Communists, too. I left for Kalimpong immediately to send the message to Tibet.

But no one was responding to my messages. Sardar Panikkar visited me at the end of August, wondering why there had been no response to Prime Minister Nehru's offer of help. The prime minister had another, more emphatic message. The mobilization of the Tibetan population was absolutely necessary to face the impending problems with China, he said. India wanted to help Tibet to prepare militarily, both by training soldiers and supplying arms. India could even serve as a base of support in case of an invasion. Nehru also suggested that the Tibetan government begin transferring some of its priceless relics and manuscripts from eastern to central Tibet for safekeeping. The monasteries in Amdo and Kham were filled with ancient manuscripts, paintings, and statues, some more than a thousand years old, and their loss to an invading army would be tragic. Mr. Panikkar asked me to transmit the advice as quickly as possible. I was off to Kalimpong again.

Then I received another message from my father-in-law, reiterating Zhu De's invitation, wondering why there had been no response, and again urging the Tibetan government to send a delegation to Beijing as soon as possible. Zhu De was now accusing the imperialists of sowing dissension between the Chinese and Tibetans and cautioned the Tibetans against listening to their propaganda about communism. Again Zhu assured the Tibetan government that

China had no intention of changing the status of Tibet. I returned to Kalimpong again.

By this time, I had sent five messages to the Tibetan government—two from Prime Minister Nehru, one from the American government, and two from Zhu De, the highest-ranking military official in the Chinese Communist Party. I had not received a single reply. The Americans wanted to help. The Indians wanted to help. The Communists wanted to talk. What was the Tibetan government doing? Sleeping? Dreaming? Why weren't they answering?

Tibet was being torn apart by its own internal power struggles, its leadership ignorant and unaware of what was happening in China and how the change in government might affect Tibet. They were not worried about the Chinese. Rumors reaching us in India were about leading officials in the Taktra government still plotting to remove the Dalai Lama and have me killed. The only foreign contact they seemed to be having was with the British, in the person of Hugh Richardson, who thought that the government of Tibet was so wonderful and unique that no reform was necessary. The Tibetan government had no idea how to respond to the Americans, the Indians, or the Communists. The ignorant lamas were convinced that China could not possibly invade Tibet. I was worried, tired, angry, and frustrated. I did not know whether to laugh or to cry. I still become indignant remembering the disastrous incompetence of the Tibetan government and its inability to respond.

Then suddenly, in July 1949, the Tibetan government ordered all Chinese expelled from Lhasa. They said they were afraid of Communist infiltrators. But they expelled all Chinese who were then resident in the city, including the Guomindang officials and Chinese shopkeepers as well. Perhaps they were afraid that the Chinese would defect to the Communists. They were given little more than a week to leave. I was shocked. I met Chen Xizhang, the Guomindang's chief representative in Lhasa, as he was passing through India en route back to China. He told me that Hugh Richardson had advised the Tibetan government to expel the Chinese, and the government had decided to follow his advice.[1]

The Nationalists and the Communists alike condemned the expulsion. The propaganda coming from Beijing radio was suddenly radically transformed. The Communists were describing the expulsion as a plot undertaken by the Tibetan government at the instigation of the British imperialists. They described Nehru as a lackey of British imperialism. After all, the British Richardson was India's representative in Lhasa, and they must have known or suspected that Richardson had advised the Tibetans to expel the Chinese. The real reason for the expulsion, the Chinese said, was to prevent Tibet from being liberated by the Chinese People's Liberation Army.[2]

This was the first mention of the possible "liberation" of Tibet by the People's Liberation Army. Until then, the talk had been about liberating Taiwan. With Communist propaganda now accusing the Tibetan government of being a tool of the British imperialists, the new Chinese government had an excuse to invade.

I received a third visit from Mr. Nehru's emissary. Ambassador Panikkar and Prime Minister Nehru were now certain that a Chinese attack on Tibet was imminent. We had the same conversation again. Ambassador Panikkar wanted to know what was happening in Tibet and whether there had been any reply from the Tibetan government. He reiterated the urgent need for an immediate mobilization of the Tibetan military. He again urged the government of Tibet to transfer important relics and manuscripts for safekeeping. He urged the government to proceed deliberately, not to panic or make hasty decisions. There was still time for the Tibetan government to build an airstrip near Lhasa, at the foot of the Sera and Drepung monasteries. In the event of a Chinese invasion, India could fly in weapons and personnel to help defend Tibet. And they could evacuate the Dalai Lama by air to safety in India if he needed to escape. But they had to begin acting soon.

I had still heard nothing from the Tibetan government. My efforts were like throwing a stone into the ocean; they had no effect. By then, the American embassy had also approached me again about whether there had been a response to their invitation. Again I had to say no. Once more I left Calcutta for Kalimpong so Thubten Sangbo could pass along the most recent messages to an unresponsive Tibetan government. Even Thubten Sangbo was frustrated by this time. Prime Minster Nehru must have been frustrated, too.

I was ashamed of my government. The Tibetan leadership had no understanding of the new Communist government in China, and no sense of what the consequences could be for Tibet. They did not even seem to know that India had gained its independence from the British. Great Britain was nearly dead at the end of the Second World War, but the Tibetan government was still listening to Hugh Richardson. Finance Minister Shakabpa seemed to think that cooperation with the British was the only route to take. Hugh Richardson must have thought that the Chinese Communist Party would never invade. Maybe he really was afraid that some of the Chinese in Tibet were Communist spies. Everywhere in China, people were taking public oaths of allegiance to the Chinese Communist Party. Maybe Richardson thought that if the Tibetans kicked out all the Chinese, the simple Tibetans would be easier to manipulate. The Tibetans did not understand their own reality.

I felt a heavy burden, a moral responsibility to do all that I could to help my brother and my people. I was afraid of what might happen if the Communists invaded. But nothing was in my hands. Taktra Regent and the ministers of the Kashag held all the power. I was desperate.

I began thinking that I should go to Beijing. I thought that maybe there I could find a way to be of service to my people. I had no particular plan of what I might do or how I might do it. I had little idea of what the Communists were thinking. The whole situation was completely unknown. But I was doing no service by staying in India.

To get to China from India I would have to pass through British-controlled Hong Kong, and for that I needed a transit visa. I submitted my application to the British high commissioner in Calcutta. But the British delayed. They sent for further instructions from higher levels. When the instructions came, my visa was denied. The British, it seemed, did not want Tibetans talking directly to the Chinese.

My plan to return to China had been an act of desperation. It was wishful thinking, a dream. I was running on hope. Looking back, I do not know what I could have done. But I did think that China could be of help to backward, incompetent Tibet.

I came up with another plan. I would go first to Manila, from there to Portuguese-controlled Macao, and then from Macao into China. By March 1950, I had a visa to the Philippines.

It was only then that the Tibetan government seemed to wake up. Just days before my scheduled departure from Calcutta, a delegation sent by Taktra Regent and headed by Finance Minister Shakabpa came to visit me. They had accepted Zhu De's invitation to visit Beijing and were on their way to China. They asked my advice. I was disgusted. For six months I had been trying to communicate with the Tibetan government, passing on messages from the Indian government, the American ambassador, and from Zhu De. Tibet had never responded. Now, they were suddenly asking me what to do.

Zhu De had invited them to China, promising that the status of Tibet could remain the same; India had offered military help; the United States had offered help. The Tibetan government had ignored them all. On October 1, 1949, Mao Zedong had stood on the Gate of Heavenly Peace and declared the establishment of the new People's Republic of China. The Communists were talking about liberating Tibet from the imperialists. The British were refusing to give visas for Tibetans to go to Hong Kong en route to China. Now representatives of the Tibetan government were suddenly asking me what to do. I did not know what to do. I refused to talk to them further. I was disgusted with the entire Tibetan government.

The tide began to turn. On April 1, 1950, the Indian government established diplomatic relations with the new People's Republic of China. Hugh Richardson finally stepped down as India's representative in Lhasa, and India's own diplomat S. N. Sinha became his country's counsel general there. With Sinha in Lhasa, the messages that the Indian government had been trying so hard to deliver by telegraph could at last be conveyed in person. But they still had no effect. That summer, when Sinha met Tibet's two foreign ministers, Surkhang and the monk official Liushar, he was still emphasizing the importance of mobilizing Tibet for an imminent Chinese attack and urging the government to build an airstrip. He was still promising India's help. But the foreign ministers assured Sinha there was no need to worry. They remained convinced that a Chinese attack against Tibet was impossible. We have too many mountains, they said. This fairy tale that the Chinese or Ma Bufang could invade Tibet has been around for a long time, Surkhang told him.

Mr. Sinha had no other channel of contact, no way to reach Taktra Regent or the Dalai Lama directly to persuade them of the folly of the government's refusal to prepare for trouble with China. He was an official of India's foreign ministry and had to go through proper channels. He was almost as disgusted as I had been with the Tibetan government's corruption and nonchalance.

I still believe that if the Tibetan government had responded earlier to the overtures from Nehru, the United States, and even the Communists, our situation today would different—at least a little bit different. We never asked the Indians or Americans for help. Those offers were unsolicited. We desperately needed help. But the people running Tibet were incompetent—not just ordinarily incompetent but absolutely incompetent. They were a national tragedy, so weak and divided that they made the job of Mao Zedong's invasion easy. The Communists could just march right in and take us over.

The Shakabpa delegation never reached China. The British would not give them a visa, either. They were still in New Delhi meeting with Yuan Zhongxian, Mao Zedong's new ambassador to India, when the attacks against Chamdo began.

11

The Chinese Invade

The attacks began on October 7, 1950, and came from multiple directions. The main goal was to capture Chamdo, the capital of Kham, and cut off any possible escape route to Lhasa. Some twenty thousand soldiers from the Eighteenth Corps of the Second Field Army of the Chinese People's Liberation Army participated in the operation. General Zhang Guohua was the commander of the troops, and his deputy Wang Qimei led them into battle across the upper reaches of the Drichu River. One of the Communists' leading military strategists, Liu Bocheng, together with Deng Xiaoping, both ranking party officials in China's Southwest Military Region and soon to become powerful leaders within the new Communist government, had drawn up the plans.

Ngabo Ngawang Jigme, the same man who had brought down my father's wrath while overseeing the construction of my family's house in Lhasa, was the governor-general of Kham and responsible for Chamdo's defense. He had assumed his new position barely a month before. Ngabo was associated with a group of young, relatively liberal, modern-minded officials who did not always see eye-to-eye with the conservative faction surrounding Taktra Regent. He had been stationed in Kham earlier in his career and had worked most recently in Lhasa with Surkhang, assisting him with a variety of military details, from managing supplies to paying the troops. Ngabo's appointment as governor-general was unexpected. His rise in rank from Tsipon to Shape, equivalent to that of a Kashag member, had been quick. Even Ngabo himself later admitted to me that he had been ill prepared for his new job.

Ngabo was replacing Lungshar's son Lhalu, who had become governor-general of Kham in 1947 a few months after joining Surkhang in the arrest of Reting Regent. Not long after the Communists declared victory in Beijing, the Taktra forces, including Lhalu, had finally awakened to the realization that the Chinese might attack after all. Belatedly, they tried to begin building an army capable of resisting a Chinese attack. But the efforts were much too little and far too late. The entire Tibetan army had only thirteen thousand troops in November 1949,[1] when the efforts to modernize began in earnest. On the eve of the Chinese invasion, some twenty-five hundred of those troops were stationed in Kham. Everyone knew that this tiny, ill-equipped, barely trained Tibetan army was no match for the vastly more numerous, better led, better trained, better equipped, more experienced, and battle-hardened Chinese. The Tibetan government did not want to be held responsible for the inevitable defeat. Ngabo saw the decision to appoint him governor-general as an attempt to shift the onus of loss away from Lhalu, Taktra, and their supporters.[2] With Ngabo in charge, the blame for military's failure would rest with him.

But Ngabo never had any intention of putting up a real resistance. He knew that defeat was certain. He wanted to avoid unnecessary bloodshed. He believed that a negotiated settlement was the best hope for Tibet, and he set about dismantling some of the defenses put in place by Lhalu, fearing they might provoke a Chinese attack. But the Chinese needed no provocation. By October 12, their troops had crossed the upper reaches of the Drichu River—known to the Chinese as the Jinsha and in English as the Upper Yangtze—and were advancing on Chamdo. Ngabo's aides began frantically radioing Lhasa for guidance. There was no response. For three days, radio messages repeatedly went out from Chamdo to Lhasa, but still there was no response. The Tibetan government was literally out to lunch. The Kashag was in the midst of one of its annual picnics, lavish outdoor affairs that went on for days. The instructions would have to wait until their picnic was over.

Ngabo and his staff fled Chamdo secretly in the night rather than staying to lead the fight. The local Khampas were left to fend for themselves. Ngabo had commandeered the horses that would have allowed them an escape.

Some say that Ngabo was just as afraid of being killed by the Khampas as he was of the Chinese. Khampas are Tibet's great warriors, renowned for their fighting prowess. They are a fierce and independent group made up of different tribes, each ruled by its own chieftain. The tribes often fought bloody internecine feuds, and enmities between them could pass from generation to generation, on through the centuries. While the Khampas revered the Dalai Lama and could be militantly patriotic, relations between the Khampas and the Tibetan government in Lhasa were rarely good. At best, the Khampas felt ignored and looked down upon by the Lhasan officials, and many resented Lhasa's demands for taxes when they were getting so little from Lhasa in return. At worst, Tibetan soldiers stationed in Kham had such a reputation for corruption and rape that the Khampas regarded them as a hostile force. Khampa loyalties were further complicated when parts of Kham were incorporated into the Manchu empire and later fell under the ostensible rule of the Nationalists. The divide and rule tactics, first of the Manchus and then of the Chinese, produced new strains. In 1939, the Khampas were administratively further split when the Nationalists set up a new province of Xikang, which was almost entirely Khampan and bordered the Lhasa-ruled province of Kham. But neither the Tibetan nor the Chinese governments were ever able to assert real control over this feisty and independent-minded group.[3]

On the eve of the Chinese attack, Khampa loyalties were still divided. Some were so angry with the Tibetan government that they preferred the Chinese, whether Nationalists or Communists, as a foil against Lhasa. Ngabo's decision to commandeer Chamdo's horses for his own escape and leave the Khampas stranded must have further enraged them. Some Khampas were prepared to welcome the Communists, and some were prepared to fight them on their own. To further complicate matters, some of the forces moving in on Chamdo from Xikang were said to be members of a Communist-led Khampa militia.

Chamdo fell quickly. By October 19, less than two weeks after the attacks began, the fighting was over. Ngabo and his fleeing troops were soon captured by the fast-moving Chinese cavalry and put under arrest in the nearby Drugu monastery. It was there, in the monastery, that Ngabo signed the official surrender. Casualties had been light. Official Chinese figures reported that only 180 Tibetans had been wounded or killed. The thousands who had been captured were given a hearty meal, a few speeches on the glories of socialism, promises of better things to come, a small amount of cash, and then they were sent home.

Word of the defeat did not reach Lhasa immediately. There was no way to communicate. Robert Ford, the Englishman in charge of radio communications from Chamdo, had been captured. His wireless system had been destroyed. Ford had come to Tibet from Bombay, where he was a sergeant in the Royal Air Force working as a radio operator. He was supposed to be a temporary replacement for Reginald Fox, who was the radio officer in the British mission headed by Hugh Richardson. But Ford fell in love with Tibet, and when no Tibetans could be found to operate the American radio that was being sent to the Tibetan governor's office in Chamdo, Robert Ford volunteered for the job. He spent nearly five years in jail following his capture there and went on to write about both the attack on Chamdo and his experience in a Chinese prison.[4]

With nothing but silence from Chamdo, the Tibetan government could only draw the obvious conclusion about what had happened there. Lhasa was plunged into chaos. The Kashag and the regent panicked. Some wanted to flee Lhasa immediately and take the Dalai Lama with them. S. N. Sinha, the Indian representative in Lhasa who had long been imploring the Tibetan government to prepare for just such an attack, now urged the officials to remain calm. Sinha wanted the government officials to remain in the city. If they fled, no one would be running the country and the people of Tibet would lose confidence in their government just at the time the government was needed most. Lhasa would be plunged into chaos. The Chinese forces were still five hundred miles away, Sinha pointed out. There was still plenty of time to prepare, time even to build an airstrip. India could help. His government was still willing to supply arms. If the Dalai Lama's safety were ever threatened, India could fly him out. But the Kashag was not listening.

Taktra Regent was paralyzed. The Chinese were making demands. They wanted the Tibetan government to agree that Tibet was a part of China. They wanted the People's Liberation Army deployed inside Tibet. The Kashag could not accept the Chinese demands. They be-haved as though compromise was still possible. Then they changed their minds. They wanted Shakabpa's delegation, still waiting in In-dia, to go to Beijing for negotiations. There, Shakabpa could accept China's demand that Tibet become part of China if China agreed that the status of the Dalai Lama and Tibetan Buddhism would not change. Then the Kashag reversed its decision again. They did not want Shakabpa to accept any of China's demands. Shakabpa was afraid to go to China in any case. The Indians wanted him to stay in New Delhi to continue discussions with Yuan Zhongxian, the new Chinese ambassador to India.

In desperation, the Kashag turned to the United Nations for help. Shakabpa wrote an impassioned plea, addressed to the UN Secretary General, laying out the Tibetan case for independence and its inabil-ity to resist the military might of China, and urging the United Na-tions to intercede against Chinese aggression. He sent the message by telegraph from Kalimpong. But the United Nations, too, was paralyzed. Neither India, nor Great Britain, nor the United States, the three countries most able to help, were willing to support the

Tibetan request. The United States was embroiled in a war against North Korea. With India's independence, the British had given up on Tibet, ceding their own interests to India. India suddenly did not want to do anything that might bring repercussions from China.

El Salvador rallied to the Tibetan cause. On November 14, it presented a resolution to the United Nations condemning China and calling for a full investigation into Chinese aggression. Ten days later, the UN General Assembly voted unanimously to postpone the decision in the hope that a peaceful, negotiated settlement could still be reached.

In Lhasa, Taktra Regent was becoming more unpopular with every passing day, openly scorned by the people. The incompetence of the Taktra government, the failure of his administration to act in the face of the growing threat from China, and the incessant internal struggles for power had brought Tibet to catastrophe. People were demanding Taktra's resignation. He could no longer cope. So he obliged. Taktra resigned his regency.

Thus it was that on November 17, 1950, in the midst of this devastating crisis, in a quiet ceremony inside the Potala Palace, with representatives of India, Nepal, Bhutan, and Sikkim looking on, my brother the Dalai Lama, then barely fifteen years old years and nearly three years short of majority, assumed the full mantle of leadership over Tibet. He appointed two acting prime ministers (*sitshab*) to assist him in running the government: the layman Lukhangwa and the monk Lobsang Tashi. Both were senior officials, widely respected and admired. They were straightforward, honest, independent, and patriotic men, not connected in any way to the factions and conspiracies that had been plaguing the government for years. There would be no more intrigues under them.[5]

It was shortly after this, as the Tibetan government was debating what to do about China's demands, that my elder brother Norbu, Taktser Rinpoche, arrived in Lhasa. Norbu was in a good position to explain what a Communist presence in Lhasa might mean. He had already experienced the Communists himself.

Norbu had been appointed the abbot of the Kumbum monastery following his return to our native village to bury our father's ashes. He was still there in 1949 when the Communists marched in declaring themselves the "liberators" of Qinghai. The Muslim warlord Ma Bufang had escaped immediately, fleeing to Saudi Arabia with five planes chartered from Claire Chennault's famous Flying Tigers who had served Chiang Kai-shek so well during the war against Japan. Four of the planes were said to be loaded with gold, and one was so heavy that it nearly crashed. In Qinghai, Communist-led mobs began a campaign of plundering and looting. The beautiful hermitage of Shartsong so near to my family's house was robbed and burned to the ground even as Communist officials were assuring Norbu that Tibetans were still free to practice their religion. Communist agents occupied Kumbum. Order both inside and outside the monastery broke down. Norbu became a prisoner in his own monastery. Communist officials interrogated him incessantly, attempting to indoctrinate him with their propaganda about the wonderful Chinese Communist Party and the great leader Mao Zedong, trying to wash Norbu's brain. They wanted him to return to Lhasa to persuade the Dalai Lama to cooperate with them. They wanted the Dalai Lama and his people to welcome the Communists as liberators, to accept their alien ideology, and to replace our antiquated religious beliefs with new socialist ones that would have the monasteries liquidate their labrangs, give up their estates, and force everyone into collectives. In the book he wrote years later, Norbu said that these officials even suggested that if the Dalai Lama did not comply with their demands, "ways and means would have to be found to get rid of him. . . . They even let me see quite clearly that if necessary they would regard fratricide as justifiable."[6] Norbu was offered a high political position for betraying, and possibly even killing, our brother. As proof that the offer was true, the Chinese listed cases of others who had been rewarded with high positions after turning on relatives and friends.

But Norbu tricked them. He set off from Kumbum for Lhasa with the summer caravan of 1950, accompanied by two Tibetan

companions and three Chinese appointed by the Communist overlords—a married couple and a radio operator. The Chinese officials
thought they had convinced Norbu to sing their praises and persuade the Dalai Lama to go along with them. But when his group
arrived at Nagchuka, the border between Qinghai and Central Tibet, the Tibetan border guards refused the Chinese entry. The siege
of Chamdo had begun while the caravan was en route, and Kham
had already fallen. But central Tibet was still under Tibetan control,
and the Dalai Lama had just assumed the mantle of temporal power.
The Chinese accompanying Norbu were arrested. They were furious
at Norbu's betrayal.

The story Norbu told when he met the Dalai Lama in Lhasa was
not the one the Chinese had wanted him to tell. Instead, he poured
out his heart, describing the turmoil within his monastery and the
falsity of Communist propaganda. Norbu did not want the Dalai
Lama to accept the Communists' demands. He wanted him to flee.

Norbu did not stay long in Lhasa. He was sure the Communists were about to march on the city. He knew he could not live
in a Communist-controlled Tibet. Given his own refusal to comply with their demands, he believed that his life could be in danger
if they were ever to see him again. He wrote later that, having already personally experienced the frustrations of a once free man cast
in chains, he knew that he could not live without liberty.[7] He fled
across the Indian border to Kalimpong and left for the United States
soon thereafter.

WEEKS LATER, the Kashag decided to send the Dalai Lama and
most of the government to safety. The young Dalai Lama, disguised
as an ordinary Tibetan layman, fled Lhasa on December 16, 1950.
The two newly appointed prime ministers were left behind to serve
as interim caretakers. Most other leading officials fled with the Dalai Lama, traveling westward by horseback some 150 miles through
Gyantse to Dromo (Yadong) just inside the Tibetan border with
Sikkim. If the Dalai Lama needed to go into exile, the border with
Sikkim was only hours by horseback away. From Dromo they

established radio contact with Lhasa and India, as the Dalai Lama and the Kashag pondered what to do.

The Chinese were insisting on negotiations, and they wanted them held in Beijing rather than Lhasa or Chamdo. The Kashag had no other choice but to agree. Ngabo Ngawang Jigme, still under house arrest in Chamdo, was appointed the lead negotiator for Tibet. Two junior officials, Sampo Tenzin Dhondup and Khenchung Thupten Legmon, were to serve as Ngabo's assistants and went to join him in Chamdo. Another two assistants, Lhautara Thupten Tender and Kheme Sonam Wangchug, then in Lhasa, were also appointed members of the negotiating team. The two groups were dispatched separately to the Chinese capital, Ngabo and his team traveling eastward overland to Beijing, the Lhasa-based team going via India. My brother-in-law Phuntsog Tashi Takla was their Chinese interpreter, and Sandu Lobsang Rinchen was their English interpreter, needed because the second group would be traveling to Beijing via English-speaking India. By early April, both teams had arrived in Beijing, ready for the negotiations to begin.

BUT THE CHINESE had another matter they wanted solved first. The would-be Tenth Panchen Lama and his entourage had just arrived in Beijing, brought at the Communists' behest and under their flag. The Communists had recognized this twelve-year-old boy from Amdo as the legitimate reincarnation of the Ninth Panchen Lama who had passed away in Jyekundo in 1937. The Dalai Lama and the Tibetan government had not. Before negotiations could begin, the Chinese demanded that the Dalai Lama and the government of Tibet officially recognize their Panchen Lama. Without the Dalai Lama's recognition, the talks could not begin.

THE REINCARNATION OF the Ninth Panchen Lama had been controversial from the beginning. The Manchu imperial court had long tried to sow dissension between the two lamas, often encouraging the Panchen Lama, whose traditional role had always been confined to the spiritual realm, to assume a political role as well. At the time of the Younghusband expedition in 1903, when the Thirteenth Dalai Lama had fled to China, some of the Ninth Panchen Lama's officials had negotiated with Younghusband at Khamba Dzong, and the Panchen Lama moved from Shigatse to Lhasa, later accepting an invitation from the British to pay a visit to India in 1905. The Thirteenth Dalai Lama saw the Panchen Lama's behavior as overstepping his religious bounds. When the Dalai Lama finally returned to Lhasa in 1913 after the collapse of the Manchus, relations were already strained.

The reform-minded Thirteenth Dalai Lama was committed to the continuing independence of Tibet and was determined to take full control of governmental as well as religious matters. In 1923, when the Dalai Lama tried to introduce a new system of taxation capable of funding both a modern military and a new educational system, the Panchen Lama's labrang at the Tashilunpo monastery in Shigatse refused to pay its allotted share. The Panchen Lama turned to the British to mediate on his behalf, and when the British refused, the Panchen Lama fled east, where he spent long periods in both the Kumbum and Jyekundo monasteries. The Chinese embraced him. For years, they sought to bring the Panchen Lama back to Tibet under their military protection, and for years the Tibetan government refused. The Panchen Lama was in flight for the rest of his life. He never returned to Central Tibet.[8]

The search team for the Ninth Panchen Lama's new incarnation was slow in getting started and even longer in making a decision. In fact there were two search committees. One was headed, as it should have been, by Lhamon, the elderly monk from Tashilunpo monastery who had served as chief secretary to the Ninth Panchen Lama. The other was led by Che Jigme, whom I had known in Nanjing when he was head of the Panchen Lama's office there. Under their direction, a young boy from my native place of Amdo had been selected, and an installation ceremony had been conducted in Kumbum monastery in August 1949 just as the Communist forces were beginning their final sweep across Gansu province and into Qinghai. Zhou Fukai, the head of the Guomindang's Office of Mongolian and Tibetan Affairs in Nanjing, was in attendance, thus signaling the Nationalist government's approval of Che Jigme's choice.

When the Communists entered Qinghai later that summer, Zhou Fukai fled, leaving the would-be Panchen Lama to seek refuge at the Shanti monastery on Kokonor Lake. After the Communists occupied Kumbum, they invited the would-be Panchen Lama to return. Lhamon and Che Jigme agreed. Thus began a long collaboration between the Communist Party on the one hand and the opportunistic, behind-the-scenes political forces of the would-be Tenth Panchen Lama on the other.

The first sign of the new Panchen Lama's professed loyalties was on October 1, 1949, the day Mao Zedong declared the establishment of the new People's Republic of China. The new Panchen Lama sent a message to Mao and Zhu De, congratulating them on their victory and calling for a speedy "liberation" of Tibet. "From now on, the realisation of the democratic happiness of the people and revival of the country are only questions of time and it will not be long before Tibet is liberated," the letter read. "I sincerely present to Your Excellencies on behalf of all the people in Tibet our highest respects and offer our heartfelt support."[9] Later, in January 1950, the Chinese published another appeal from the Panchen Lama, again claiming to speak on behalf of all the people of Tibet and begging the Communists to send troops "to wipe out reactionaries, expel the imperialists, consolidate the national defences . . . and liberate the Tibetan people."[10]

The Panchen Lama's calls for liberation were a sham. How could a twelve-year-old boy claim to represent the people of Tibet? The child was incapable of drafting such letters. And he was too young and unschooled to understand how ridiculously inappropriate his pleas to the Communists were. Lhamon and Che Jigme were behind the letters, selling the unwitting child to the Communists. Neither the Tibetan government, nor the Dalai Lama, nor the people of Tibet recognized this would-be Panchen Lama as legitimate.

NOW, BEFORE NEGOTIATIONS could begin, the government of Tibet was being ordered to recognize this Chinese-appointed

Panchen Lama. But Ngabo had no authority to agree. This was a question for the Dalai Lama and the religious authorities of Tibet to decide, and they had another candidate. Ngabo and Li Weihan, China's lead negotiator and director of the United Front Work Department, locked horns, and Ngabo threatened to return to Lhasa with the agreement unsigned. For several days, telegrams went back and forth between the negotiators in Beijing and the Tibetan government in Lhasa and Dromo. Finally, the Dalai Lama asked for a divination to be performed. He accepted the result and agreed to accept the Tenth Panchen Lama in Beijing as legitimate.[11]

THE PANCHEN LAMA remained under Communist control for years. Only much later did he gain the respect of the Tibetan government, the Dalai Lama, and the people of Tibet. Many referred to him as the Chinese Lama.[12] But with his acceptance by the oracle in Lhasa in April of 1950, the negotiations with the Chinese could begin.

Ngabo was in an impossible position. He had authority to negotiate but no authority to make big decisions without consulting the Kashag in Dromo first. His instructions from the Tibetan government were not to accept the claim that Tibet was part of China, not to agree that Chinese troops could be stationed inside Tibet, and to insist that Tibet would be free to conduct its own foreign relations, especially with nearby India and Nepal. But these were points upon which the Chinese lead negotiator would brook no compromise. In fact, there were no real negotiations. Lead negotiator Li Weihan had drawn up the Seventeen Point Agreement under the direction of Mao Zedong himself. The Tibetan delegation was read the agreement point by point and asked to sign. The words coming from the Chinese mouths were polite, but they were in command. Even the position of Li Weihan was a signal to the Tibetans that the Chinese were in full control. The United Front Work Department is an organ of the Chinese Communist Party and not the Chinese government, and it is charged with managing relations with friendly non-party organizations. The whole structure of the negotiations left no room for compromise.

Signing of the Seventeen Point Agreement, May 23, 1951.
Ngabo Ngawang Jigme is standing third from the left.

Ngabo had no way to communicate this fully to Lhasa or Dromo. His communications with the Tibetan government were being transmitted through the Chinese telegraph system. He did the best he could. He tried to resist. He refused to sign the agreement at first, and negotiations temporarily broke down. Li Weihan ordered him to sign the agreement. Chinese troops would march on Lhasa if they did not, Li threatened. The threat was real. The Chinese army had already taken over Chamdo. They were in Tibetan territory. Ngabo delayed, claiming that he did not have his official seal to stamp the document. The Chinese made a new one. Actually Ngabo did have his own seal, as governor general of Kham.[13] He just did not want to use it. So Ngabo was forced to sign at gunpoint. The "Agreement of the Central People's Government and the Local Government of Tibet on Measures for the Peaceful Liberation of Tibet," later known simply as the "Seventeen Point Agreement," was signed in Beijing on

May 23, 1951. Ngabo stamped it with the Chinese-made seal, forced to agree that Tibet was a part of China.

The Dalai Lama was still in Dromo when the agreement was signed. He was shocked when he learned the news from a radio broadcast from Beijing. "We were appalled at the mixture of Communist clichés, vainglorious assertions which were completely false, and bold statements which were only partly true," he wrote later. "And the terms were far worse and more oppressive than anything we had imagined."[14]

Ngabo's stamp was not enough. Despite the public Chinese hoopla about the signing of the agreement and the pretense that Ngabo was acting under the direction of the Dalai Lama and his government, the Chinese knew that the agreement would never be considered legitimate by the people of Tibet, the Tibetan government, or the larger world beyond unless it really did have the blessing of the Dalai Lama.

But the government of Tibet was still divided. Many of the powerful lamas from the leading monasteries took at face value the promise that the power and position of the Dalai Lama would remain intact and that Tibet's traditional religious and political systems would be respected. For them, these were the crucial aspects of the agreement. They thought that the Chinese were sincere. The fact that China would be managing Tibet's relations with foreign countries was not important to them; foreign relations had never been important to the Tibetan religious orders. And even after the successful attack on Chamdo, few imagined that the Chinese would really send troops to occupy Lhasa. If the Chinese wanted to say that Tibet was a part of China, but Tibet remained free to maintain its own culture and traditions, then what China called Tibet did not much matter to these monks.

Others, however, saw the Seventeen Point Agreement as an ominous first step in the intrusion of a Communist-led China into Tibet. Some of the people with the Dalai Lama in Dromo, fearing the worst, wanted to get him out of Tibet to somewhere he could claim political asylum and work in safety for a better agreement. My brother Norbu, Takster Rinpoche, then just over the Sikkim border in Kalimpong, was one of them. So was Shakabpa, who was also in Kalimpong at the time. Liushar, Tibet's foreign minister, made a visit from Dromo to Sikkim's capital of Gangtok to meet with the Indian political affairs officer, Harishwar Dayal, to explore the possibility of India granting the Dalai Lama asylum.

The choice was so hard. The Dalai Lama was still so young. The mantle of temporal power had been thrust upon him so suddenly. Some of the high officials surrounding him were opportunists. Others were elderly lamas with no understanding of the outside world. What kind of decision could he have made?

I think the Dalai Lama would have gone to India if asylum had been granted. Otherwise, Liushar's visit to Harishwar Dayal would have been superfluous. But the Indian government balked. They refused to grant him asylum. Prime Minister Nehru himself had to have made the decision. Suddenly, India was no longer offering to help. I can only speculate as to why. The Indians had tried so hard to help. Their offers had been sincere. Nehru was conscientious about Tibet. Tibet was important to India. Nehru knew that. But his offers of help had been ignored. Nehru must have been disgusted with the behavior of the Tibetan regent and his cabinet. He must have seen them as incompetent and out of touch. The Kashag and the regent understood neither the Chinese threat nor the offers of help from India. So Nehru did not know what to do. He changed his mind. He decided he had to deal with the Chinese. He concluded that good relations with China were essential to India's own development.

In the end, the Dalai Lama had no other alternative. He had nowhere else to go. He had to return to Lhasa and he had to accept the Seventeen Point Agreement. Those were not decisions he chose. They were conclusions that were forced upon him.

IN MID-JULY, just before the Dalai Lama began his trip back to Lhasa, Zhang Jingwu, recently appointed as Mao's representative in Tibet and soon to become the highest ranking Chinese official there, met the Dalai Lama in Dromo and handed him a copy of the Seventeen Point Agreement. At the end of September and back in Lhasa, the three-hundred-member Tibetan National Assembly, which meets only in emergencies to consider the most important and difficult issues, convened to discuss the Seventeen Point Agreement. Ngabo, having just returned from Beijing, spoke first, explaining the process of negotiations, arguing in favor of accepting the agreement, and declaring himself willing to accept whatever punishment, even the death penalty, that might be meted out against him if the agreement failed to be ratified. Most important to Ngabo, and the reason he gave for accepting the agreement, was that it left both the status of the Dalai Lama and the political and religious systems of Tibet intact.

In the end, the Tibetan National Assembly supported Ngabo and the Seventeen Point Agreement. The promise that Tibet could maintain its political and religious systems unchanged was the most important reason for that support, and the religious leaders of Tibet were the strongest advocates for accepting the proposal. They believed the Chinese promise that nothing would change after Tibet became part of China.

The National Assembly's vote to accept the terms of the agreement was followed by a final test of divination conducted by the religious leaders. Two balls of tsampa, one with a slip of paper favoring acceptance of the agreement inside and another with a slip of paper opposed, were placed in a bowl and spun until one of the balls flew out. The slip of paper inside concurred with the National Assembly's decision. Tibet would accept the Seventeen Point Agreement.

What remained was only for the Dalai Lama himself to inform Communist Party Chairman Mao Zedong. At the urging of Zhang Jingwu, and under his direction, a letter was prepared stating that the Tibetan "local government" unanimously supported the agreement and "under the leadership of Chairman Mao and the Central People's Government, will actively support the People's Liberation Army in Tibet to consolidate national defence, drive out imperialist influences from Tibet and safeguard the unification of the territory and the sovereignty of the Motherland."[15] Even the Dalai Lama's acceptance had to be written by the Chinese. We Tibetans never considered China our motherland. Tibet is our motherland, and Tibetans are not Chinese. Tibetans had no need to drive imperialists out of Tibet because there were no imperialists in Tibet. We wanted independence, not unification with some other country. The Chinese were putting words into our mouths. They were bitter words to taste.

My brother-in-law, Phuntsog Tashi Takla, translated the Dalai Lama's acceptance into Chinese. The telegram was sent to Mao on October 24, 1951.

Today, some Tibetans still regard Ngabo as a traitor, a collaborator with the Chinese. But that is not entirely true. Ngabo had no choice. Very few Tibetans ever collaborated with the Chinese from their hearts, completely and blindly. Collaboration was always forced. If Ngabo had had the freedom to make a different choice, perhaps his choice would have been different. But he did not have an alternative. Ngabo was not a traitor. He was out to save his own skin. He did not want to risk his own neck. He was an opportunist. He wanted to survive.

Ngabo was a good and honest person, very straightforward, unlike so many other members of the Tibetan cabinet, who could be so sly. He had a mind of his own. When I met him the year after the Seventeen Point Agreement was signed, he was very disturbed about the situation in Lhasa, openly complaining to me about the corruption of Tibetan officials and distressed that some of the Kashag members were informing the Chinese about the content of their meetings.

Ngabo went on to become a high-ranking official, not only in Lhasa but at the central level as well. He was a made a vice-chairman of the National People's Congress and came to be based in Beijing. I did not see him for almost thirty years, but in 1979, I met him again in Beijing, and we continued to meet often after that. As a high official, he was constrained as to what he could say. But he had much he wanted to tell me, and what he said impressed me. Deep in his heart, he never bought the Chinese view of Tibet. He often reminded me that throughout Chinese history, whether during the time of the Manchus and imperial China or during the rule of the Guomindang, Tibet had never paid taxes to China. Never. What that meant to him was that Tibet had never been part of China. If Tibet never paid any taxes, Tibet could not have been part of China.

He also took exception to the Chinese argument that the Tibetans' claims to independence were something new. The Tibetans had long talked about independence, he said. Those claims were nothing new. Especially during the time of the Thirteenth Dalai Lama, Tibetans were always proclaiming their independence.

And he did not believe the Communists' claims that the Fourteenth Dalai Lama had been officially recognized and certified by the Nationalist government of the Guomindang. He had spent months digging into the Nationalists' archives in Nanjing searching for evidence of the Communist government's claim. He found nothing to support it. The Communists' claims were false. They were using them in an attempt to undermine the Dalai Lama's legitimacy and denounce the Nationalist government. So I believe that Ngabo was a Tibetan patriot at heart.

But he was also something of a rubber stamp. Even as other Tibetans who had been supporters of the Communist government were denounced and put into jail, Ngabo never got into much trouble. The Chinese needed him as their rubber stamp and therefore had to protect him. I used to joke with him, accusing him of being too scared to stand up to the Chinese. He responded with a Tibetan proverb, that you only die once. "I have only one life, and I have lived it as a Tibetan," he said. "So what is there to worry about death?"

Ngabo received an official funeral when he died. Rubber stamps are useful in death as well as in life. They make good propaganda. In Beijing, all the high-ranking officials attend the big state funerals to show how honorable and important the deceased had been. All the politburo members pay their condolences and cry to show their grief. It is a message to the world that they are showing the deceased respect. Maybe it is not really propaganda. Maybe all this grief is sincere, and all the respect is real. Maybe the big state funeral they held for Ngabo Ngawang Jigme was not propaganda. Maybe the Chinese leadership really respected him. But I doubt it.

12

The Long Journey Home

I was in Taiwan when China invaded Tibet. I learned about the Tibetan defeat and the Dalai Lama's escape to Dromo, land reform in the Chinese countryside, and all the liquidations and shootings of the landlords while still in Taipei. The information was coming from the Nationalist press, and reports were sketchy at best.

I had left India with my wife and three-month-old daughter in April 1950, in an ill-fated attempt to get to China via the Philippines and Macao. We faced obstacles at every step. In Calcutta, just before our Manila-bound plane was about to pull back from the gate, four Indian immigration officers, apparently alerted by the British, came on board to demand that we get off. We refused. Our tickets were valid, and we had already passed through immigration. There was no reason to kick us off. We refused to budge. After a few angry exchanges, the Indians gave up. We landed in Manila a few hours later.

Then we were stuck in Manila. The Portuguese refused to give us a visa for Macao.

A correspondent for China's Central News Agency, the Guomindang newspaper then based in Taiwan, soon learned of our plight. He invited us to stay at his home, and he introduced us to Shen

117

Jian, the representative of the Chinese Nationalist government in the Philippines. Shen suggested that we go to Taiwan to visit Chiang Kai-shek. Obtaining a visa was no problem. We were traveling on our Guomindang-issued passports, and the Philippines still had diplomatic relations with the Nationalist government.

President Chiang's staff met us at the Taipei airport and put us up in the Taipei Guest House, where most of the occupants were Nationalist military officers and government officials on short term stays in Taipei. We paid a pleasant call on the president and his wife. They encouraged us to stay in Taiwan. President Chiang even offered me the job of running the Office of Mongolian and Tibetan Affairs. I demurred, explaining that I wanted to continue my studies. I was only twenty-two years old.

Then we were stuck in Taiwan. The Guomindang government refused to give us an exit permit. I was not exactly under house arrest. We were free to go anywhere in Taiwan and were treated very well. But I was not allowed to leave the island.

I think Chiang Kai-shek was worried that I was young and impressionable and might fall under the Communists' spell. I had not told him or his staff about my aborted plan to go to China. But his government found out anyway. They had learned about the letter Marshal Zhu De sent to me in India via my father-in-law, promising that nothing in Tibet would change after the Communists came to power and inviting the regent and Kashag to send a delegation to visit Beijing. Officials in Taiwan told me privately that they had a photograph of the letter. When my father-in-law went to Hong Kong to mail it, he had stayed at the home of my wife's aunt, who was married to Luo Gan, the powerful head of Guomindang intelligence in Hong Kong and a close associate of Taiwan's chief of intelligence Dai Li. Somehow Luo Gan found out about the letter. Perhaps my father-in-law inadvertently left it lying on a table. Perhaps he told Luo Gan about it himself. We were not so careful about keeping secrets then.

President Chiang and his staff were dead set against my going to China. They did not want this impressionable young man to fall for

Gyalo Thondup and his wife Zhu Dan at the Taipei Airport, 1951

their Communist propaganda and land in their trap. So they refused to let me leave.

Everyone in Taiwan seemed to be stridently anti-Communist, and the media was saturated with anti-Communist propaganda. Chen Guofu, the former head of the Guomindang's Organization Department, onetime right-hand man of Chiang Kai-shek, and one of the most powerful leaders in the Guomindang, seemed dedicated to disabusing me of any illusions I might have about the Communists. Chen's virulence traced back to 1926 and the failed plot against Chiang Kai-shek by the leftist-leaning Wang Jingwei, then Chiang's leading contender for control of the Guomindang. Chiang had declared martial law in Guangzhou when he learned that Wang Jingwei was about to betray him, and Chiang used the plot as an excuse to

Taipeh (Taipei) Guest House

end the already rocky alliance between the Nationalists and the Communists. Chen Guofu and his younger brother Chen Lifu together made up the famous CC Clique and were given the task of purging the Communists from the Guomindang after Wang's betrayal. Dozens of Communists were arrested, and the CC Clique became renowned for their ruthlessness in subduing the Communist foe.

I had met Chen Guofu when I was a student in Nanjing and knew him not for his ruthlessness but as a learned and cultured man who had been educated in the United States. He was bedridden with tuberculosis when I met him in Taiwan, but he still made sure his cook filled my stomach with delicious home-cooked meals whenever I visited, even as Chen filled my head with stories of the dangers of communism. Chen compared the Communist Party, with its false propaganda and broken promises, to a beautiful young woman ridden with a dangerous disease and warned me to be careful of that beautiful, poisonous woman. Only later, after my own personal experiences, did I fully appreciate his caution.

Being stranded on Taiwan was pleasant enough. There was nothing much to do except pay occasional visits to the few friends—Mongolian, Tibetan, and Chinese—we had on the island. I took up fishing to while away the time. The Danshui River flowed just behind our guesthouse, and I bought a fishing rod to try my luck, befriending a seasoned fisherman who was at the riverbank every day. He used a net to bring in generous catches of shrimp and introduced me to the basics of fishing with a rod and reel. Fortunately, he was there to help me through my frightening first catch. I thought the big eel I was reeling in was a snake and had no idea what to do with it. But the light-colored eel was a nutritious delicacy to the fisherman. We traded catches, my ugly eel for his batch of shrimp. Our trades became frequent in the ensuing months, even as the fish on my hook grew more varied.

We were stuck in Taiwan for sixteen months. Generalissimo Chiang Kai-shek paid for every one of our expenses, every bite we ate.

One day, an American with whom I had become friendly offered to transmit a letter from me to President Truman. He thought the American president could get me out of Taiwan. Maybe I could study in the United States. So I wrote a letter to President Truman and Secretary of State Dean Acheson.

The answer was not long in coming. Three weeks later, George Yeh, the Nationalist government's learned and charming foreign minister who had taken a particular liking to me and often invited me to join him for breakfast, paid me an unexpected call. The Nationalist government had just received an inquiry from the United States government about my stay in Taiwan. The Nationalist government had agreed to let me leave.

We did not depart right away; there were still formalities to go through. Mr. Armstrong, the American charge d'affaires in Taipei at the time, issued visas to me and my wife in our Guomindang-issued passports. My wife and daughter visited Hong Kong to say good-bye to my wife's family. I stayed behind to become one of the first guests in the newly opened Grand Hotel, an ornate imperial-style building originally conceived by Madame Chiang Kai-shek and well befitting its name.

*Gyalo Thondup with his wife and daughter in
front of their San Francisco hotel*

President Chiang and his wife were pleased that we were going to the United States. Even in Nanjing, the president had wanted me to study there. He had even offered to pay. Now he made good on his offer. After a farewell dinner to bid me good-bye, encouraging me to study hard, President Chiang sent me off with a check for $50,000.

MY LITTLE FAMILY arrived in Washington, DC, at the end October 1951. We stayed with my older brother Norbu, who had already been there for several months. Norbu had gone to the United States as the guest of the American Committee for Free Asia and was living in Fairfax, Virginia, in a large wooden farmhouse that reminded me of Lincoln's log cabin. Only later did I understand that the American Committee for a Free Asia, later to become the Asia Foundation, was then an arm of the recently established Central Intelligence Agency. It seemed that many of the Americans Norbu had met in Kalimpong had connections to the CIA. Norbu had fallen under their spell.

Robert Ekvall, an American who had lived in Amdo with his missionary parents and was fluent in my native Amdo dialect, made all of Norbu's arrangements. A Mr. and Mrs. Duncan, also former missionaries in the Tibetan part of Sichuan, lived with my brother in the farmhouse, taking care of him and cooking his meals. Norbu had his own car and driver and an assistant, Thondup Gyantsen, who had accompanied him from Tibet. The CIA was treating him well.

Most of my contacts in Washington were with State Department officials from the China desk. They offered me a four-year, fully paid scholarship to Stanford University. It was a wonderful opportunity. My wife and daughter and I took a train to San Francisco, where we spent several months living in a five-dollar-a-day room on Bush Street and eating Chinese food in San Francisco's Chinatown. We visited the redwood forest. I met with James Ivy, the director of the San Francisco office of the American Committee for Free Asia. And I visited the Stanford campus in Palo Alto to meet with university staff. They encouraged me to enroll.

But I decided not to go to Stanford. I no longer wanted to be a student. I was grateful for the help of so many kind and well-intentioned people. But I had to return to Tibet. I had studied in China in order

Wooden farmhouse in Fairfax, Virginia

to help my brother, my family, and my country. My mind was made up. I had to return home.

Some of my American friends tried to persuade us to stay. They warned me that Tibet under Chinese occupation would be dangerous. They said that my return could serve no useful end. Norbu was adamantly opposed to my return. He himself had felt like a prisoner in his own country after the Communists came to the Kumbum monastery, and he did not want that to happen to me. He never relented in this opposition. But I knew that I would never find peace with myself unless I went home to do what I could to help.

I deposited what was left of Chiang Kai-shek's $50,000 after our travels in the United States in a Wells Fargo bank and flew with my wife and daughter to London and then on to Calcutta and Darjeeling, where my mother was waiting. She had made a pilgrimage to India when the Dalai Lama returned to Lhasa and had later taken refuge in Darjeeling where she was receiving medical treatment

Gylo Thondup with his wife and daughter in Washington, DC

following a mild stroke. Several other members of my family were with her as well. Seeing her for the first time in more than seven years was indescribably special. I had been fifteen years old when I left for China. Now I was twenty-two, married, with a two-year old daughter and another child on the way.

My mother and I would be returning to Lhasa together with my older sister Tsering Dolma and my youngest brother, Tenzin Choegyal, who had been born after our move to Lhasa, and whom I was meeting for the first time. My wife was to stay behind in Darjeeling with our daughter to wait for the birth of our next child and look after my younger sister, Jetsun Pema, and my niece and nephew,

Gyalo Thondup and his wife in Darjeeling, 1952

Tsering Dolma's children. The youngest members of our rapidly expanding family were all in school in Darjeeling, the girls in the Loreto Convent, run by Irish nuns, and the boys at St. Joseph's North Point, run by Canadian Jesuits. We expected my wife to join us in Lhasa after the baby was born.

I returned to Lhasa by horseback, just as I had left it in 1945. We followed the same route that Younghusband and his soldiers had taken on their 1903–1904 expedition to Lhasa, leaving from Darjeeling and going through Sikkim to cross the 14,140-foot-high Nathu La pass that serves as the border with Tibet. Dromo is the first town on the other side.

It was snowing heavily and bitterly cold as we crossed the Nathula pass. But word of the imminent arrival of a group of travelers that included the Dalai Lama's mother and siblings had preceded us.

Even in the bitter cold, the people of Dromo came out to greet us. They were still celebrating Losar, the Tibetan New Year, and were in a festive mood. The Chinese had not yet arrived to disturb their peace. We, too, were happy to be back on Tibetan soil. The scenery at that time of year was beautiful, the villages in the distance like tiny specks on the pure white snow. In Phari, said to be the highest inhabited place in the world (at 15,000 feet), the local officials and monks also came out to welcome us. The sight of the Jomolhari Mountain piercing the sky as it stood watch over the vast Tibetan plateau was spectacular.

Further on, in Guru, we were reminded that it was there, in March 1904, that the ill-equipped, ill-trained Tibetan soldiers armed only with primitive muskets had confronted Younghusband's troops for the first time. The result was a bloodbath. Over five hundred Tibetan soldiers died in the massacre.

Approaching Kala, colorful birds were circling the frozen lake, and the moon was bright against the night sky. The peace was broken the next day by our first glimpse of the Chinese troops who had already occupied Gyantse and were then marching west. Suddenly there they were, maybe 150 of them, staring straight ahead, walking silently in single file in the direction of Guru, a soldier carrying the Chinese flag with its red background and five yellow stars in the lead. No Chinese army had ever made it this far into western Tibet. We, too, were silent as we watched in fear, not yet able fully to grasp the reality that Tibet was now occupied by the Chinese.

At Gyantse, staying with a Tibetan family, we were again warmly received. The Tibetan officials came out to welcome us, and local people lined the streets as we came in. Gyantse is Tibet's second most important city, both militarily and economically. Its large hilltop fortress stood guard over western Tibet, and the city was a major stop on the trade route, particularly famous for the quality of its carpets. It was there that Tibet suffered its second major defeat from Younghusband's expedition. When the local Tibetan soldiers surrendered following the bombardment that finally breached the thick fortress walls, the way was open for the British to march on

Lhasa. The Chinese had already set up a military base in Gyantse by the time we arrived. A small contingent of Chinese officers came to greet us.

Our next encounter with the Chinese military was less pleasant. In the small village of Ralung, we were rudely awakened in the middle of the night by seven or eight armed soldiers kicking open the door of the home where we were staying. We were shocked when they began searching the house. They were shocked, too, when I demanded in Chinese to know what they were doing. Just following their superior's orders, they told me. I explained that I was a Tibetan and that the elderly lady with me was my mother. We were returning home from India.

Suddenly embarrassed, they began complaining about life in Tibet: they had still not acclimatized to the altitude; they had constant headaches; they had difficulty sleeping. They soon left us alone to go back to sleep.

The closer we got to Lhasa, the more people came out to greet us. At Nyethang, two days outside the city, officials of the Tibetan government and hundreds of ordinary Lhasans came to welcome us home. On the surface, nothing about Lhasa had changed since I had left some seven years before. In fact, nothing had changed since I had first arrived with the caravan from Qinghai in 1939. Even the people on the street looked the same. Whatever changes there may have been were still hidden from view.

13

Home Again

I returned to Lhasa because I thought I could help. I was still optimistic about the future. I had believed for years that Tibet was badly in need of reforms, and had some ideas of my own about how to bring them about. I believed that the time had come for a major restructuring of Tibet's thousand-year-old system of land ownership. Monasteries and the wealthy aristocrats needed to begin dividing up their estates, giving land to the people who farmed it. Peasants needed to be relieved of the onerous debts that were passed from one generation on to the next. With a redistribution of land and forgiveness of debt, the lives of the ordinary people would improve. The unity of the Tibetan people would be restored. I wanted to use my own family as an example. We had five estates. We did not need so much land. I wanted to give our land to the people who were farming it. We did not need such a big house, either. Our house in Lhasa could become a school.

I had read in Taiwan about the land reform the Communists had carried out immediately after they came to power, with every rural family being categorized into classes, ranging from poor peasants and tenant farmers at the poorest end of the spectrum to rich peasants and landlords at the richest. Land and farming equipment had been seized from the landlords and redistributed to the poor and landless peasants. The process had often been violent. Hundreds of thousands, perhaps millions, of landlords had been killed.

But in Taiwan, another type of land reform was being implemented. Based on Sun Yat-sen's principle of land to the tillers, the process was peaceful and gradual, bringing greatest benefit to the poorest farmers while not greatly reducing the incomes of the landlords. Through a process of gradually reducing the amount of rent paid by tenant farmers and selling off government land, all of rural Taiwan came to benefit.

I admired the way Taiwan had undergone land reform and knew that if we Tibetans did not begin our own land reform now, the Chinese Communists would carry theirs out later, on their own, without us. Surely it would be better for us to implement land reform ourselves than to leave it to the Communists. Ordinary Tibetans would welcome the move. The disruption and violence of the land reform that had taken place in China—the riots, the peasants killing landlords, and the landlords taking up arms in their own defense—could be avoided.

At first I saw the Chinese as our allies in the effort to reform, not because they were Communists but because they were Chinese, and China was so much more modern than isolated, ignorant Tibet. We needed to bring scientific methods to our agriculture and animal husbandry. We needed to expand our educational system with a greater focus on the secular rather than the exclusively religious education that took place inside the monasteries. The curriculum needed to be modernized. Our standard of living needed to be raised. I thought that the Chinese could help. Mao Zedong had promised to help the poor and to lift the Tibetan people out of their backwardness and underdevelopment. I believed his propaganda. I still thought he was a great man.

I also thought that I could serve as a bridge between the Tibetans and the Chinese. The Chinese presence was completely new to Tibetans. We were different nationalities with different cultures and mutually incomprehensible languages. Neither side understood the other. We had no way to communicate. Many did not even want to communicate. I thought that my facility with the Chinese language could help improve communications between Chinese and Tibetan officials. None of the Chinese officials spoke any Tibetan, and only a small handful of Tibetan junior officials, such as my brother-in-law Phuntsog Tashi Takla, spoke any Chinese. The Chinese had brought in a few interpreters, mostly Tibetans from Amdo and Kham, but their numbers were limited. At least I could serve as an interpreter.

I was delighted during my first, day-long meeting with the Dalai Lama that the conversation soon turned to questions of how to reform Tibet. The Dalai Lama quickly embraced my ideas. More than that, he wanted me to meet with ranking officials in the Tibetan government to persuade them to accept my proposals. My brother had been a little ten-year old boy when I left. Now he was a young man of seventeen, with full religious powers and the responsibility for governing his country. He was intelligent, enthusiastic, and full of curiosity. His religious education had clearly been rigorous. I viewed him with a mixture of reverence and affection, revering him as the Dalai Lama and loving him as my younger brother. My other younger brother, Lobsang Samten, joined us at the meeting and was the same gentle, easy going, humble soul of his childhood. But he also had assumed responsibilities beyond his years. He was only nineteen years old, but was already serving as the chief of staff (the chikyab kenpo), in charge of the Dalai Lama's personal treasury and responsible for overseeing the monk attendants.

From this point on, my relationship with the Dalai Lama was forever changed. He was my brother, but we never talked about personal or family matters. My mother and other brothers and sisters might get together with the Dalai Lama for dinner, but we talked about the issues facing Tibet, not about family matters. The Dalai Lama had no private life. His whole being was focused on serving the people of Tibet. His religious training instilled him with remarkable discipline and control over his emotions. Many people close to him died over the years. I am sure that he said special prayers for my mother on the occasion of her death, and he must have had feelings as one after another of his closest aides and attendants passed away. But he never expressed these emotions. He was much too disciplined. I came to see myself as an ordinary Tibetan serving under the leadership of the Dalai Lama, working for him dutifully and loyally. My role was to serve and obey him. His wishes were my orders.

At his direction, I began paying courtesy calls on the leading Tibetan officials, beginning with the two prime ministers. I tried to convince them of the need for Tibet to reform. The prime ministers, Lukhangwa and the monk official Lobsang Tashi, listened politely as I presented my case. But they did not agree. They saw no need for change and wondered what my children would think if I gave my family's land away. My land was meant to be passed on to my children, they said, and they would surely both want it for themselves and for the generations that would follow them. They did not believe that the Communists would carry out land reform in Tibet, even if they were doing so in China. The two prime ministers were as honest and upright as officials could be. They were true Tibetan patriots who had opposed the Seventeen Point Agreement from the beginning and continued to oppose it even after its ratification by the General Assembly. They spoke frankly to the Chinese and openly disagreed with them, often ignoring their orders. But they had been educated in the traditional Tibetan style and remained unalterably conservative and opposed to any major changes. Lukhangwa was already a wizened old man with stark white hair and a long, wispy white beard. His mind was made up—it was not about to change. The Tibetan prime ministers were never going to accept my plans for reform.

I had understood from the beginning that many monks and aristocrats would need to be persuaded of the wisdom of reform, particularly any reform that would see the dismantling of their estates. I thought initially that such objections could be met by providing financial compensation for their land. But the aristocrats and government officials were not to be convinced. They had been doing quite well since the Chinese arrived. The Chinese were cooperating with the Tibetan elite, trying to win them over, giving them positions in the new organizations they were setting up. Somewhere between 50 and 80 percent of the Tibetan aristocracy and officialdom were on the Chinese payroll. Even my elder sister, Tsering Dolma, had been appointed chairman of the recently established Tibetan League of Women and was getting seven hundred silver dollars a month from the Chinese. So was her husband, Phuntsog Tashi Takla. The Chinese called it a subsidy.

And the arrival of the Chinese was providing many of the Tibetan elite with new opportunities for enrichment. The population of Lhasa had grown enormously with the Chinese arrival. Some eight thousand Chinese troops were suddenly stationed in and around the city, together with their horses and pack mules. The troops and their animals had to be sheltered and fed. Much of the food had to be cooked. Food and firewood could not be brought in from China. Everything, including housing, had to come from the local economy. There was money to be made. Lhasan aristocrats like Yuthok and Sandutsang readily rented their homes at exorbitant prices to the Chinese military elite. Estates with large reserves of grain opened their warehouses and sold their surpluses at a profit. The most enterprising went into the construction business, building new housing for the expanding numbers of Chinese. Traders thrived on importing goods for sale to the Chinese.

But the ordinary people of Lhasa were suffering. The huge number of Chinese troops, together with all their horses and mules, put a terrible strain on the local economy. Before their arrival, the total population of Lhasa was thought to be somewhere between fifteen and twenty-five thousand, the higher number being reached during some of the traditional festivals, such as Monlam and Losar, when thousands of people from all over Tibet flocked in. Never in history had such a large foreign military force occupied Tibet. The Younghusband expedition, with its four thousand troops, had come and gone. They had wanted trade, not military control. Historically, Chinese had barely set foot on Tibetan soil. The Manchus sent a couple of officials (*ambam*) and two thousand troops to Lhasa. But we quickly drove them out. They never occupied Tibet or sought to govern.

Lhasa could not accommodate the huge new demand from the Chinese. Inflation was rampant. The price of food jumped 200–300 percent, and even so there was a shortage of food. Rising food prices were a heavy burden for ordinary Tibetans, and many did not have enough food to eat. Their livelihood was badly affected. People were unhappy and afraid. The ordinary Chinese soldiers could not really be blamed for the inflation and scarcity of goods. Of course prices shot up.

Many Tibetans deeply resented the Chinese presence. The Tibetan economy was far from modern, but people had always eked out a satisfactory existence. Now some people were going hungry.

As the situation in Lhasa continued to deteriorate, angry citizens set up a "people's council" (*mimang*), joining together to write letters and sign petitions demanding the withdrawal of Chinese troops. Slogans began appearing on the walls of shops and teahouses: Tibet Belongs to the Tibetans! China Get Out of Tibet! Long Live His Holiness the Dalai Lama! Some Tibetans began demonstrating in the streets.

The Chinese leadership in Lhasa was furious, Mao's own representative and ranking general, Zhang Jingwu, above all. My initial meetings with General Zhang had been cordial. Since many patriotic overseas Chinese students were returning home to serve their newly Communist motherland and I had just returned home from the United States, General Zhang and his associates, Zhang Guohua and Tan Guansan, seemed to think that I, too, was one of the young, pro-Communist leftists. They wanted to win me over to their point of view. They listened patiently, nodding without comment, to my views about rural reform. But Zhang Jingwu's overwhelming preoccupation at the time was not with reform but with the demonstrations then taking place in Lhasa. Zhang insisted that American, Guomindang, or Indian imperialist agents were organizing the protests. I could only sit quietly and listen as he ranted on.

The Chinese were afraid of outright Tibetan revolt. Instead of withdrawing their troops to meet the protesters demands, they sent in more. Another eight thousand soldiers arrived in Lhasa in early 1952, shortly after I arrived, doubling the original number, and thus further worsening the economic crisis and enraging the local people.[1] Now the sights on the streets did begin to change. We saw more and more Chinese soldiers. As the opposition from the people of Lhasa grew, the Chinese military officials grew increasingly vexed. They labeled the people's council a "reactionary rebel organization" and seemed to genuinely believe that the demonstrations and petitions were being instigated by foreigners, that the Tibetan people were incapable of organizing such protests themselves. They began threatening to shoot the demonstrators and to use military force to put them down. They put up barbed wire barricades on the streets of Lhasa. Troops on the streets were equipped with heavy machine guns.

I tried to reason with Zhang Jingwu and his generals, to convince them that the protesting Tibetans were not foreign agents. I pointed out that historically, Chinese and Tibetans had had good relations. We had lived in harmony for a thousand years. We Tibetans were not anti-Chinese. We were antiforeign. We felt the same way about the Americans, the Indians, and the British. I asked the Chinese to be patient, to treat us Tibetans as their younger brothers, to use peaceful methods of persuasion. I pointed out that if they resorted to violence, the harmony between Tibetans and Chinese would be destroyed. And that harmony could not easily be restored.

Then suddenly the Chinese target of attack shifted from the demonstrators to the two Tibetan prime ministers, Lukhangwa and Lobsang Tashi. The Chinese generals accused them of being American agents. An encounter between Zhang Jingwu and Cabinet Minister Surkhang prompted the charge. Surkhang early on had become something of an informer, allowing himself to be exploited, currying Chinese favor. Surkhang told Zhang Jingwu that directing his anger toward the Tibetan people or the Tibetan People's Council was pointless. He likened the demonstrations in the streets to directing a film. "Do you blame the actors in a film for what happens, or do you blame

the director?" he had asked. "What reason is there to be angry with
the actors? You need to know who is directing the film." He accused
Lukhangwa and Lobsang Tashi of directing the demonstrations. According to Surkhang, they were the conspirators behind the protests.

I urged General Zhang Jingwu not to believe this two-faced
Tibetan official. It was not true that the two prime ministers were
Americans spies or that they were directing the demonstrators. How
could they be American agents? Neither of them had ever been to
America. They didn't even know where America was. Was it somewhere in Tibet? Where on earth was it? I urged Zhang Jingwu to be
careful, begging him to remain calm.

But Zhang Jingwu's agitation continued unabated. He was a
coarse and uneducated man and was often impulsive. Sometimes he
became violently emotional, jumping up and down, walking back
and forth, swinging his arms and pounding the table. Tibetan officials were all reactionary, he said. He wanted to get rid of them all.
He was furious with me, too, for having a different point of view.

Zhang Jingwu and his generals wanted the two prime ministers
to resign. If they did not, Zhang Jingwu threatened to have them
killed. The terms of the Seventeen Point Agreement specified that
China would not alter the Tibetan political system, that officials
would continue to take and hold office as usual. The Chinese themselves had written the agreement. Tibetan proposals for modifica-
tions had been ignored. The Tibetans had agreed under duress. But
now the Chinese were threatening to violate the terms of their own
invention. They were openly interfering in Tibetan affairs. It was
armed occupation.

The Dalai Lama was ensconced in the Potala Palace with no
power to act. He could not govern Tibet. And the two prime ministers had no control either. Neither the Dalai Lama nor his prime
ministers could do much of anything. Patriotic Tibetans were suffering, from both inflation and from the high-handedness of the occupying Chinese. Gun-toting Chinese troops were everywhere. The
people of Lhasa were demanding the withdrawal of troops and a re-
negotiation of the Seventeen Point Agreement.

Gyalo Thondup in front of the Potala in 1952

I was listening to people from both the Chinese and Tibetan sides. I could not support the Chinese, and I could not join the Tibetan people to fight against them. I sympathized with the Tibetan people and with my brother the Dalai Lama, so isolated in his palace and not knowing what to do, with his two prime ministers suspected of being American spies and 80 percent of his officials collaborating with the Chinese. But if I publicly supported the Tibetan people in their protests, I could bring harm to the Dalai Lama. No one had questioned me yet, but if the situation continued, I would have to declare publicly whether I stood with the Tibetans or the Chinese— or whether I was a two-faced collaborator playing both sides.

The Chinese wanted me as their tool. They wanted me to become one of their puppets. In fact they wanted the Dalai Lama and eventually the entire Tibetan population to be their puppets, dancing to the Chinese tune. They began hinting that they would support me politically, and even militarily, if I supported them in their efforts to wipe out their opposition, the so-called reactionary aristocracy.

And they hoped I could get the Dalai Lama to go along. Their offer revealed their true intention of wiping out the Tibetan political elite. Implicit in that revelation was the threat that if I did not go along, I would be wiped out, too.

The Tibetan prime ministers were forced to resign. The Chinese forced the Kashag and the Dalai Lama to ask them to step down. Lukhangwa fled to Kalimpong, and Lobsang Tashi returned to his monastery. The situation was chaotic and ominous. We were heading toward disaster. If nothing changed, bloody conflict could break out between the Chinese army, the Tibetan people, and the Dalai Lama. The Dalai Lama's life could be in danger. And if disaster struck, we were locked inside Tibet with no connections to the outside world. We did not even have any real connections with India, our next-door neighbor. The Chinese could arrest us and kill us all without our being able to receive outside help, maybe without anyone outside even knowing.

My position was increasingly untenable. Tibet was indeed a backward, conservative country. I had returned hoping that the Chinese Communists could bring progress, that they could serve as a force for the good. I had hoped that the Chinese would take a patient, tolerant, go-slow approach to bringing about change. But the reality was just the opposite. The Chinese army was an occupying power, treating ordinary Tibetan people as their enemies, using colonial, imperialist tactics of divide and rule. After six months of listening to the Chinese, my hopes had flown out the window like the wind. I did not want to be a collaborator. But I did not know what to do.

14

Escape from Tibet

An unexpected invitation from Chinese Communist Party Chairman Mao Zedong forced me to decide. Mao wanted me to head a Tibetan delegation to a conference of the Communist Youth League in Beijing and from there to join an all-China delegation to an international youth conference in Vienna. Zhang Jingwu and the other Chinese generals encouraged me to go. Actually, the invitation was yet another order, prettified as an invitation, another effort to manipulate me into collaborating against my will. I had no choice but to say yes.

The invitation became the straw that broke the camel's back. I could no longer allow myself to succumb to this type of manipulation, nor could I put myself in a position of continual confrontation with the Chinese military officials in Lhasa. To stay and fight would make the Dalai Lama's position even more difficult and risk bringing him harm. I decided I could be of more help to the Dalai Lama and my people from outside Tibet. I had to escape. I would go to India, contact Prime Minister Nehru, and elicit his help. Perhaps other governments could also be persuaded to join the Tibetan cause. My mother and younger brother Lobsang Samten concurred with my decision. Indeed, they encouraged me to go.

I presented my dilemma to S. N. Sinha, the Indian counsel general in Lhasa who had given such good advice to the Tibetan government and then been so frustrated when his warnings about the impending Chinese attack seemed to evaporate into thin air. I told him my plan. I would escape to India, present the Tibetan case to the Indian government, perhaps be in contact with representatives of other governments, too, and live with my family in Darjeeling. Mr. Sinha immediately sent a private message to Prime Minister Nehru, explaining my situation and requesting that I be granted asylum.

The reply arrived the next evening. Mr. Nehru welcomed me to stay in Darjeeling to do whatever I wanted. He asked me to inform him when and where I would be crossing into India so that he could alert the border guards to expect me. I was not sure exactly when I would be crossing, but I knew I would be entering through Tawang, near Burma and Assam, along one of the old, well-traveled trade routes.

I had already promised General Zhang that I would attend the conference in Beijing. For my escape to succeed, I needed an excuse to leave Lhasa without arousing suspicion. I told the general that before I left, I wanted to finish implementing the reforms on my family's estates. On my own, without consulting the Chinese, I had already introduced reforms in Ramagang and Tolung Seshin, the two estates just across the Kyichu River from Lhasa. Now I wanted to implement the same reforms for the two in southern Tibet—Jora and Chayul. I assured General Zhang that I would return in time for the trip to Beijing. He was delighted.

The Dalai Lama knew nothing of my plans. We never told him. So long as he remained ignorant of my intended escape, he could honestly claim later not to have known and thus could not be blamed. Only my mother, Lobsang Sampten, S. N. Sinha, and Lhamo Tsering, my longtime, trusted deputy who was escaping with me, knew of the plans. Even our three traveling companions—two family servants and a lama from the Kumbum monastery—did not know.

The Chinese generals held a banquet to send me off. They urged me to come back quickly, and I promised to join the youth delegation in Beijing as soon as I returned. But I was playing tricks. I kept my promise to reform our estates. At Chayul, I burned generations of promissory notes, forgiving all debts and interest. I cancelled the taxes the four hundred families on the estate ordinarily paid on the land they farmed. The land became theirs. I opened the granaries and distributed our reserves for free. Later, at our estate in Jora, close to the Assam border, I again burned the promissory notes, cancelled the tax on land, and distributed grain to the two hundred or so families there. As the newly freed Jora farmers were preparing a banquet to celebrate, butchering pigs and sheep, my traveling companions and I quietly took our leave, promising to return within the week. I did not like having to lie, but we had no time to linger. We had to pass through Tsona en route to India, and the Chinese were already setting up a military outpost there. We wanted at all costs to avoid a confrontation with the Chinese troops. We traveled by dark and hid by day, going some sixty hours without sleep until we finally arrived at the Indian checkpoint along the border of the North-East Frontier Agency, what is today called Arunachal Pradesh.

The Indian soldiers were shocked, even frightened, to see us. We looked like a band of soldiers ourselves, six able-bodied young men on huge, spirited Amdo horses, toting guns and carrying maps, binoculars, and compasses. Only after I offered to turn our guns over to the soldiers did they breathe a sigh of relief.

But they did not know what to do. They had had no notice that a group of Tibetan men would be crossing the border. The officer in charge of the post was at a dinner party in a nearby monastery and was not expected back until late. We would have to await his return.

We had prepared our dinner and were looking forward to sleep when the officer rushed in to confront us. He was agitated and rude, demanding to know who we were and where we were headed. I told him we were refugees from Lhasa, escaping to Darjeeling. He accused us of being Chinese spies. I protested, taking out my pen and writing my name: Gyalo Thondup. I asked if he had received any instructions from the Indian government about Gyalo Thondup. He still thought I was lying and wondered what kind of message he could have received. I asked him to leave us alone. We had gone too long without sleep. We were exhausted. We could talk in the morning. He was still angry when he left, but we fell quickly asleep.

At two in the morning, the officer and his soldiers were back, rushing in and shaking me awake. The officer was trembling and apologetic. He had gone through his files. He had located official instructions pertaining to Gyalo Thondup, received over a month before. He wanted to take us immediately to the military guesthouse, where we would be given proper accommodations. He could not stop apologizing and begging my forgiveness.

I urged him to calm down, not to be scared. I wanted to sleep where I was. I was exhausted. I did not blame him. We could move to the guesthouse in the morning.

The next morning the Indian officer served us a hearty breakfast of tea and fried eggs. The traveling companions who had had no idea of my plan to escape were stunned. The night before, they were expecting to be jailed; now, suddenly, we were honored guests.

A ten-man military escort accompanied us from the border post to the town of Tawang in the southern foothills of the Himalayan Mountains. Tawang, the site of an ancient monastery, was a beautiful place, filled with fragrant magnolias and colorful rhododendrons. The population of some three hundred or four hundred families was entirely Tibetan. Tawang was south of the McMahon Line and thus had been formally ceded to British India as part of the Simla Convention of 1914. While representatives of China, Tibet, and Great Britain had participated in the Simla negotiations, only Tibet and Great Britain had signed the final agreement establishing the border between southern Tibet and northern India that came to be called the McMahon Line after the British plenipotentiary who negotiated the treaty. But the British had never actually taken control of the area. The commissioner of Tawang had always been Tibetan. With Indian independence in 1947, all previously British-held territories were inherited by India. The Indian government waited until February 1951 to take actual control of Tawang. Then they finally chased the Tibetan commissioner away and hoisted the Indian flag.

The residents of Tawang were still wary of Indian rule. When they learned that the Dalai Lama's brother was in town, they first thought that I had come to reclaim the place for Tibet. The village chieftains showered me with gifts of eggs, cheese, meat, and the hand-carved wooden bowls for which the town is famous. We received more than a thousand eggs. I had to explain that I was running away from the Chinese occupiers of Tibet and was in no position myself to help free them from Indian rule. We were in Tawang for about ten days, staying with a trader from my native Amdo, getting a good rest before setting out for the final week-long leg of the journey through the tropical jungles of Assam.

From Tawang, another military escort sent us through Assam to the Indian town of Jaswant Garh, the first place inside the border with a railway connection. From there, we sent two of our traveling companions back to Lhasa with our horses and equipment. When they wondered how to break the news of my escape to my mother, I told them to tell her that I had duped them. My mother put on a great show of anger and dismay when they told her the story. They never knew that she had known all along.

After two days of meetings with Indian officials, Lhamo Tsering, the Kumbum lama, and I left by train for Siliguri and from there took a taxi to Darjeeling, arriving so early in the morning that my little sister Jetsun Pema was not yet awake. My wife was no longer there. She had gone to Calcutta to await the birth of our second child. Medical facilities were better in Calcutta.

I quickly caught a private cargo flight to join my wife, arriving to find her at the stove cooking dinner in an advanced stage of pregnancy. She was so shocked to see me that she thought she must be dreaming. She had never imagined that I would leave Lhasa. A few days after celebrating my return, she was rushed to the hospital in labor. Our son Khedroop was born the next day, on June 24, 1952.[1]

I entered the hospital myself only a few days after my wife and infant son were discharged. Somewhere in the jungles of Assam, while drinking water from the mountain streams, I had contracted both typhoid fever and malaria. My fever was so high that the doctors immersed me in ice to bring it down. Except for a piece of toast and a small scoop of ice cream every couple days, they would not let me eat. When I finally returned home two and a half months later, I had lost some forty pounds.

15

Beginning Life in India

Generals Zhang Jingwu and Tan Guansan were so shocked to learn of my escape that they sent two emissaries to Darjeeling to convince me to return. They still wanted me to lead the Tibetan youth delegation to Beijing, still wanted me as their collaborator and slave. When I refused, they apparently concluded that my return from the United States was not evidence of my patriotism and devotion to the "motherland" after all but an indication that I must be an American spy. Had I not returned to Tibet from the United States and then escaped to India? Later, they publicly branded me a traitor and took away my citizenship. I was even worse than a "reactionary rebel."

My efforts to bring the plight of Tibet to international attention began while I was still recovering from my illness. My wife helped me write a letter to American President Truman describing the political situation in Tibet, the suffering of the Tibetan people, and the plight of the Dalai Lama. I urged the United States government to help. It was a short letter, only two or three pages long. We were not asking for weapons or military assistance then. The armed resistance in Tibet had yet to begin. We wanted the United States to use its good offices to convince the Chinese to withdraw their military from Tibet. In those days, people like me thought that the United States was so great and powerful that it could make almost anything happen.

I wrote a similar letter to my old friend President Chiang Kai-shek. He was the first to respond to my call for help. He sent a woman disguised as a tourist to tell me that the Republic of China on Taiwan was prepared to contribute arms and money, whatever we required, to help the Tibetan cause. But Tibet's cause and the goals of the Nationalist government were not the same. We wanted Chiang Kai-shek to support our struggle for a free and independent Tibet and saw the removal of Chinese troops as the means to secure that goal. Chiang Kai-shek and the Nationalist government wanted us to fight to overthrow the Communists and bring the Nationalists back to power. We could not accept their terms. The Communists were already putting out their propaganda saying that we were tools of the Nationalists. We never refused the Nationalists' help outright. We simply did not respond.

The Indian government gave me my first glimmer of what the American response to my letter might be. India was not meant to know about my letters to Taiwan and the United States, but they found out anyway. Balraj K. Kapoor, the new Indian political officer in Sikkim handling his country's affairs with Tibet and Bhutan, visited me in Darjeeling to tell me that the American embassy in New Delhi was seeking official permission from India to meet with me to discuss the letter I had written to President Truman. Mr. Kapoor had instructions from Prime Minister Nehru to request a copy of my letters to both Chiang Kai-shek and the American president. And he had additional instructions from the prime minister. He was to inform me that I was no longer allowed to carry out political activities in India.

I was shocked that Nehru should prohibit me from engaging in politics. I had escaped from Tibet in order to seek outside help. Mr. Sinha had assured me before I left that Nehru had given his permission for me to do whatever I wanted in India. My reasons for going had been very clear to him. I protested to Mr. Kapoor, railing against these new instructions. Why had the prime minister changed his mind? I refused, with apologies and an effort to remain polite, to give him copies of the letters.

Mr. Kapoor was unfailingly polite. He offered to help me with whatever I needed. He soon proved useful beyond all expectations. He knew of my financial difficulties. I had no steady income. My mother was sending me money through the traders in Kalimpong, and both my wife and I had small savings. But I needed work to support my family. In addition to my wife and two children, my youngest sister Jetsun Pema and Tsering Dolma's two children were still in school in Darjeeling. I was responsible for supporting them all.

Mr. Kapoor suggested that I go into the import-export business. His office could help with the required permits. Some Indian merchants in Kalimpong suggested that I import liquor from Europe and sell it in Lhasa. I was soon importing White Horse and Johnny Walker Red Label whiskey from Scotland and three-star Hennessey and Martel brandy from France, exporting the alcohol back to Tibet through the traders in Kalimpong. I also had a license to import tea from Yunnan, which I sold at a one-time profit to some Tibetan traders. My trade in liquor did remarkably well. The bottles I bought for 32 rupees sold for 100 or more in Lhusa. The Chinese military leaders in Lhasa were my best customers. They often threw parties for the Tibetan aristocrats, where the alcohol I supplied them flowed freely. The traders transporting the liquor confessed to me that they also occasionally imbibed from their cargo. Crossing the mountains on cold snowy nights, they sometimes took a few swigs from a bottle or two, replacing the alcohol they had consumed with their own urine. The Chinese never seemed to notice, and my business was never affected.

The ban on my political activities did not last long. In April 1953, I received a visit from V. Kumar, whom I had known in Nanjing when he was the number three secretary in the Indian embassy there. He had since become an official with Calcutta's national security control responsible for foreigners in West Bengal, where Kalimpong and Darjeeling are located. Kumar had instructions to arrange for me to meet Bhola Nath Mullik, the director of Indian intelligence. Mullik was asking to meet me at the instruction of Prime Minister Nehru. The prime minister had rescinded his earlier order forbidding me to engage in political activities. I could do whatever I wanted in India. In return, I was to stay in close contact with Indian intelligence. Mr. Mullik assured me that the Indians were ready to help the Tibetan cause, and he appointed his deputy in Calcutta to give me whatever assistance I needed. I had no particular requests for assistance then. Only when the resistance began in earnest, and we needed radio equipment and weapons, would I turn directly to Mullik for help. But my long and close association with B. N. Mullik and Indian intelligence began at that point.

In 1954, Apa Pant, an able and loquacious diplomat with strong political views, replaced Mr. Kapoor as the political officer in Sikkim. Pant was an ardent follower of the late Mahatma Gandhi and tried to convince me that we Tibetans could win our struggle against China through emulating the same nonviolent resistance that India had practiced against the British. For several years, I spent almost every weekend in the Sikkimese capital of Gangtok, driving from Darjeeling in my Ford station wagon, playing tennis with Pant on the private court outside his home, and listening to his advice about how to use nonviolent resistance to bring independence to Tibet. I became a pretty good tennis player, but found his political suggestions to be naïve, unrealistic, and impractical—nonsense, in fact. What had worked against the British in India could not possibly work against the Chinese in Tibet. Tibet was under military occupation, and Chinese soldiers would have no scruples about shooting nonviolent resisters. But I needed the cooperation of the Indians in our struggle for Tibet, and Aba Pant could help.

By this time, a small number of Tibetans, including some who had been ranking government officials in Lhasa, had taken up residence in the Himalayan hill stations of Kalimpong and Darjeeling. One of them was Tsepon W. D. Shakabpa, the former finance minister who had tried to get me back to Lhasa by inviting me to join his trade delegation while I was still a student in Nanjing. Shakabpa had been in Kalimpong since 1950, after failing to get to Beijing to negotiate on behalf of Tibet as the Chinese were preparing to attack. He had refused to return to a Chinese-occupied Tibet, where he had reason to fear for his life, and he remained a prominent and ardent advocate for Tibetan independence.

Khenchung Lobsang Gyaltsen, another ranking official, was also in Kalimpong, serving both as the unofficial Tibetan trade representative there and in charge of the gold bullion then held in Sikkim through the good offices of the chogyal. The bullion had been purchased during Shakabpa's visit to the United States under instructions from the Tibetan government with funds from the lord chamberlain's treasury. He had spent about a million dollars, buying the gold at forty dollars an ounce. The gold was meant to be held in safekeeping for the Tibetan government in case of emergency.

The Chinese had found out about the bullion and were lobbying Khenchung Lobsang Gyaltsen to send it back to Lhasa. As the Dalai Lama's new chief of staff, my brother Lobsang Samten believed that the bullion was better kept in Sikkim, where the Chinese could not get hold of it. One of my tasks in India was to make certain that Khenchung Lobsang Gyaltsen did not cave in to Chinese demands.

As the Tibetan community in Darjeeling and Kalimpong kept growing, all sorts of small organizations and committees were springing up. Shakabpa, Lobsang Gyaltsen, and I met frequently to discuss the situation in Tibet and to consider what we could do to help. We persuaded Tharchin Babu, a Tibetan Christian who had been publishing a monthly newspaper, *The Tibet Mirror,* to increase production to once a week, so Tibetans in India could receive regular news of what was happening inside Tibet. In July 1954, when a terrible flood in Gyantse killed hundreds of people and left thousands of others homeless, we raised money to help in the relief efforts there. We gathered to celebrate Tibetan holidays, especially the Dalai Lama's birthday and Losar, the traditional Tibetan lunar New Year. In Lhasa, Losar begins with the Dalai Lama making offerings

to our protective deity Palden Lhamo and sending best wishes—
tashi delek—to everyone. The Losar celebrations combine religious
ceremonies with secular feasting and can last for days.

Shakabpa, Lobsang Gyaltsen, and I came to serve as the unofficial
leaders of the Tibetan community. We never considered ourselves a
real organization, but our activities sometimes took place under the
informal rubric of the Tibetan Welfare Association (*Dedon Tsogpa*).
Some came to refer to us as *jhenkhentsisum*—*jhen* meaning elder
brother and referring to me, *khen* referring to Lobsang Gyaltsen's
title of *khenchung* (a monk official of the fourth rank), *tsi* referring
to Shakabpa's official title of *tsipon*, and *sum* denoting the number
three.

I had often disagreed with Shakabpa when he was serving the
Taktra regime. He had actively opposed Reting Regent and must
have played a role in the demise of both my father and Reting. Many
among the Tibetan community in India still remembered his abuse
of power during that time and cautioned me against working with
him. Some prominent Tibetans, including Yuthok and Raga Pandatsang, openly urged me to expel Shakabpa from our circle. But I
thought we Tibetans needed to cast aside our differences during this
period of struggle. We were politically united in our goal of a free
and independent Tibet. We wanted to bring the Dalai Lama out. We
needed to publicize the plight of Tibet and win international support for our cause. I believed that if the outside world understood
what was happening inside Tibet that the truth would ultimately
prevail. We could do our work effectively only if we put aside our
quarrels. Our likes and dislikes did not matter in our struggle. What
mattered was that we had found common ground and were joining
forces to pursue our cause. Our mission on behalf of Tibet stood
above all else.

In September 1954, Apa Pant provided us our first opportunity
to present our case to the Indian government. He arranged for me,
Lobsang Gyaltsen, and Shakabpa to travel to New Delhi, where we
briefed Indian officials and politicians, beginning with Prime Minister Nehru and ranging from Foreign Secretary S. Dutt and the

Home Minister Pandit Pant to members of Parliament. We talked to politicians on all sides of the Indian political spectrum, including members of the dominant Congress party, opposition members from the Communist Party and from the Socialist Party, and independents. Our message was always the same. We described the terrible problems the Dalai Lama and the Tibetan people were facing under the Chinese occupation and told them about the growing opposition to Chinese rule. We warned the prime minister and his officials that if China succeeded in Tibet today, India would face problems with China tomorrow. We wanted Mr. Nehru to intervene on behalf of Tibet. We hoped he would use his good offices to persuade the Chinese to withdraw, or at least drastically reduce, their military presence there. Mr. Nehru was attentive and sympathetic, just as he had been at our first meeting after my return from Nanjing, and he asked many questions. But he never offered his opinion.

Everyone we met, including Ashoka Mehta, one of India's most distinguished scholars, was unfailingly hospitable, listening closely to our views. Everyone was sympathetic to the problems of Tibet. But few fully agreed with our argument that China could become a threat to India. China and India had signed the Panchsheel Treaty several months earlier, in April 1954, proclaiming the five principles of peaceful coexistence—mutual respect for each other's territorial integrity, mutual nonaggression, mutual noninterference in each other's internal affairs, equality and mutual benefit, and peaceful coexistence. Only a few rare political independents such as Acharya Kripalani were openly critical of the treaty, describing it as "born in sin to put the seal of our approach on the destruction of an ancient nation."[1] This was the heyday of Chini-Hindi Bhai Bhai, the brotherhood of India and China. The Indian government, with Nehru at the helm, was not prepared to be openly critical of its new Chinese brother.

16

The Dalai Lama Visits China

Even as we were in New Delhi warning the Indian government of the perils of China, the Dalai Lama himself was in China at the official invitation of Mao Zedong and the Communist government. The first session of China's National People's Congress was about to convene, and the Dalai Lama was to serve as the head of the Tibetan delegation to the meeting. He traveled with an entourage of some five hundred people, including my mother, my older sister, two younger brothers, several of the Dalai Lama's tutors, the Panchen Lama, members of the Kashag, and many high-ranking Tibetan officials. General Zhang Jingwu accompanied the Dalai Lama, sticking close by his side everywhere he went.

Many Tibetans had opposed the Dalai Lama's visit to China. Some had even described it as an abduction. They believed that he had been taken there against his will and feared that the Chinese would hold him hostage and refuse to allow him to return. The crowds who lined the streets of Lhasa to bid the Dalai Lama goodbye had wept as his palanquin passed. They were afraid that they would never see him again.

Traveling by car, horseback, airplane, and train, the Dalai Lama had arrived at the Beijing train station on September 4, 1954, to an enthusiastic welcome from Chinese Premier Zhou Enlai, military chief Zhu De, and an applauding crowd of ordinary Chinese. Party Chairman Mao Zedong honored him with an elaborate reception in the Great Hall of the People. The Chairman's welcoming speech was warm. He was a gracious host. During his stay, my brother visited Mao privately at his residence in Zhongnanhai and saw him also at public events, meeting the party chairman more than a dozen times in all. They discussed everything from Tibetan culture and religion to problems with the Chinese troops then stationed in Lhasa. Phuntsok Wangyal, a Khampa from Batang who had been an early and enthusiastic member of the tiny Tibetan Communist Party, served as their interpreter. Even today, the Dalai Lama still views Phuntsok Wangyal with respect and considers him a friend.

Throughout the visit, Mao continued to reassure the Dalai Lama that the Chinese troops were in Tibet to help, not to rule. If the troops did not behave, Mao said, he would pull them out. Tibet would become an autonomous region rather than a province of China. Mao proposed the establishment of a Preparatory Committee for the Autonomous Region of Tibet (PCART). The committee would ensure that the Tibetan people themselves, not the Chinese, would dictate the pace of future reforms. The Chinese leader was full of reassurance.

The Chinese also introduced the Dalai Lama and his delegation to some of China's recent economic accomplishments. They visited China's northeast (Manchuria), where they saw a newly built hydroelectric project and visited numerous industrial factories that had been built with loans and technical assistance from the Soviet Union. They went to Shanghai, the most modern and cosmopolitan of China's cities. They stayed in China until Losar, the Tibetan New Year, of 1955.

Only on the eve of the Dalai Lama's departure did the visit turn sour. After behaving so politely to my brother, evincing such respect for Buddhism and promising regional autonomy for Tibet, the chairman's attitude unexpectedly changed. In their final meeting, Mao suddenly declared that Tibetan Buddhism was poison.

Dalai Lama with Mao (Xinhua)

"Firstly," Mao said, "It reduces the population because monks and nuns must stay celibate, and secondly it neglects material progress."[1] The Dalai Lama was shocked. Later he said that he was suddenly afraid when Mao spoke those words. He felt a burning sensation all over his face. He concluded that Mao was "the destroyer of the Dharma after all."[2] Mao had completely misunderstood him, the Dalai Lama concluded, failing to understand that the very essence of his purpose and being was spiritual and religious. Mao meant to destroy religion, not protect it.

On their way back to Lhasa, the Dalai Lama, together with other members of my family, visited the Kumbum monastery and our ancestral village of Taktser. Again, thousands of monks and ordinary people came to greet them, just as they had some fifteen years before when we set out from the Kumbum monastery to Lhasa. By the time of this visit, Amdo had already begun the process of rural land reform and collectivization that the Communists had started in most parts of China just after taking power but had yet to implement in Central Tibet. In Amdo, land and property had been seized from the so-called landlords and redistributed to poor farmers. Many of the landlords had been put on public trial and violently struggled against. Some had been executed. Chinese officials accompanied the Dalai Lama and members of my family to every visit they made in Amdo. They were never allowed a private conversation with their fellow Tibetans, not even with close relatives and friends. People were afraid to speak freely. In Taktser, when my mother asked our relatives and friends how they were faring after land reform, everyone said the same thing. They were very happy. They thanked Chairman Mao Zedong and the Chinese Communist Party. But they were weeping as they spoke. They were supposed to be in heaven but all they could do was cry. Their lives were tortured, and they were afraid to tell the truth.

17

The Dalai Lama Visits India

The Dalai Lama was still in China when Apa Pant raised with me the possibility that His Holiness might make a visit to India. Prime Minister Nehru had also been in China while the Dalai Lama was there, and the two had met for the first time. The Buddha Jyanti celebrations in honor of the 2,500th anniversary of the Buddha's birth were to be held in the fall of 1956 in Bodh Gaya, the town where the Buddha attained enlightenment. The celebration would be a joyous occasion, bringing together thousands of Buddhists from all over the world. The Indians wanted the Dalai Lama to attend. The Maha Bodhi Society of India would issue the invitation, and Thondup Namgyal, the crown prince of Sikkim and president of the Maha Bodhi Society, would travel to Lhasa to present the invitation in person. The Buddha Jyanti celebration was a strictly religious occasion. The Chinese government could not reasonably object.

Apa Pant asked Shakabpa, Lobsang Gyaltsen, and me to serve as intermediaries in the secret negotiations that would be required to bring the visit to fruition. We made clear from the beginning that the Dalai Lama's visit was contingent upon two prior assurances: a grant of political asylum once the Dalai Lama was inside India, and

Dalai Lama speaking at the Buddha Jyanti celebrations

Prime Minister Nehru's promise that he would use his good offices to persuade the Chinese government to remove, or at least significantly reduce, the number of troops in Tibet. On these two issues, the Dalai Lama's advisors and I stood united. Without first receiving these assurances, the invitation could not be tendered.

The negotiations went on for more than a year, with messages going quietly back and forth through trusted intermediaries in Kalimpong to the Dalai Lama's closest, most trusted advisors in Lhasa—his lord chamberlain Phala above all. Neither Shakabpa nor Lobsang Gyaltsen nor I was ever in direct contact with the Dalai Lama. Nor was the Dalai Lama ever directly in contact with us. Tibetan government procedures require all communications with the Dalai Lama to go through his leading staff. As his brother and a member of his family, I could contact the Dalai Lama directly. But the arrangements we were making with India were official rather than familial.

The political situation in Tibet was deteriorating even as the negotiations continued. After the Dalai Lama's visit to our native village in early 1955, resistance to Chinese rule in Amdo and Kham began to grow. The Chinese were in the process of implementing their so-called reforms. When the Chinese convened meetings to convince the farmers of the benefits that land reform could bring, many countered by arguing that reform was unnecessary and refused to go along. When Chinese cadres and People's Liberation Army soldiers insisted on implementing the reforms nonetheless, some angry farmers turned against their would-be liberators and killed them. That agricultural villages were organized into cooperatives, with land taken away from individual families and turned into collectives, was bad enough. But people were devastated when the monasteries, too, were attacked, their traditional estates dissolved and their land taken away to be distributed to the poor. Ordinary Tibetan people could not comprehend why their revered lamas were being declared enemies of the state, dismissed from their monasteries, struggled against, and sometimes even imprisoned and killed. Tibet's traditional way of life was under violent attack.

Incidents of violent resistance increased in proportion to the unpopularity of the Chinese "reforms." Local people began organizing teams of guerrilla fighters. In 1955, Goloks in Amdo attacked a Chinese military garrison. In 1956, people of Lithang in Kham rose up in resistance. Many of the resisters were monks and some of them had guns, though their weapons were usually old and ineffective compared to those of the Chinese. As the fighting worsened, people began fleeing to the monasteries both for their own protection and to defend them from Chinese attack.

The monasteries made easy targets for the Chinese army. The Changtreng Sampheling monastery in Kham, whose leading lama was Trijang Rinpoche, the Dalai Lama's junior tutor, was one of the first to be bombed. Lithang, where the Chinese bombed the ancient monastery and killed hundreds of monks, was next. Each retaliation by the Chinese further fueled the popular flames of Tibetan outrage and violence.[1] As order broke down in the face of violence, families from Amdo and Kham began fleeing the chaos. Many were headed west, toward Lhasa.

In Lhasa, the Preparatory Committee for the Autonomous Region of Tibet, formally established after the Dalai Lama's return, had soon become a sham. While the Dalai Lama was the ostensible chairman of the committee and most of its members were Tibetan, the Chinese had made most of the appointments, and they were decidedly in control. The committee had no power. Decisions were made by the Chinese leaders of the Communist party in Tibet. Their decisions were sent to the preparatory committee only to be rubber-stamped.

Word of the growing resistance in Amdo and Kham came to Kalimpong and Darjeeling. Some of the resisters were fleeing to India. The new arrivals were a constant source of discouraging news about what was happening inside. Getting my brother safely into India with a clear guarantee of political asylum was becoming all the more urgent.

After months of negotiations, we finally reached an agreement with Apa Pant representing the government of India. The Dalai Lama would be granted political asylum once he arrived in India, and Prime Minister Nehru would negotiate with the Chinese for a withdrawal of Chinese troops.[2] Everything seemed to be in order. I looked forward to my brother's arrival with anxious anticipation.

I WAS WITH APA PANT and the maharaja of Sikkim to greet the Dalai Lama as he crossed the border into Sikkim on November 24, 1956. He had traveled by car from Lhasa to Dromo, where the paved road ended, and then made the final stretch of his journey over the Nathula pass on horseback. The next day, he flew in an Indian military aircraft directly from Siliguri to Delhi, where Prime Minister Nehru officially welcomed him in a quiet, dignified ceremony. The rest of the family—my mother, me, my two younger brothers, Lobsang Samten and ten-year-old Tenzin Choegyal, and my sisters Tsering Dolma and Jetsun Pema—flew via Calcutta to join the entourage. Later, our brother Norbu, Taktser Rinpoche, joined us, too. For the first time in our lives, my mother and all the siblings were together at the same time. Families such as ours rarely had occasions to meet. A spread of twenty-seven years separated

*The Great Mother with her seven children, from left: Great Mother,
Tsering Dolma, Thupten Jigme Norbu, Gyalo Thondup, Lobsang Samten,
His Holiness the Dalai Lama, Jetsun Pema, Tenzin Choegyal.*

Tsering Dolma, the oldest of the children, born in 1919, from the
youngest, Tenzin Choegyal, born in 1946. My sister Jetsun Pema,
born in 1940, was attending school at the same time as the children
of my eldest sister, Tsering Dolma. Except for me, the other male
children had become monks and left the family for monasteries at
a very early age.

ZHANG JINGWU had briefed the Dalai Lama carefully before the
trip, instructing him on what and what not to say. Other officials
further warned him to beware of the omnipresent foreign reactionaries who might seek to corrupt his thought. They encouraged him
to praise China's great progress in improving the well-being of the
people. They wanted him to assure the skeptics that religious freedom was alive and thriving in Tibet. Ngabo even prepared a draft
of the speech the Dalai Lama was expected to give at the Buddha

Dalai Lama and his entourage in India, 1956. Ling Rinpoche,
the Dalai Lama's senior tutor, is on the Dalai Lama's right.
Trijang Rinpoche is on his left. Lhasa-based family members
are in lower right of photo.

Jyanti. The Dalai Lama threw it away. He talked instead about the
history of Buddhism and how it had come from India to Tibet and
of the historical importance of the religious and spiritual ties between the two countries. He particularly emphasized the peaceful
nature of the Buddhist faith and called for a spread of religious belief
beyond Asia to the West. Religion was a means of ending war and
bringing forth a new era of world peace.

Later, the Dalai Lama made pilgrimages to other of India's most
sacred Buddhist sites—to Sanchi, where the relics of the Lord Buddha are contained in a great stone stupa commissioned by Emperor
Ashoka in the third century BCE; to Ajanta, where Buddhist paintings and sculptures tracing back to the second century BCE survive
intact in stone mountain caves; and to Benares, the ancient city on

the Ganges where the Lord Buddha is said to have delivered his first sermon.

During his meeting with Nehru in China, the Dalai Lama had been impressed by the Indian prime minister's honesty and sincerity. In India, the contrast between closed and ever suspicious China and democratic India, so open and at peace with itself, was even more stark. Soon, my brother was opening his heart to the prime minister, explaining to him how desperate things had become in eastern Tibet and how he had come to believe that the Chinese were intent on destroying Tibet's religion and culture forever. He told the prime minister that he had decided he ought not to return home. He felt he could no longer either do any good for his people or stop them from resorting to violence. He told Nehru that he wanted to stay in India until Tibet could win back its freedom by peaceful means.[3] He asked for Nehru's help and brought up the question of political asylum.

But the Chinese had gotten wind of our plan. As the Dalai Lama was traveling in India, Premier Zhou Enlai arrived there, too, and set about trying to force my brother's return. The Chinese premier turned on his charm. He promised Nehru that he would convince Mao to remove the offending troops from Lhasa and make sure that the Seventeen Point Agreement was respected. Zhou met with the Dalai Lama, too, to convince him to return, promising that no new "reforms" would be introduced in Tibet until the people were ready. He urged him to return to his homeland where he was needed. He also issued a threat. The situation in Tibet was deteriorating, Zhou said. The Chinese were prepared to use force if the popular resistance continued.

In early January 1957, Zhou Enlai invited my brother Norbu and me to join him, Field Marshal He Long, and Chinese ambassador to India Yuan Zhongxian for dinner at the Chinese embassy. Norbu and I made no effort to soft-pedal our criticisms of the Chinese presence in Tibet and the havoc it was wreaking. The huge number of unnecessary troops had led to such a shortage of food and high inflation that some people were facing starvation. Noble, kind-hearted people who had worked for the good of Tibet were being treated like enemies. Evil people were being appointed to high office. The Chinese generals were trying to stir up discord, pitting the Panchen Lama against the Dalai Lama. The Chinese should respect the fundamental rights of the Tibetan people and treat Tibetans as equals, we said.

I had first learned about Zhou Enlai during the negotiations between the Communists and the Nationalists at the end of the Second World War. Zhou was already doing Mao's bidding by then, even when following Mao meant betraying his own closest comrades. But Zhou was sophisticated and suave. He admitted to my brother and me that perhaps some Chinese officials had not fully understood the situation in Tibet. They did not understand the Tibetan language and culture and had made little effort to learn, he said. He promised to report our concerns to Chairman Mao. He said he would persuade Mao Zedong to withdraw his troops and told us that China did not want to interfere in the internal affairs of Tibet or to undermine the local economy. He wanted us to persuade the Dalai Lama to return to Lhasa, repeating his false promises about convincing Mao to reduce the number of troops. He even said that if he went back on his word, we should feel free to speak out publicly against him. Neither Norbu nor I believed him. Zhou was a deceitful man, spewing sweet talk and spouting lies. I have a word for Zhou. I call him *xiao bailian* (小白脸), little white face. Chinese use the term to describe someone who is understanding and sincere on the outside but inwardly crafty, sly, and full of tricks.

THEN SOMETHING shocking happened. Nehru changed his mind. He went back on his promise. He refused to grant my brother the political asylum we had so desperately wanted and negotiated so long to secure. He told my brother that he should go back to Tibet and work peacefully to try to carry out the Seventeen Point Agreement. [4] He even told the Dalai Lama that I, Gyalo Thondup, was unreliable and warned him not to trust his own brother.[5] He told the

Dalai Lama not to believe what I was telling him. He started pushing the Dalai Lama to return to Tibet.

Intelligence chief Mullik and Sikkim political officer Pant broke the news to me. They tried to assure me that the Dalai Lama would be safe in Tibet. Zhou Enlai, after all, had given assurances.

They were naïve. How could they believe that my brother would be safe? The Dalai Lama had spoken publicly in India, openly expressing his dissatisfaction with the Chinese government, the lack of freedom he had in his own country, and his desire to remain in India. I accused the Indian officials of pushing my brother into a dungeon, into the butcher's hands, into the fire. This was murder. I wept as I accused them. Where was their compassion, their morality, their principles? I had been foolish to believe Nehru's promises, and the Indian prime minister had been naïve to believe Zhou Enlai. Maybe he had simply been overpowered by the Chinese premier. Zhou's promises were empty talk. The Chinese would never withdraw their troops.

I WAS TERRIFIED about what might happen to my brother. Norbu and I tried to persuade him to stay. Everyone wanted him to stay. But once again he had no choice. Nehru would not give him asylum. He had to return to Lhasa.

Shakabpa, Lobsang Gyaltsen, and I accompanied the Dalai Lama on the last leg of his Indian journey, when he spent a week at Bhutan House in Kalimpong before moving on to Gangtok.[6] The Chinese had tried to prevent the Dalai Lama from visiting Kalimpong. They knew that many disaffected Tibetans who had fled to India were congregated in Kalimpong and nearby Darjeeling. Surely the refugees would try to meet the Dalai Lama and plead with him to stay. And Nehru, during one of his meetings with Zhou Enlai, had described Kalimpong as a den of spies.[7]

At first Nehru agreed to respect the Chinese wish that the Dalai Lama not visit such a place. But he soon changed his mind, pointing out that India is a free country after all. His staff arranged the Dalai Lama's visit to Kalimpong and Gangtok.[8]

Thousands lined the streets of Kalimpong to welcome the Dalai Lama, and a huge crowd assembled to hear his teachings in the outdoor stadium on the grounds of Dr. Graham's school on the outskirts of the town. The same scenes were repeated several days later, when the Dalai Lama delivered teachings in the nearby Sikkim capital of Gangtok.

AS I ACCOMPANIED my brother to the Sikkim border to say our good-byes, I had no doubt that he was returning to a horrible fate. I was convinced that I would never see him again.

My brother was utterly serene. I stood in awe watching him take his farewell. He told us not to worry. "I am facing the truth," he said. "I am facing the Lord Buddha. I am going for the people of Tibet. I am not frightened. My people are there."

I felt something indescribably unique and special about my brother then, something I had first begun to feel in Lhasa returning after so many years away. He was not an ordinary man. His equanimity, I thought, must be rooted deep in his Buddhist learning and faith.

Two years later, Nehru would change his mind and welcome the Dalai Lama back. I would come to thank him and the people of India for providing shelter to our people and helping us to survive. Eventually I would come to consider Nehru a great leader. But at the time, I felt outrageously betrayed.

18

The CIA Offers to Help

Weeks after the Dalai Lama returned to Tibet, I delivered the first group of resistance fighters to the Mahanandi River that divides India from what was then East Pakistan and is now Bangladesh. Inside East Pakistan, the six young Tibetans were met by Pakistani and American officials and flown to the island of Saipan. The CIA took over from there. Four months later, the recruits and their equipment were loaded on an unidentified aircraft and dropped back inside Tibet.

My brother Norbu had arranged my first official encounter with the CIA. He had left the United States and taken up residence in the Hongunji monastery in Japan[1] after some sort of falling out with his American sponsors. In 1954, the CIA contacted him there and asked him to introduce me to some of their operatives in India. Until then, unnamed Americans had occasionally visited me in Darjeeling and Kalimpong, wanting to know what was happening in Tibet, expressing concern and saying that they wanted to help. But they had never offered anything concrete. No one used name cards then, and some people did not even go by their real names, so I did not always know the true identities of everyone I met. In retrospect, Nehru was

167

probably right that the Kalimpong was a den of spies. Some of the Americans I met there must have been from the CIA.

Kalimpong was full of colorful foreigners then. The multi-talented Russian painter, scholar, ethicist, and pacifist, Dr. Nicholas Roerich, lived with his beautiful mystic wife Helena in a hilltop abode they called Crookety House. Helena stayed there after her husband's death, continuing to write her Agni Yoga books until she died in 1955. The anthropologist Prince Peter from Greece and Denmark, a student of the great anthropologists Branislow Malinowski and Sir Raymond Firth, was also a presence. Unable to enter Tibet following the Chinese invasion, he undertook anthropological research on the Tibetans in Kalimpong, taking thousands of photographs, measuring thousands of Tibetan heads, and interviewing polyandrous Tibetan women who had more than one husband. Zhou Enlai himself may have convinced Prime Minister Nehru that Prince Peter was a spy, which ultimately led to his expulsion from Kalimpong and India. The Mongolian monk named Dawa Sangpo also frequented Kalimpong without arousing any discernible suspicion. Only later did he reveal himself in print as a Japanese spy whose real name was Hisao Kimura.[2] I reached my own conclusions about the British scholar Marco Pallis, who had traveled inside Tibet as an explorer, pilgrim, and scholar and was so deeply immersed in the study of Tibet and its Buddhist religion that he dressed in the traditional chuba.[3] Sometime in the early 1960s, Pallis took me to meet the director of MI6 in London to solicit the help of British intelligence. The director soon disabused me of any notion of getting anything from the British and told me not to believe those fellows who thought that England might help. "We have already withdrawn from everywhere east of the Suez," he told me. He suggested I talk to the Americans instead.

When Norbu flew to Calcutta to take me to meet Miss Terry at number 2 Victoria Terrace, I was well aware of her credentials. Indian intelligence had apparently gotten wind of our meeting, too. Leaving Miss Terry's apartment building just as dark was about to descend, I caught a glimpse of Mr. Kumar from Calcutta's foreign registration office sitting with several other men in a car across the street. He ducked from view just as he caught sight of me, but by then it was too late. That was not the last time I discovered Indian intelligence agents at a meeting that was meant to be secret.

Miss Terry knew about my still unanswered letter to President Truman and explained that she was meeting me under her government's instructions. She said that the United States wanted to help the Tibetan cause in whatever way we needed. We met frequently thereafter, and she introduced me to some of her colleagues as well. But it was not until John Hoskins took over her post in September 1956[4] that the CIA's offers became more concrete. By then, the resistance movement in Tibet, especially in Kham, was well under way. The CIA was prepared to train some of the freedom fighters as radio operators and guerrilla warriors. John Hoskins wanted me to introduce him to some of the Tibetan fighters. I was happy to oblige.

I did not have to go to Tibet to find young men eager to be trained to fight on behalf of their country. A number of resistance fighters who had taken up residence in Kalimpong and Darjeeling had already come to me for help. Until the CIA made concrete offers, I had nothing to offer but words of encouragement.

Most of the resisters in India were followers of Andrug Gompo Tashi, a wealthy, patriotic Kham trader from Lithang where the resistance had begun with the introduction of China's so-called reforms. Popular outrage had been further fueled with the death and devastation unleashed when the Chinese attacked and bombed the local Lithang monastery. Gompo Tashi had established a resistance organization called Chushi Gangdruk, meaning "Four Rivers and Six Ranges," the ancient Tibetan name for Kham. He was financing many of the freedom fighters and was soon to become their undisputed leader. Another group of resistance fighters who had fled to Kalimpong were monks from the Labrang monastery in Amdo (Gansu). Thonden Rinpoche was their leader, and Gunthang Tsultrin was his deputy and the manager of his labrang. Both were active resistance fighters themselves.

What the resistance fighters wanted most was weapons and training. What Hoskins and the CIA were proposing was a three-step process. First, the CIA wanted direct word from the Dalai Lama that he wanted and welcomed American help. With the Dalai Lama's support, the CIA would begin the second step, which was training a group of resistance fighters in Morse code and radio communications and then dropping the trained radio operators back into Tibet, together with CIA-supplied equipment. Inside Tibet, they would communicate directly to the CIA in Washington, providing information about the location and size of the various groups of resistance fighters and detailing the number and type of weapons at their disposal. On the basis of that information, the CIA would begin the third step, which was training more resistance fighters in guerrilla warfare and providing them with arms, ammunition, and other material support.

The training would take place in some remote part of the world, and the fighters would then be secretly dropped back into Tibet with weapons and radios. Airdrops of more weapons and equipment would follow. If all went well, the trained recruits could then both train and equip the local resistance fighters. The radios would allow them to coordinate their actions across Tibet as well as to provide intelligence about the resistance to the CIA in both the United States and India.

The Americans were slow to understand that their first consideration, a direct request from the Dalai Lama for help from the American CIA, was impossible. The Dalai Lama was never part of any decision to involve the CIA in the struggle for Tibet. The US government never received any request or go-ahead from him. The Dalai Lama's religious training prohibited him from sanctioning the use of violence. And His Holiness was still officially working under the terms of the Seventeen Point Agreement in cooperation with the Chinese. No one who was part of the Tibetan government could risk China's ire by being seen to support the resistance. Any overt violation of those terms could pose terrible problems for the Dalai Lama and the Tibetan government. The Dalai Lama was even more vulnerable following Nehru's refusal to grant him asylum. After so openly speaking out about his problems with the Chinese, any contact with the Americans would render him open to charges of collaboration with the imperialists. The Dalai Lama's staff made sure that the Chinese could never accuse the Dalai Lama, his secretariat, or the Kashag of supporting the resistance or working with the CIA.

The resistance movement was completely spontaneous and independent, both from the Tibetan government in Lhasa and from any foreign power. Some high-ranking officials in the Tibetan government, including people close to the Dalai Lama, knew about the resistance from the beginning and were sympathetic to its cause. When the Dalai Lama was passing through Amdo on his return to Lhasa from China, resistance fighters from Kham had managed to make contact with lord chamberlain Phala and other members of the secretariat and the Kashag. From the beginning, Phala, and surely some others, privately supported the resistance and were kept well informed about its progress. Phala encouraged them to continue their struggle.

But neither the Kashag nor the secretariat were ever actively involved in the resistance. The Tibetan government never gave the freedom fighters any financial support or direction. The people surrounding the Dalai Lama made sure that he remained carefully shielded from news about the resistance. Gadrang Lobsang Rigzin, the ranking monk official (*chikyab kenpo*) in charge of the Dalai Lama's staff, was the final arbiter of whom the Dalai Lama might meet. Even lord chamberlain Phala, who was also very close to the Dalai Lama, had to go through Gadrang to meet him. The protection of his staff guaranteed that no one directly connected with the CIA would ever meet the Dalai Lama. His visitors were too well-screened. Whatever the Dalai Lama may have known about the CIA came largely from Phala and Gadrang.[5]

Though they never received approval from the Dalai Lama, the CIA finally decided to go ahead without his okay. The Dalai Lama was still in India when the CIA asked me to choose the first batch of six young men to receive their training. I turned to Gompo Tashi and my deputy, Lhamo Tsering, for help. Gompo Tashi and his nephew, Wangdu Gyatotsang, a former monk turned freedom fighter, selected the volunteers. Wangdu was one of four sons of the wealthy Lithang-based Gyatotsang family. He had fled to India shortly after the communist takeover, taking with him his three brothers and much of the family's wealth, including gold, silver, and an array of weapons transported by horses and mules. Wangdu was anxious to return to Lithang to fight. He became the leader of the first group of CIA-trained recruits. The other five young men selected to join his team were Athar, also from Lithang, Lhotse, Dharlo, Tsewang Dorje, and Baba Changtra Tashi.

Lhamo Tsering introduced the newly selected group to John Hoskins and served as their interpreter. Khenchung Lobsang Gyaltsen and I met with the young men in Kalimpong to brief them on their mission and swear them to secrecy. Not even their families could know what they were about to do. I had made a promise to B. N. Mullik to keep Indian intelligence informed of my political activities, but we could never let the Indian government know that we were using their country as a recruiting ground for the American CIA. Our work had to be carried out in the strictest of secrecy.

The Chinese government inadvertently helped us in our recruiting efforts. Chinese radio had often criticized me after my escape to India, so many people knew that the Dalai Lama's elder brother was in India actively opposing Chinese rule. It was shortly after the Dalai Lama's return to Lhasa that China publicly branded me a traitor. They took away my citizenship and officially cast me out from the Tibetan community, accusing me of joining with the American imperialists to cause trouble in Tibet. The denunciations against me on Chinese radio broadcasts alerted some of the resistance fighters to my presence in Darjeeling. Several of them came to me to volunteer for the Tibetan cause.

SMUGGLING THE TRAINEES out of India was not so difficult. Relations between India and the United States were strained. Nehru had joined the Badung Conference in April 1955 where such diverse leaders as Egypt's Abdul Nassar, Indonesia's Sukarno, and President Tito of Yugoslavia joined together to declare a set of international principles based on nonalignment, neutrality, and noninterference in the others' internal affairs. Nehru's policy of nonalignment and neutrality in the midst of the cold war did not sit well with the United States. In June 1956, American Secretary of State John Foster Dulles publicly labeled Nehru's policy immoral.

But America's relations with Pakistan were good. And India's border with East Pakistan was the Mahanandi River, just behind Bagdogra Airport near Siliguri, a three-hour drive from Kalimpong. The Pakistani government agreed to allow the United States to use one of its deserted airports as the jumping off point for the trainees. If we could get the fighters across the Mahanandi River, Pakistani soldiers and officials would pick them up on the other side to take them to the secret airport where an American transport plane would ferry them to the designated training spot.

We chose the night of March 20, 1957, when the moon would still be full, to send the first group across the border. I was to pick them up in my Ford station wagon as they were walking, spread out and in single file, along Kalimpong's main road. Wangdu was the first to be picked up. He knew everyone in the group and could point them out to me as we drove. We laughed and joked as we made our way to Siliguri. The young men were honest and intelligent and excited about their adventure. I teased them about the crocodiles they might meet crossing the river. They were not afraid to die.

I dropped them at the Mahanandi River together with Gelong, a Hindi-speaking member of my household staff familiar with the terrain. He was to serve as their guide. The water was still low at that time of year, so the men were able to wade across the river. They walked the whole night before linking up with the Pakistani officials, the CIA operative, and Thondup Gyantsen, my brother Norbu's assistant, who was to serve as their interpreter during the training. I was back home in Darjeeling before the sun came up. Gelong took a taxi home after leaving the group, arriving back the next day.

From Pakistan, the group was flown in an unmarked plane to the island of Saipan in the Marianas archipelago somewhere in the Western Pacific. Saipan had been the scene of many bloody battles during the Second World War, and the detritus of war was still there—from the bones of dead soldiers to unexploded bombs and all kinds of guns and artillery. For four months, ten CIA instructors trained the six resistance fighters in radio communications and Morse code, taught them how to read and draw maps, and introduced them to the fundamentals of intelligence gathering and reporting, guerrilla warfare, and a variety of weapons and explosives.

By July, they were ready to return to Tibet. The group was divided into two teams, one to be dropped near Lhasa, the other into Kham. Athar (known to his American teachers as Tom) and Lhotse (otherwise known as Lou) made up the Lhasa team. They were the first to jump, in the light of a full moon, parachuting down near the ancient Samye monastery about eighty miles from Lhasa in southwestern Tibet along the Tsangpo River, known in India as the Brahmaputra. Their equipment included a radio transmitter, binoculars, a few handguns and rifles, and some ammunition. The weather turned foggy before the four men scheduled to parachute into Kham could jump. The plane returned to base with them still on board. They would try again later, during the full moon of September.

DAYS PASSED BEFORE Lhotse and Athar were able to make radio contact, but the two men were safe, and their radio worked. Their communications were sent in Tibetan in Morse code in relays via India to the CIA in Washington. There, Geshe Wangyal, an English-speaking Kalmuck-Mongolian monk who had spent years in the Sera monastery outside Lhasa and had passed the highest Geshe exams, translated the messages from Tibetan Morse code into Tibetan and then from Tibetan into English. Geshe Wangyal had moved to the United States in 1955, at the age of fifty-four, to establish a Tibetan Buddhist monastery in New Jersey, where he was to become the spiritual teacher to several leading American scholars of Buddhism, including such luminaries as Robert Thurman and

Jeffrey Hopkins.[6] From the beginning, he was a vital part of the CIA operations, serving as an interpreter, teaching the illiterate trainees how to read and write, as well as introducing them to the Tibetan Morse code. His English translations of the radio transmissions were then sent to John Hoskins in the consulate in Calcutta, who then met with Gompo Tashi and other members of the Chushi Gang-druk to analyze what was happening on the ground inside Tibet and formulate furthur plans.

The first task of Athar and Lhotse was to make their way to Lhasa in what was to be the final but still unsuccessful effort to get some direct word from the Dalai Lama requesting American government help. After being air-dropped near Samye, they gradually made their way to Lhasa and entered the city disguised as pilgrims. They met with Gompo Tashi and with Phala to inform them of their work and request a meeting with the Dalai Lama.

But they did not meet with His Holiness. Phala was still shielding the Dalai Lama from direct involvement with anything having to do with the American CIA or weapons and fighting.

Unable to meet the Dalai Lama or get a direct request from the Tibetan government for American help, Athar and Lhotse linked up with other would-be resistance fighters, leaving Lhasa to join Gompo Tashi in Lhokha in southern Tibet along the Indian border just as the resistance was entering a new phase. Months earlier, Gompo Tashi had traveled through Tibet soliciting donations on behalf of the construction of a spectacular golden throne to be presented to the Dalai Lama with wishes for his long life on the occasion of his twenty-second birthday. The Tibetan people had given generously of their gold, jewelry, and cash to pay for the building of the throne. According to the CIA's John Kenneth Knaus, its construction required forty-nine goldsmiths, five silversmiths, nineteen engravers, eight tailors, six painters, three blacksmiths, three welders, and thirty assistants.[7]

On July 4, 1957, thousands of people gathered at the Norbulingka summer palace to witness the presentation of the throne to the Dalai Lama and participate in the religious ceremonies beseeching the protective deities to grant him a long and prosperous life. The outpouring of donations from so many Tibetans and the aura of the ceremony itself brought a new sense of unity to the Tibetan people, particularly to the Khampas who were the main force of the resistance. Their devotion to the Dalai Lama as the spiritual and temporal leader of Tibet was reaffirmed, and their commitment to resist the Chinese was given new strength. Gompo Tashi, as the force behind the golden throne, became the indisputable leader of the Khampas.[8]

ON SEPTEMBER 13, 1957,[9] the four CIA trainees who had not been able to make the jump on the first try were air-dropped over Lithang into the very heart of the resistance. Only three of them, Wangdu Gyatotsang (Walt), Tsewang Dorje, and Dharlo, actually made the jump. Baba Changtra Tashi (Dick), one of the two radio operators, panicked when his time came, and could not bring himself to jump. He returned with the crew and later made his way back to Lithang on foot.

Wangdu and his small team quickly linked up with the resistance leaders in Lithang. By the second day, Tsewang Dorje, the radio operator, had established contact with Washington. Wangdu reported that up to thirty thousand resisters were actively fighting in Lithang, armed with whatever primitive weapons they had, from rifles to knives and spears.[10] They were up against a vastly better armed and trained Chinese communist force. The Lithang resisters were desperate for arms. Wangdu wanted an immediate airdrop of weapons from the CIA. He hoped that with enough weapons, the number of resistance fighters would rapidly increase as well.

Wangdu's requests for an immediate airdrop went unheeded. The CIA wanted more information about the number of Tibetan guerrillas, where they were, who was leading them, and how many weapons and how much ammunition they had. They apparently did not believe that thirty thousand resisters could be fighting the Chinese in Lithang.

The Chinese military stationed in Lithang soon learned of Wangdu's return. They had heard the plane in the night and knew that it was not one of theirs. They apparently also learned that Wangdu had been trained by the Americans. The Chinese army closed in on Wangdu's team from all directions, demanding their surrender. The team managed to evade the army for nearly three weeks and finally escaped through their lines with a band of nearly four hundred resistance fighters.[11] In the ensuing months, Wangdu's tiny army fought numerous battles against the Chinese. The hoped-for airdrops never came.

As the resistance continued, so did the descent into chaos of parts of Kham and Amdo. In the ongoing upheaval, thousands of Khampas were fleeing west as far as Lhasa, setting up their tents on the outskirts of the Tibetan capital in hopes that the Tibetan government there could protect them. From their encampments outside, they were visiting the city often. Thousands more refugees moved to the area of Lhokha. By early 1958, some fifteen thousand people had sought refuge in Lhasa and its environs and an equal number had moved into Lhokha. It was in Lhokha, on June 16, 1958, that Andrug Gompo Tashi, with incense burning and a new flag of Tibetan resistance unfurled, formally proclaimed the transformation of the Chushi Gangdruk into the National Volunteer Defense Army. The new name was meant to signify that the resistance movement was no longer confined to the Khampas but had become nationwide in scope. Most of those involved with the resistance, including me, continued to refer to the resistance fighters as Chushi Gangdruk. Whatever its name or membership, the new organization was about to become the main army of the resistance and the major recipient of the CIA's support.

As news of the growing resistance reached Kalimpong and Darjeeling, a thousand men who had fled to India from the turmoil in Kham set out for Lhokha to join the Chushi Gangdruk. Suddenly everyone seemed to be joining the Chushi Gangdruk. Under the leadership of Gompo Tashi, the once ragtag group of freedom fighters became better trained and disciplined, and was organized into twenty-three units based on their native locale. By the middle of 1958, the resistance had driven the Chinese troops from almost all of southern Tibet and had established effective control over the entire area of Lhokha. Only a small garrison in Tsetang, with a few thousand soldiers at most, remained under Chinese control. Then the resistance expanded back eastward. Neither the Tibetan government nor the Chinese army seemed able to control them.[12]

Still, the Khampas were desperately in need of arms and ammunition. In July, just after the establishment of the National Volunteer Defense Army, Athar made a secret visit to Kalimpong to report to Lhamo Tsering and me, representing Gompo Tashi and the Chushi Gangdruk in Lhokha. They needed weapons.

At last the CIA was willing to supply them. The first load of CIA-supplied arms, ammunition, hand grenades, medical kits, binoculars, and Indian rupees was air-dropped into Drigu Thang in Lhokha shortly after Athar's visit.[13] A second drop followed not long thereafter.

In September 1958, Chushi Gangdruk got an additional influx of weapons when, with the tacit approval of the abbot, some six hundred resistance fighters raided the monastery in Shang Gaden Chokhor near Tashilhunpo, where the Dalai Lama had stayed upon his return from India in 1957 and the Tibetan government had a hidden armory.

Neither the air-dropped equipment from the CIA nor the confiscated equipment from the monastery could begin to meet the real needs of the resistance.[14] But the Chinese generals in Lhasa did not know this. They were worried that they were losing control and that Tibet was heading toward war. In August 1958, Zhang Jingwu demanded that the Tibetan cabinet take active measures to quell the revolt. He wanted the Kashag to order the Tibetan military to subdue the resistance. And he wanted the cabinet to expel the Khampas who had been pouring into the city. The Chinese troops were afraid to arrest the new arrivals or to force them out themselves. Some of the Khampas were armed. They wanted the Tibetan government to use its own soldiers to put down the resistance and drive the Khampas out.

The Kashag refused. The Tibetan government could not use Tibetan soldiers to disarm Tibetan resisters. It could not turn its troops against its own people. Nor was the Tibetan government willing to order the refugees pouring into the city to leave. Why should the Tibetan government drive fellow Tibetans out of their sacred city?

But there was a more practical reason for the Kashag's refusal. The Tibetan army in Lhasa numbered no more than 2,000 men. If the Dalai Lama's bodyguards were added in, the total figure would rise to 2,500. The number of resistance fighters then totaled some 35,000–40,000 men. The Chushi Gangdruk had driven the Chinese out of almost all of southern Tibet. The resisters were in control there. The Tibetan military was no match for the freedom fighters. More importantly, if the Tibetan military had been ordered to turn on the resistance fighters, the vast majority would have joined the resistance instead. Even if the Tibetan government had wanted to put down the revolt, they had neither the manpower, the equipment, nor the will to succeed.

Some twenty thousand Chinese soldiers were garrisoned in Lhasa. With the population of the city continuing to swell, the Chinese concluded that the newcomers vastly outnumbered their troops. They needed more soldiers, but sending in new reinforcements by air was impossible. Bringing troops in overland by truck and by foot from Kham would take time. The Chinese tried to trick the people of Lhasa into believing they had more troops than they really did. They began repeatedly moving trucks loaded with soldiers out of the city by night while the city slept and driving the same trucks and troops back into the city by day, thus creating the illusion of a steadily growing number of soldiers.

By the beginning of 1959, another wave of newcomers began to arrive in Lhasa from all over Tibet. The traditional yearly festival of Monlam was approaching. Control of the city is turned over to the monks of Sera, Drepung, and Ganden during this three-week holiday, as prayers are offered on behalf of Tibet and Buddhism. The Dalai Lama himself presides over the festival. The population of Lhasa always swells at that time of year with monks and ordinary people alike.

The Monlam festival of 1959 was particularly important. It was then that the Dalai Lama was to take his final examination for the Geshe degree, the highest level of learning in the Tibetan Buddhist faith. If the population of Lhasa, including the monks in the surrounding monasteries, was ordinarily around fifty thousand people, by the Monlam festival of 1959 it may have been double that. The streets were crowded with monks and colorfully dressed pilgrims from all over Tibet, circumambulating the Barkhor, prayer wheels spinning, endlessly chanting the sacred mantra *Om Mani Padme Hum*. Never before had the city held so many people.

Everyone was nervous. The situation was tense. Chinese troops began withdrawing into safe enclaves, concentrating their forces in scattered pockets around the city, keeping out of sight, afraid of being attacked. As the Dalai Lama was later to write, "everyone knew that something momentous was about to happen."[15] With tensions running so high, any spark could break the uneasy peace.

19

The Dalai Lama's Escape

The spark was an invitation to the Dalai Lama from the Chinese political commissar, General Tan Guansan. The general wanted the Dalai Lama to attend a cultural performance at the Chinese military headquarters.[1] Tan Guansan and the Dalai Lama had met before. The Chinese general had often visited the Dalai Lama at his palace. In the midst of the unfolding crisis, his visits had become more frequent, as he berated His Holiness about the resistance and continued to demand that the Tibetan army be mobilized against the rebels. The Dalai Lama had come to dread and loathe his meetings with the uncouth and ill-mannered man.[2]

With popular suspicions running high, many in Lhasa saw the general's invitation as a trick. When the Chinese further instructed the chief of the Dalai Lama's security, my brother-in-law Phuntsog Tashi Takla, to leave the usual contingent of bodyguards behind, popular suspicions were confirmed. The Dalai Lama never ventured forth without an entourage of officials and bodyguards. Pomp and circumstance accompanied him wherever he went. What reason could there be for leaving his bodyguards behind? Many believed that the Chinese were about to kidnap the Dalai Lama and hold him hostage. This would be one way for the Chinese military to protect itself. With the Dalai Lama inside the Chinese military camp, the Tibetan resisters would never dare attack it.

Word of the invitation and the accompanying order to dispense with the bodyguards spread quickly. By early in the morning of March 10, the day the cultural performance was to take place, people began converging on the Norbulingka Palace, knowing that the Dalai Lama was inside. In a matter of hours, quickly and spontaneously, thousands, then tens of thousands of people[3] had surrounded the palace, simultaneously attempting to protect the Dalai Lama from a Chinese attack and to prevent him from leaving to meet the Chinese officials. Soon the entire population of the city seemed to be outside the Norbulingka.

With the Dalai Lama sealed inside, messengers continued to go back and forth between the palace and the Chinese military headquarters. One of the messengers from Tan Guansan's side, Kunchung Sonam Gyantso, was stoned to death by the crowd just in front of the Norbulingka gate. Kunchung Sonam Gyantso was the brother of Pakpala Kunchung, then the second highest ranking Tibetan official in Lhasa and notorious for his collaboration with the Chinese. Other collaborators, including Ngabo, then the highest ranking Tibetan official in Lhasa, went into hiding to protect themselves from the angry crowd. Ngabo had become a member of the cabinet after signing the Seventeen Point Agreement and was seen by many as a Chinese sympathizer. He took refuge inside their military compound.

When the crowd demanded assurances that the Dalai Lama would not attend the performance, his staff conveyed the Dalai Lama's promise that he would not go.[4] But the crowd could not be assuaged. The Dalai Lama sent three of his ministers to explain the situation to Tan Guansan, but the Chinese general accused the ministers of promoting the resistance and refusing to disarm the Tibetan "reactionaries." He threatened drastic action to crush the opposition to Chinese rule.[5] Some of the Tibetan government's younger officials and the newly elected leaders representing the protesters wrote a public denunciation of the Seventeen Point Agreement and declared it null and void. On March 12, in an act unprecedented in Tibetan history, the women of Lhasa took to the streets to protest.

The standoff continued for several days, with the crowds growing larger and angrier with every passing day. They were crying for independence, demanding the repeal of the Seventeen Point Agreement, and calling for the Chinese to leave. The Dalai Lama met personally with the seventy leaders of the new *mimang* (representative committee), warning them that the Chinese were likely to use force if the crowd did not disperse. Some of the demonstrators shifted their protest to Shol, the village just under the Potala, but the crowd outside the Norbulingka was still huge.[6] By March 16, reports of troop movements in and around Lhasa were taken as signs that the Chinese military was about to move against the demonstrators—and against the Norbulingka with the Dalai Lama still inside. When two heavy mortars landed harmlessly just outside the Norbulingka, no one doubted that an assault was imminent.

The situation was explosive. The demonstrators were not to be stopped. In these precarious circumstances, the Dalai Lama had three choices. He could stay with his people and risk perishing with them in the inevitable Chinese attack. He could go to the Chinese military headquarters and risk being taken hostage. Or he could try to escape from the Norbulingka and cross the Kyichu River to southern Tibet.[7]

He chose to escape. Very few people were involved in the decision—the Dalai Lama's chief of staff Gadrang Lobsang Rizen, Kashag members Surkhang, Shasur, and Liushar, lord chamberlain Phala, His Holiness's chief bodyguard Phuntsog Tashi Takla, and, above all, the Dalai Lama himself. The escape would never have been possible without the additional, remarkable help of the three personal attendants closest to His Holiness, the Simpon Khenpo (master of the robes), the Chopon Khenpo (master of the rituals), and the Solpon Khenpo (master of the kitchen). These were the men closest and most important to the Dalai Lama's everyday life. They were involved in all of his decisions, in every move he made.

They left the Norbulingka in three separate groups. The Dalai Lama's tutors and four members of the Kashag went first, hidden under a tarpaulin in the back of a truck. My mother, my younger brother Tenzin Choegyal, and my sister Tsering Dolma left, unnoticed, in disguise. Then, a couple of hours before midnight on March 17, the Dalai Lama, without his glasses and dressed as an ordinary Tibetan solider with a rifle slung over his shoulder, slipped out of the Norbulingka with only chief of staff Gadrang, his chief of bodyguards Phuntsog Tashi Takla, lord chamberlain Phala, and two soldiers at his side. No one recognized them as they passed through the crowd.[8]

The Kyichu River that runs just south of Lhasa was less than two kilometers away. A coracle was waiting to ferry them across. The two other escape groups and a contingent of the Tibetan military met them on the other side. Horses and ponies from a nearby monastery were saddled for the flight.[9]

They traveled by horseback all night. By noon the next day they had scaled the Che La pass and crossed the Tsangpo (Brahmaputra) River into Lhokha in southern Tibet. Only then could they begin to feel safe. There were no Chinese troops in Lhokha. The Chinese military had withdrawn. The Tibetan resistance controlled the entire territory from there to the Indian border, some three hundred to four hundred square miles.

By then there were about one hundred people in the escape party. Beyond the Dalai Lama and members of my family, most were government officials, men with only the clothes on their backs. They had left their families behind without even saying good-bye. About three hundred and fifty Tibetan soldiers escorted the escape party, along with another fifty or so guerrillas.[10] Invisible to the escape party, but fully mobilized to defend the Dalai Lama to the death, were thousands of Gompo Tashi's resistance fighters posted at every pass, sending messages back and forth. There was still some danger that the Chinese military could outflank the fleeing entourage.

Phala had sent a messenger ahead to warn the Chushi Gangdruk that the Dalai Lama might flee. Athar had quickly put together a force of one hundred of their best soldiers and horses and set out with Lhotse and their radio to link up with the Dalai Lama. My mother and elder sister, Tsering Dolma, were the first members of the escape party the resistance fighters met. They had gone by a different, faster route and were well ahead of the larger entourage. It was Athar who sent the first message to the CIA that the Dalai Lama had escaped and was safely across the Tsangpo River. The message went from Tibet via India to the CIA in Washington.[11]

I was in Darjeeling when the crowds began gathering around the Norbulingka. I knew nothing of what was going on there. It was only from Athar's first message that I learned of the Dalai Lama's escape. After the message was received in Tibetan Morse code in Washington, it had been translated into English by Geshe Wangyal and sent to John Hoskins at the CIA office in Calcutta. Hoskins flew with the message from Calcutta to Bagdogra and then on to Darjeeling by taxi to deliver it to me. From then on, reports continued to come in almost every day for the rest of the Dalai Lama's flight. It was only a matter of hours between the time the radio dispatches were sent and the time I received them. Most of them were simple statements giving the Dalai Lama's current location and offering assurances that he and his entourage were safe. There was not much we could do but wait. We were receiving reports without being able to send them ourselves.

The original plan was for the Dalai Lama to stop at Lhuntse Dzong, a stronghold of the Tibetan resistance some sixty miles from the Indian border (though double that on foot) but still inside Tibet. From there, they hoped to negotiate the withdrawal of Chinese troops, the safe return of the Dalai Lama, and the continuation of his position as head of the Tibetan government. But by the time the entourage arrived in Lhuntse, they were beginning to learn what had happened in Lhasa after the Dalai Lama's flight. So many people were fleeing in face of the violence, linking up with various contingents of the Dalai Lama's entourage, that he was receiving a steady barrage of dismal news.

It was two days before the Chinese realized that the Dalai Lama had fled. The shelling of the Norbulingka began when the Chinese still believed that the Dalai Lama was inside. Lhasa degenerated into bloodshed. The crowd surrounding the Norbulingka had grown to tens of thousands by then. The Tibetan crowd was hopelessly primitive against the Chinese troops. The Tibetans surrounding the Norbulingka had never been well organized or armed. They were not much more than an empty-handed mob of angry, ordinary citizens and monks. Within the crowd were some armed resistance fighters. Some of the Khampas had outmoded, primitive rifles. But most of the people were defenseless. They had used stones to kill Khunchung Sonam Gyantso, and some people still used stones to fight the Chinese troops. Faced with Chinese machine guns, canons, and rockets, most of the Tibetans ran, scattering in panic. Thousands were killed in the area around the Norbulingka, in the streets of Lhasa, and as they tried to escape across the Kyichu River. The streets were filled with bodies. People were shouting, running from body to body, looking into the faces of the dead, searching for missing relatives. Thousands of people were taken prisoner. It was chaos. No one had expected the Chinese to mow the demonstrators down. The resistance in Lhasa quickly collapsed. In only a couple of days, the city was back in the hands of the Chinese.

Later I learned that after the Chinese attack began, Peng Dehuai, the Chinese minister of defense, sent a radio communication to Tan Guansan, the official whose invitation to my brother had sparked the popular revolt and who was then in charge of the assault. "*Bu yao dong*," the message said. Do not move. Peng Dehuai thought that the Tibetan resisters so greatly outnumbered the Chinese troops that the army could easily be overwhelmed. But Peng's message was too late. The attack had already begun. And the unarmed Tibetans, whatever their numbers, were no match for the Chinese canon fire. The Tibetan resistance had crumbled. Many had already died in the attack. Others were surrendering or running away.

In 1962, the Tibetan resistance captured a document published by the political department of the Eighteenth Army of the People's Liberation Army headquarters in Lhasa, saying that between March 1959 when the Dalai Lama fled and October 1960, the People's Liberation Army had "wiped out" eighty-seven thousand Tibetan "bandits" in Central Tibet alone. These were the People's Liberation Army's own figures, and they did not include Kham and Amdo where the resistance had been most fierce and where many more people must have been killed. The killing continued well into the 1960s. Imagine, if the casualties in Amdo and Kham were added in, how many people must really have died.

His Holiness and his advisors knew by the time they reached Lhuntse that there was no longer any way to negotiate with the Chinese. The Chinese had already announced the dissolution of the Tibetan government. So the Dalai Lama and the officials accompanying him set up a temporary government there, and he formally repudiated the Seventeen Point Agreement. The Tibetan army and the Chushi Gangdruk were joined into a single fighting force. Gompo Tashi became part of the new government with the official rank of Dzasak. From Lhuntse, I received a different message. The Dalai Lama and his entourage wanted political asylum in India. They asked me to make the request. I flew immediately from Bagdogra to New Delhi to meet with Prime Minister Nehru.

Mr. Mullik, the director of Indian intelligence, set up the appointment. I met the Indian prime minister in his office in the Parliament House.

As I entered Mr. Nehru's office, he asked, "How is the Dalai Lama? Where is he? Is he safe?" I told him that he had reached Lhuntse safely and explained that I had requested the meeting upon the Dalai Lama's instructions. I had received a message by wireless requesting me to ask Prime Minister Nehru to grant His Holiness political asylum. The Dalai Lama and the Tibetan government had concluded that it would be impossible to remain in Lhuntse. They wanted to cross the border into India.

The prime minister's response was immediate. "Of course," he said. Then he turned to the practical questions of where and when His Holiness would be crossing. We talked about where the Dalai Lama would stay.

The last leg of his journey took the Dalai Lama through Jora, where I had stopped to implement reforms on our estate when I fled in 1952. My mother spent a couple days there resting. The Dalai Lama's last stop was in the small village of Mangmang, where he became ill with dysentery and had to spend a couple of days recovering. It was there that he received the message that Prime Minister Nehru had granted political asylum to him and his entourage.

From Mangmang, Athar and Lhotse prepared to turn back to Lhoka to rejoin Gompo Tashi and the resistance. They were expecting another arms drop from the CIA, and another ten thousand more men had fled to Lhokha to join the freedom fighters there. The resistance would continue even after the Dalai Lama's escape. Athar and Lhotse met Phala once more before returning. In exchange for 180,000 of the 300,000 rupees[12] that had been in the first arms drop to the resisters, Phala gave Athar and Lhotse 10.8 million Tibetan srang. Indian rupees would get the fighters nowhere in Tibet, but they would be useful to the Dalai Lama and his party once inside India. The fighters kept 120,000 rupees just in case they were needed.

Later, some Tibetans in Kalimpong began circulating a rumor that I had taken the rupees. But I was in Darjeeling then, not Tibet, and had never seen the money. The airdrops containing the money were flying from East Pakistan, and I had nothing to do with them. The four men who had started the rumor were subsequently expelled from India not for their false accusations but as Communist agents. Intelligence agents from all sorts of places were stirring up rumors and fostering dissension then.

The Dalai Lama writes of meeting some of the Khampa fighters toward the end of his journey, though he does not mention their names. He says that "in spite of my beliefs, I very much admired their courage and their determination to carry on the grim battle they had started for our freedom, culture, and religion. I thanked them for their strength and bravery, and also, more personally, for the protection they had given me. . . . By then, I could not in honesty advise them to avoid violence. In order to fight, they had sacrificed their homes and all the comforts and benefits of a peaceful life. Now they could see no alternative but to go on fighting, and I had none to offer."[13] On March 30, 1959, two weeks after his flight from Lhasa, the Dalai Lama crossed through the Sela pass (Se La to the Indians) and arrived in Tawang in the North-East Frontier Agency (later to become the Indian state of Arunachal Pradesh), where I had been so warmly greeted by the local people during my own escape some seven years before. There he was greeted by Indian foreign ministry official P. N. Menon, formerly India's consul general in Lhasa and soon to become the Indian government's chief liaison with the Dalai Lama. Menon formally made the grant of political asylum to His Holiness and officially escorted him to Tezpur. Shakabpa, Lobsang Gyantsen, and I were in Tezpur to welcome him and other members of my family.

Even after all these years, I am still amazed when I think about the escape. A superstitious person could easily believe that it was a miracle. But the escape was not a miracle. It was a human effort by the few people closest to the Dalai Lama, Phala, his lord chamberlain, a couple of cabinet members, his personal attendants, advisors, bodyguards, and the resistance fighters. They were willing to sacrifice their lives, their families, everything, to protect the Dalai Lama. Their plans never leaked out. They never told their families, never even had a chance to say good-bye. They arranged everything without outside help. The CIA did not help. The CIA did not even know about the escape until several days after the Dalai Lama was gone. Nor did I. The escape had nothing to do with the CIA, nor, indeed, with me.

20

From Mussoorie to Dharamsala

The Dalai Lama's escape was making international headlines even before he crossed the border into India. Hundreds of reporters were waiting for him when he arrived in Tezpur. All of them wanted to interview him and hear his story.

The Chinese government had already put out its own story. The Dalai Lama had not left Tibet of his own free will, they said. He had been abducted by reactionary bandits and taken away by force. They blamed the kidnapping on the Tibetan nobility and slave owners, the people they dubbed the "reactionary elite." Zhou Enlai announced to the world that the Chinese government had declared the Seventeen Point Agreement null and void, dissolved the Tibetan government, and appointed the Panchen Lama as the new head of the Preparatory Committee for the Autonomous Region of Tibet.[1]

China's alleged evidence that the Dalai Lama had been kidnapped was to be found in the notes he had exchanged with Tan Guansan while the protesters were surrounding the Norbulingka. In an effort to bide time and avoid bloodshed, the Dalai Lama's communications had attributed his inability to attend the cultural performance to the crowd of "reactionary" demonstrators outside. He expressed his regrets to the Chinese general for not being able to attend the performance that he had very much hoped to see. Based on these exchanges, the Chinese publicly announced that he had been held against his will and forcibly transported to India.

China's concocted story that the Tibetan aristocrats had kidnapped the Dalai Lama put a bizarre twist on reality. In fact, from the time the Chinese army marched into Lhasa in 1951 until the Dalai Lama's escape in 1959, the most faithful collaborators with the Chinese government had been members of the Tibetan aristocracy. Many of them were still on the Chinese government's payroll receiving hundreds of Chinese silver dollars a month.

The real opponents of Chinese rule were not the aristocrats but ordinary Tibetan people. The tens of thousands who gathered outside the Norbulingka in March 1959 were ordinary farmers, nomads, and merchants. The entire resistance was made up of ordinary, unknown, nameless Tibetans. While they were fighting and dying for Tibet, the nobility were hiding in their homes or taking refuge in the Chinese military headquarters. Today, when young Chinese-educated Tibetans come to meet with me in India, they sometimes wonder how China was able to take over Tibet so easily. We Tibetans are not stupid, they say. How did we let this happen? To that I respond that they should ask the aristocrats and the lamas. They were the ones responsible.

Even as the Chinese continued day after day to broadcast their concocted story of the Dalai Lama's kidnapping, the Indian government remained reluctant to allow the Dalai Lama to present his explanation of why he had fled. By the time the Dalai Lama arrived in Tezpur, the Indian foreign ministry had already crafted a carefully worded press statement, perhaps written but certainly approved by Prime Minister Nehru himself. Surely Nehru's staff consulted with the Dalai Lama first, but the statement was written in the third person and read by an Indian official.

The Tezpur Statement noted that Tibet, historically, had always been autonomous and that the Seventeen Point Agreement had been signed under pressure. Despite the promise of autonomy, all important decisions in Tibet since the signing of the agreement had been made by the Chinese government. Following the resistance in Kham, the statement noted, the Chinese had destroyed many monasteries and killed or imprisoned many lamas and monks. The statement contained a brief description of the protests in Lhasa that had led to the Dalai Lama's escape and stated categorically that the Dalai Lama had "left Lhasa and Tibet and come to India of his own free will and not under duress." It stated that he expressed his regret over the tragic bloodshed in Lhasa.[2] And the statement expressed the Dalai Lama's gratitude for the Indian government's welcome and for all the messages of goodwill awaiting him when he arrived.

We were angry then that the Indian government seemed to have spoken in the Dalai Lama's name. Reading the text more than fifty years later, I see the Tezpur Statement as a masterpiece of dignity and discretion. Nehru wanted neither to insult the Chinese nor to sever relations with them. The Chinese government was already denouncing India for giving the Dalai Lama refuge. They saw the grant of asylum as a case of interference in China's internal affairs and hence a violation of one of the five principles of peaceful coexistence as stated in the Panchsheel Treaty agreement of 1954. Nehru still held out hope that the Dalai Lama's differences with China could be resolved and that some form of peaceful settlement could be reached. Before knowing more about the Dalai Lama's own views, he was reluctant to let representatives of the Tibetan government speak. In retrospect, the Tezpur Statement was an act of skillful diplomacy. Nehru still held out hope for some sort of accommodation with China.

But the Indian government was also worried about all the international attention His Holiness was receiving. Everyone wanted to meet this charming young man. Nehru was still worried about what he might say, especially about his intention to establish a government in exile in India and seek international support for the Tibetans' right to self-determination. Nehru described the Dalai Lama as his honored guest, but he wanted his honored guest's asylum to remain humanitarian rather than political.

Nehru wanted the Dalai Lama out of the limelight. One way to do that was to move him to an obscure, out of the way place, one not easily accessible to the international press. I initially hoped that the Dalai Lama might settle in Darjeeling, where the Thirteenth Dalai Lama had stayed and many Tibetan refugees already lived. Shilong, the capital of the Indian state of Assam near Kohati, was another possible site. The Americans were suggesting Thailand or Switzerland as alternatives to India, and they were willing to shoulder the cost. But I felt strongly that the Dalai Lama should stay in India as close to Tibet as possible. I wanted him just across the mountains from our homeland, no matter how difficult the circumstances. Perhaps physically, he might be more comfortable in some other place, but psychologically, being close to home and knowing that the lamas and his people were nearby would be a source of comfort.

The Dalai Lama had a moral responsibility to remain in India as well. Thousands of refugees were pouring into India all along the border, through Bhutan, Sikkim, and Assam. They were sacrificing everything to be near His Holiness. The Dalai Lama was duty-bound to stay in India to look after his followers.

When I met Prime Minister Nehru to discuss a longer-range living arrangement, he suggested the Himalayan hill station of Mussoorie, some seventy miles south of the Tibetan border and two hundred miles from New Delhi. There, the Dalai Lama would be relatively isolated from the media but still close enough to New Delhi for occasional visits from Indian officials.

The Dalai Lama made the move from Tezpur to Mussoorie by train, a trip of several days. Every stop found swarms of ordinary Indian people surrounding his train in welcome.[3] In Mussoorie, the Dalai Lama was put up in a charming, comfortable bungalow called Birla House. Prime Minister Nehru paid his first visit to the Dalai Lama there on April 24.

In Mussoorie, the Dalai Lama was still under pressure from the Indian government not to meet the press. At first we succumbed to their wishes, but as weeks passed and thousands of Tibetans were still pouring into India with only the clothes on their backs and their

stories of the persecution and violence at home, our own people began urging us to speak out. The refugees genuinely feared that the
annihilation of Tibet was at hand. They wanted the truth to be told.
Finally we could no longer remain silent. On June 20, 1959, we held
a press conference for the international media, speaking from the
porch of our Mussoorie bungalow. We did not request Prime Minister Nehru's permission. We did not much care what his reaction
might be.

Press conferences were an entirely new phenomenon for the Tibetan government. We called upon our legal advisors Purushottam
Trikamdas, a former secretary to Mahatma Gandhi, and D. K. Sen
to help prepare the English version of what we wanted to say.[4] The
Mussoorie Statement was read by a junior official, with the Dalai
Lama standing by. More than a hundred journalists from all over the
world attended as members of the Kashag and other leading Tibetan
officials looked on. As the newly appointed foreign minister of the
Tibetan government in exile, I was one of those responsible for responding to the questions that followed.

The June 20 statement adamantly refuted the Chinese story that
the Dalai Lama had been abducted by a group of reactionary rebels.
We also refuted the Seventeen Point Agreement. Since the Chinese
had violated the terms of the agreement that they themselves had
drafted, the Tibetans would no longer abide by it either. We said
that Tibet was a sovereign nation that had never been part of China,
that we had been invaded and forced under duress at the point of
a bayonet to sign the agreement. We pointed out that the Chinese
themselves never had any intention of carrying it out. They had broken their own agreement almost immediately when they forced the
Dalai Lama's two prime ministers to resign or face execution without
trial. We accused the Chinese of instigating a reign of terror and carrying out wanton persecution and plunder. We explained once more
what had happened when the Dalai Lama visited India in 1956 and
Zhou Enlai promised Prime Minister Nehru and the Dalai Lama
that the number of Chinese troops in Tibet would be drastically
reduced and economic conditions would improve. The Mussoorie

Statement reaffirmed the Dalai Lama's own commitment to political and economic reform, including land reform on the monastic and aristocratic estates. He accused the Chinese of deliberately blocking his efforts in carry out reform and called for an international body to conduct an impartial investigation of our allegations against the Chinese and of the ongoing situation in Tibet. At the same time, the Dalai Lama assured the world that we Tibetans had no feelings of enmity or hatred toward the great Chinese people.

It was during this press conference, in the question and answer session that followed, that the Dalai Lama said that "wherever I am, accompanied by my government, the Tibetan people recognize us as the government of Tibet." The Tibetan government in exile was thus implicitly and informally established.

And the Tibetan position had been made known to the world. We had successfully countered China's false propaganda. D. K. Sen became a trusted advisor to the government in exile and helped His Holiness write his first book, *My Land and My People*. His English was beautiful.

Nehru was angry about the press conference, both with the Dalai Lama and with me. We had defied his admonition not to speak publicly. He regarded me and my colleagues, Shakabpa and Lobsang Gyaltsen, as troublemakers. The Chinese were angry, too. They began openly denouncing the Dalai Lama. But to the Tibetan government in exile, the benefits of presenting our point of view to an international audience were clear. The Fourteenth Dalai Lama was to become the most public of all dalai lamas and the most accessible. As refugees continued to stream into India and seek him out, he met personally with each and every one.

In the meantime, we were receiving offers of help. Generalissimo Chiang Kai-shek made a public statement expressing sympathy for the Dalai Lama, condemning the Communist Party's atrocities in Tibet, and offering assurances that when the Guomindang returned to govern China again, he would support self-determination for the Tibetan people. He sent a letter to the Dalai Lama offering to help. We did not respond. President Chiang's own public statement was fine, but the Guomindang's official propaganda machine still insisted that the Tibetans were fighting for the return of the Nationalists to the mainland and intimated that the Tibetan resistance movement was receiving support from Taiwan. At the same time, on the other side of the Taiwan Strait, the Communists were still talking about liberating Taiwan and were using the Guomindang's propaganda to accuse the Tibetan resistance of being supported and led by the Nationalists. I wanted to establish a clear Tibetan identity, free of any Chinese influence. Until their propaganda changed, we could not accept help from the Nationalists.

The Geneva-based International Commission of Jurists, composed of eminent lawyers from around the world, and led by Purshottam Trikamdas, took up the Dalai Lama's suggestion in his June 20 statement to conduct an impartial international investigation of the situation in Tibet. The Commission reported that China had systematically violated the terms of the Seventeen Point Agreement, thus rendering null and void any obligation for Tibet to adhere to its terms. It noted the restrictions China had placed on religious practices by ordinary Tibetan people and the widespread killing of Tibetan monks and lamas, arguing that such acts constituted genocide against Tibetans as a religious group. And the commissioners accused the Chinese of massive violations of the fundamental rights and freedoms of the Tibetan people, including the wanton killing of ordinary Tibetans. The report thus set forth in vivid detail the substantive basis for its conclusion that horrible human rights abuses were still being perpetrated in Tibet.

We used the report from the International Commission of Jurists as evidence in a series of appeals to the United Nations accusing China of invading and occupying Tibet, reiterating that we had never been part of China and accusing China of massive violations of the fundamental rights of the Tibetan people. The CIA introduced me to the American lawyer Ernest Gross and paid for him to help us develop our case. In the fall of 1959, I traveled to New York with former finance minister Shakabpa, the Dalai Lama's private secretary Rinchen Sandutsang, and our advisor, the Indian lawyer and writer D. K. Sen, to plead the Tibetan case.

Our efforts had only limited success. In 1959, a mildly worded UN resolution sponsored by Ireland and Malaya condemning China's violations of the Tibetans' human rights passed with forty-five countries voting in favor, nine opposed, and twenty-nine abstaining. The next year, 1960, a majority of voting countries agreed to discuss the issue of Tibet, but the international crisis that erupted after the Soviet Union shot down an American U2 spy plane over Soviet territory diverted attention away from Tibet and toward a ratcheting up of the cold war. Thus, instead of pleading the case of Tibet, I was in the visitors' gallery to witness Soviet leader Nikita Kruschev's dramatic performance in the UN General Assembly, when he took off his shoe and pounded it on the table in denunciation of the United States. In 1961, after Kennedy's assumption of the American presidency and in the wake of a new international wave of anti-Communism, a more strongly worded resolution, sponsored by Thailand and Malaya, also passed in the United Nations, but it had no practical effect on the situation in Tibet.

The international community was long on expressions of sympathy toward Tibet but short on concrete actions. Even India, which had given the Dalai Lama refuge, did not support our resolutions in the United Nations. The United States, which was clandestinely providing training and arms for the underground guerrillas, was publicly vague about its support. The Dalai Lama, as Nehru's honored guest, was in a difficult, awkward position. He had to respect the wishes of his host. He could not use India as his staging ground to call for international recognition of Tibetan independence.

Sometime in 1960, Prime Minister Nehru suggested that the Dalai Lama move to another Himalayan hill station—Dharamsala, in Himachal Pradesh, some five hundred miles from New Delhi. I had reservations about the move. The scenery in the hills of Dharamsala and the Kangra Valley below is far more beautiful than Mussoorie's. But Dharamsala was a sparsely populated area far from any city. It was difficult to get to. The roads were terrible and the living accommodations almost nonexistent. And it rained in Dharamsala—not just ordinary showers, but rain pouring from the sky in buckets. The monsoons lasted for months. The place felt haunted when I first visited. The houses were dilapidated and leaky. Even the Dalai Lama's quarters leaked. There were no hotels, or even a building that might conceivably serve as a place for guests.

But after the Dalai Lama's move, thousands of refugees from Tibet still found their way to Dharamsala. They wanted to be near him. They wanted to tell their stories of the killings, arrests, and torture still being perpetrated by the Chinese.

Hundreds of people in Tibet were still dying every day. People were being hunted like wild animals and tortured. Many were put in prison and forced into slave labor. Some committed suicide. People's homes were searched, and their property was confiscated or destroyed, everything from jewelry and cooking pots to the family's religious artifacts. Even the poor nomads were robbed. Granaries were taken over by the Chinese. So was the treasury of the Tibetan government and the Dalai Lama's two palaces, the Potala and the Norbulingka. The leading monasteries outside Lhasa—Sera, Ganden, and Drepung—were occupied by the military, their sacred relics and books either taken away or burned. Similar things were happening in thousands of other smaller monasteries across Tibet. Soldiers desecrated the sacred scriptures by throwing them on the ground and stamping on them with their dirty boots. Cauldrons ordinarily used in the monasteries for tea were used to hold fodder for the Chinese military's horses. Grain grown by the monasteries and butter meant to be burned in their lamps was fed to the Chinese animals. The monks were arrested or sent away. Tibet was becoming a giant concentration camp. And the resistance continued.

21

Mustang

The uprising in Lhasa had been easy to quash. The resistance crumbled in a matter of days. The movement there was never well organized. The protesters were fighting with their bare hands. While the people of Lhasa and Central Tibet deeply resented the Chinese military presence and the damage being done to their traditional way of life, they were never either as rebellious or as well organized as the people of Amdo and Kham. In other parts of Tibet, the fighting continued long after the Dalai Lama's escape. So did our support from the CIA.[1]

From that night in March 1957 when I sent the first group of freedom fighters across the Mahanandi River until sometime in 1963, more than two hundred and fifty young Tibetans received CIA training, first in Saipan and later, beginning in 1958, in Camp Hale, Colorado.[2] Camp Hale was a top-secret, deserted military training base high in the Rocky Mountains where the altitude and mountain conditions more closely approximated the geography and weather of Tibet. The first recruits sent to Camp Hale soon dubbed it *Dumra,* meaning "garden." Their training continued to be secret.

During the course of the resistance inside Tibet, eight CIA-trained teams were air-dropped into areas where the resistance was strong.[3] Most drops of men were followed by drops of CIA-supplied weapons, ammunition, radios, and other military equipment. But the guns supplied by the CIA were nothing but a tiny drop compared to China's endless ocean of arms. They were never enough. My deputy, Lhamo Tsering, made a list of every piece of equipment the CIA supplied us, rifle by rifle, hand grenade by hand grenade, bullet by bullet, and radio transmitter by radio transmitter. For the twenty-five thousand resistance fighters on the ground in Lhokha, the CIA supplied about seven hundred guns. For the five thousand fighters active in Amdo, the CIA dropped maybe five hundred or six hundred rifles. An area with two thousand fighters got maybe three hundred or four hundred. Most of the rifles were old and outmoded, leftovers from the Second World War. Many had been captured from the Chinese. None of the CIA-supplied equipment was made in the United States. They did not want any evidence that America had been involved in the Tibetan cause. Militarily, the Tibetan resistance fighters never stood a chance.

I still believe that if the CIA had given us enough weapons, the resistance would have had a chance. Had I understood how paltry the CIA's support would be, I would never have sent those young men for training. Mao was not the only one to cheat the Tibetans. The CIA did, too.

Organizationally, the challenges faced by the resistance were enormous. The CIA had trained the fighters in guerrilla warfare, but actually becoming guerrilla warriors inside Tibet was a different matter altogether. Much of Tibet was in turmoil. Order had broken down. Tens of thousands of people were in flight, and the Chinese military was moving in everywhere to wipe out the bandits and establish control.

The Chinese had an extensive intelligence network that allowed them to maintain constant contact with their own forces and protect their troops from surprise attack. They had plenty of radios. They controlled all the roads and continued to build more. They could observe from the air what was happening on the ground and could launch coordinated attacks by air and on land. But there was no way for the tens of thousands of scattered guerrilla fighters to maintain contact. The Tibetan resisters had only a few CIA-supplied radios. They had to remain on constant alert and in combat readiness and got so little sleep that they were always exhausted.

Food for the fighters was hard to come by. Food for everyone was hard to come by. The Chinese military was requisitioning everything for itself, using a strategy of starvation against the Tibetan resistance. Theft of food was common, and the guerrillas sometimes raided the Chinese army's stores. Local people took the law into their own hands and hunted down thieves. Killings and fighting were frequent. Displaced people were turning to the guerrilla fighters for protection from the Chinese. Sometimes, when local people learned that a guerrilla band was camping nearby, whole families, together with their possessions and animals, would move in to set up camp beside them. Battles were fought in the midst of women, children, and livestock. At other times, local people, even friends and relatives, reported the presence of the freedom fighters to the Chinese, afraid for their lives if the Chinese ever learned that they had known that the resistance was there and had not told. The Chinese had good propaganda. They used cunning tricks to lure the Tibetan fighters into their traps. They dropped tens of thousands of leaflets assuring the Tibetans that the "bandits" were on the verge of annihilation. Those who surrendered were promised leniency.

But still many of the resisters fought on. Some had only knives or stones for weapons. Some began each battle with a pledge to fight to the death for the protection of the Buddha dharma, the Dalai Lama, and the independence of Tibet. Some of the Khampas pledged to fight until not a single Khampa remained. Many carried a cyanide tablet around their necks and pledged to swallow it when their ammunition was depleted and defeat was certain.[4] Many of the resistance fighters knew they had no chance of winning, but believed that to fight and die was better than not to fight at all. Having fought and died for truth and justice in this life, they knew they would be free from suffering in the next.[5]

Many of the resisters died, and many were captured by the Chinese and imprisoned. Some died in combat. Some killed themselves at the end of battle when defeat was certain and escape was no longer possible. They swallowed their cyanide capsules. Some died in prison. The conditions inside Chinese prisons were unbearably inhumane, and helping one's fellow inmates was a crime.[6] Some of the prisoners, including those trained by the CIA, broke under torture, finally confessing to their help from the United States and identifying me, Gyalo Thondup, as the organizer of the resistance.[7] Some who confessed really were given leniency and were let out early. Others were let out early only to be put into labor reform camps. Many were imprisoned for more than twenty years.

The resistance fighters were brave and heroic young men. But the challenges they faced were ultimately insurmountable. They held out for as long as they could. They won many battles and killed thousands of Chinese, forcing thousands more to retreat. They were true Tibetan patriots and heroes. More than a year went by before the Chinese military could begin to establish control. But in the end, the resistance fighters were overwhelmed. By 1960, the resistance inside Tibet was slowing down.

One by one, those among the CIA-trained groups still alive were forced to concede defeat and flee. Of the six original CIA-trained fighters, only three were alive by 1960. Athar and Lhotse had returned to Lhokha after meeting the Dalai Lama only to discover Chinese troops moving in on their camp. The Lhokha freedom fighters did not have enough weapons to resist. Instead of fighting with no hope, many were fleeing across the border to India. Athar and Lhotse soon decided they had no choice. They buried their radio equipment on the top of a mountain and set off for India too, linking up with resistance leader Gompo Tashi en route. They crossed into India together. Their remaining rupees must have come in handy after all.[8]

Of the four freedom fighters dropped into Lithang, only Wangdu, the leader, survived. Tsewang Dorje disappeared not long after the drop, never to be heard of again. Dharlo was killed in the fighting. Baba Changtra Tashi, who had panicked and refused to jump, never found Wangdu after his overland return to Lithang. He died there in a short battle during which he killed two Chinese soldiers and was killed in turn by a hand grenade thrown by a third.[9] Wangdu stayed in Lithang, joining with other resistance fighters, attacking and being attacked, until April 1959, when he fled with his elder brother and a few others to India, traveling through Jyekundo and the Changtang, finally reaching Lhokha and crossing the border from there.

A third group of CIA trainees had been dropped into the nomadic area of Shentse (Ratsogen) in northern Tibet (near Jang Namtso, Jang Ringtso Lake) on September 19, 1959. The nomads there had fought the Chinese Communists bravely on their own. Several of their leaders had become national heroes when news of their deaths spread far and wide. The CIA trainees had hoped to give new direction and fresh weapons to the movement in Shentse, but by the time they were air-dropped in, the nomads' resistance had crumbled. The Chinese were in command, carrying out their mopping up operations. Joining with the nomads was impossible. There were no forces left to join. Nor could they begin afresh. No one among the trainees was familiar with either Shentse or its people, and the local people did not make them welcome. Food was scarce, and every new mouth to feed was that much less food for the nomads. The CIA-trained warriors stayed out of sight, hiding in the mountains and subsisting on the local wildlife, for fifty days. Finally they declared failure and gradually moved west, arriving in Mustang in early November 1959.

Mustang lies about three hundred and fifty miles southwest of Lhasa and is a rugged, poor, several hundred square mile, barely inhabited area of Nepal that juts like a tongue north into Tibet and once was a part of it. Even in this remote and mountainous part of the world Mustang is particularly isolated and inhospitable. At thirteen thousand feet high, it is cut off from Nepal in the south by some of the world's highest mountains. In 1959, the government of Nepal had only nominal control over the area and received minimal taxes from its local elite. But Mustang was quite accessible to Tibet. For Gompo Tashi and his resistance fighters, the place offered new possibilities.[10] Communist troops had yet to penetrate the Tibetan areas along the Mustang border, and Mustang's tiny population was militantly anti-Chinese. Mustang's climate and geographic conditions were congenial. It was a perfect place to establish a guerrilla base. Another chapter in the history of Tibetan resistance was about to begin.

In 1960, CIA representatives met with Gompo Tashi, then in India and still the leader of the Chushi Gangdruk, to discuss the possibility of setting up an intelligence gathering and reconnaissance force in Mustang. The CIA secretly broached the issue with Nepali King Mahendra and he, apparently, agreed.

The CIA proposed beginning the secret operation with one thousand men and asked Gompo Tashi and me to do the recruiting. My deputy, Lhamo Tsering, oversaw the day-to-day work of the Mustang operation. He had been in the third group of men to be trained by the CIA and was a dedicated, hardworking man. I admired him greatly and depended on him to get things done.

Many of the former resistance fighters who had fled from China's rule had been put to work on road construction crews inside Sikkim. We sent out feelers to see if some of them would be interested in a new type of resistance based in Nepal. The response was immediate and overwhelming. Young Tibetan men by the hundreds began leaving Sikkim, passing through Darjeeling en route to Nepal. For the next several weeks at least two hundred Tibetan men were transiting through Darjeeling every day. The media soon got wind of the exodus. When news of the sudden migration of hundreds of Tibetan men hit the press, both the Indian and Sikkimese governments were alarmed. So were we. The operation was meant to be secret, and we adamantly denied any role in the flight. By the time we were able to stop the flow, two thousand men had arrived in Mustang. The CIA

only had funds for one thousand, and we were unable to raise any
more.

The Mustang operation that was supposed to be highly confiden-
tial turned out to be an impossible secret to keep. Both the Indian
and Sikkimese governments soon learned why so many Tibetan men
had fled. The Sikkimese government complained to the Indians.
Nehru and his government complained to me. They forbade me
from crossing the Teester River. I was banned from both Kalimpong
and Sikkim for a decade.

Former soldiers in the Tibetan army and the Dalai Lama's bodyguards were also angry with me. All 2,500 of them had escaped from
Tibet and were anxious to join the new resistance. But word of the
new venture in Mustang reached them too late to join. I could not
let them go. I could only promise to let them know if any other new
opportunities arose.

THE MUSTANG PROJECT got off to a difficult start. With two
thousand new recruits and funds for only half of them, the would-be
resistance fighters spent a miserable first winter, constantly hungry
and cold and without material support. Eventually, though, the
Mustang operation had a series of successes. Sneaking clandestinely
across the border into Tibet, the resistance was able both to interdict
Chinese trucks along the Tibetan-Xinjiang highway and to gather intelligence the old fashioned way, by hooking up listening devices to
cables and telephone lines, tapping phones, and monitoring broadcasts. Over the years, we captured quite a rich collection of Chinese
military documents. It was from one of the raids in Mustang that
we learned the official figures from the army headquarters in Lhasa
putting the number of deaths in Central Tibet between March 1959
and October 1960 at eighty-seven thousand. In 1961, an ambush of
a truck en route from western Tibet to Xinjiang captured a vast set
of documents from the People's Liberation Army's secret *Bulletin of
Activities.* That catch was probably the biggest, richest set of intelligence materials ever captured from the Chinese. Meant to be read
only by senior military officers, the bulletins revealed the serious

difficulties experienced by both the military and ordinary citizens in the face of the massive famine then gripping China. They detailed the tensions within the Chinese military and between the military and the people's militia and touched on the growing conflict with the Soviet Union. Some reports contained the Chinese leadership's evaluation of the United States and Taiwan.

We never kept those documents, though. They were sent immediately to the CIA in Washington. The only document I still have is the one revealing the number of Tibetans killed after the Dalai Lama's escape.

Even as the reconnaissance and interdictions continued, the situation in Tibet grew increasingly worse. In the early 1960s, the Chinese set up people's communes. Tibetans were no longer allowed to grow barley. They were forced to grow grain. But grain is impossible to grow in Tibet. So when harvest time came there was nothing to eat. In Lhasa, people ate dead horses that the Chinese military had buried in fields. Some ate boiled shoe leather or the bark of trees. People dug in the soil to find earthworms. People's faces and stomachs grew swollen from eating such terrible things. Then people starved. Thousands and thousands of people starved. Traditionally, Tibet had plenty of inequality. Many people in rural areas were poor. In some villages, some people may have had only enough income to survive. But never in the history of Tibet had we experienced famine. In thousands of years, the Tibetan people had never died of starvation.

When I first heard these stories, I did not believe them. I thought they were exaggerated. Only later did I discover that they were true. Even hell might not be as bad as what Tibetans experienced then. Maybe hell is better.

The Chinese blame the Cultural Revolution for everything bad that happened in Tibet. But that is not true. Most of the damage was done before the Cultural Revolution. All the wealth that the Tibetans had accumulated over the generations had already been vacuumed away. After 1959, the Chinese destroyed everything inside the monasteries. There were more than six thousand monasteries in

Tibet and some of them were a 1,000 and up to 1,500 years old. The newest was at least three hundred years old. Over the centuries these monasteries had acquired priceless antiques, thangkas, and statues from Nepal, India, and China. All of Tibet's wealth was in those monasteries. And all of them were looted, emptied before the Cultural Revolution began. Everything was gone. When the Cultural Revolution started in 1966, everything had already been stolen. The dead were already dead. What was left were skeletons. During the Cultural Revolution, they pulled down the monasteries, too, tore down the walls, got rid of the skeletons. It was a premeditated act organized by the leadership of the Chinese Communist Party over a twenty-year period. It was not, as the Chinese say, just an "incident."

And it was not carried out by ordinary Chinese people. The Chinese are wonderful people. They also suffered terribly during those twenty years, and they were completely in the dark about what was happening in Tibet. Deng Xiaoping was in charge of the Chengdu military region then. When Tan Guansan and Zhang Guohua asked Deng what to do about the empty skeletons, Deng instructed them to be careful of the border regions with India and Nepal. He did not want people on other side of the border to know what was happening in Tibet. But inside Tibet, around Lhasa and Shigatze, in Kham and Amdo, sending in youngsters to tear down the monasteries was fine. If the buildings were not pulled down, maybe people would ask why the insides were empty. The Red Guards could do whatever they wanted inside Tibet. So the Red Guards from China came to Tibet to mobilize the young Tibetan Red Guards, and together they pulled down the buildings.

22

Settling Down in India

The Dalai Lama arrived in India with most of his government intact. His most capable and trusted officials had fled with him. But their responsibilities for helping eighty-five thousand refugees begin new lives in a strange and different land presented the new government in exile with previously unknown challenges. Both the physical and psychological dislocations faced by the newly arrived Tibetans were profound. The refugees needed places to live and work. Their children needed schools. The lamas and monks wanted to reestablish their monasteries. The elderly needed homes for the aged. Everyone needed clinics and hospitals. While offers of assistance began coming to us from governments and international aid organizations from many parts of the world, we could not have survived without the help provided us by the Indian government.

We set up different departments to carry out the variety of official tasks—a home department to find housing and work for the refugees, an education department to find and train teachers and to set up new schools, a religious department to help the lamas and monks regroup and reestablish their monasteries, and a health department to set up clinics and hospitals and train new doctors and nurses.

We also had a publicity department. Much of our work with foreign countries was focused on educating the international community about the situation in Tibet. Very few governments or international organizations had more than a passing understanding of either the Dalai Lama or Tibet, and those who had been exposed to the Chinese message had been badly misinformed. Through the publicity department, we tried to project ourselves internationally, correcting the Chinese picture and informing the world of the Chinese invasion, the atrocities the Chinese were still committing in Tibet, the ongoing violations of our basic human rights, and the Chinese attacks on our culture, religion, and language.

One of my responsibilities was dealing with foreign governments and international organizations. Before the Dalai Lama's arrival in India, I had no position in the Tibetan government. Even my work with the CIA was done in my private capacity. With the establishment of the Tibetan government in exile, I was put in charge of foreign affairs. For several years, Shakabpa, I, and several other colleagues traveled to the United Nations to present the Tibetan case and garner international support for the protection of the human rights of the Tibetan people and for Tibet's status as a free and independent country. I traveled to Switzerland, England, and Japan and met with a variety of international organizations—the International Red Cross in Switzerland, CARE, Catholic Charities, and Oxfam, among others. My new role also put me in charge of security both for the Dalai Lama and for all the Tibetans in exile. And I continued to oversee our clandestine intelligence and resistance activities with the CIA and various Indian intelligence agencies. Much of my work remained highly secret, though keeping those secrets was never easy.

I tried from the beginning to shield the Dalai Lama from the CIA and anything having to do with our clandestine activities. As part of my work, I made regular reports to him and the Kashag, but I made a strict distinction between government officials and intelligence officials and never spoke to the Dalai Lama about our secret work, never reported on the reconnaissance missions, the fighting, or the deaths that were part of my job. I never used the word CIA.

I spoke instead about American government support. I saw intelligence work as dirty and felt it would be dishonorable for the Dalai Lama or the Kashag to be involved with it. I assumed sole responsibility. At some point, yes, my brother knew something about the clandestine side of what we were doing. But we never spoke about it together.

Those early years in India were difficult, and we faced a number of conflicts. Some of the difficulties were financial. Shortly after the Tibetan government in exile settled in Mussoorie, the Kashag recommended to the Dalai Lama that he ask Prime Minister Nehru for a loan of some 200 million rupees to cover our expenses. Shakabpa, Khenchung Lobsang Gyaltsen, and I sat in on the meeting. The sum seemed extraordinarily high, a reflection perhaps of the lavish lifestyles some of the wealthy aristocrats in the Kashag had led in Lhasa. I raised the question of the loan privately with P. N. Menon, then the Indian government's official liaison with the Dalai Lama. Mr. Menon thought it highly unlikely that Nehru would agree to a loan for so much. He suggested instead that we prepare a budget for our expected yearly costs and ask for a loan to cover actual expenses. Something in the range of 800,000 rupees a month or 10 million rupees a year would be appropriate, he thought.

When I reported to the Kashag on my meeting with Menon, two members in particular—Surkhang and Yuthok, both wealthy members of the aristocracy—objected. They thought we should insist on the 200 million. The Dalai Lama followed their advice and met personally with Nehru to make the request. Nehru flatly refused, saying that the Indian government simply did not have 200 million rupees to loan. And he warned the Dalai Lama to be cautious about listening to such advice from his ministers.

Surkhang and Yuthok were so embarrassed when the Dalai Lama reported his conversation to the Kashag that they fled Mussoorie and never returned. Perhaps they had suffered an irreparable loss of face when the loan they had so adamantly sought was so curtly refused. Perhaps they believed that the government in exile would collapse without it. They soon fled India and later fell in with Guomindang intelligence and moved to Taiwan, where they set up what they called an office of the Kashag. But their office was fake. The Kashag in India had never approved it. Surkhang and Yuthok had no contact with the Dalai Lama or the Kashag after fleeing from Mussoorie and had no right to portray themselves as representatives of the Tibetan government. Their new office did not last long.

Their defection was a blow to the government in exile, straining relations among some of its members. Guomindang intelligence continued its efforts to undermine our unity. They were still angry with the Dalai Lama for refusing their help and insisting that we Tibetans were struggling for independence rather than the return of the Nationalists to the mainland.

THE HUGE FINANCIAL LOSS we suffered with the sale of the gold bullion that we were holding in case of emergency was our largest early scandal. In 1950, following Shakabpa's return from the United States, we had deposited the gold bullion he had purchased there in a Gangtok warehouse under the protection of the chogyal of Sikkim. Later, after the Chinese invasion of Chamdo and the Dalai Lama's escape to Dromo, additional gold from the Dalai Lama's treasury had been placed in safekeeping in Sikkim. With the Dalai Lama's escape to India in 1959 and Nehru's refusal to provide the Tibetan government a loan, the emergency that the bullion was meant to help us confront had finally come to pass. We needed money to support the Dalai Lama and the Tibetan government in exile. And we had to provide for the refugees.

We decided to sell the bullion. Prime Minister Nehru offered to buy it all, but we thought we could get a better price on the open market, where gold was then selling at much higher than the $40 an ounce we had paid for it.

Four leading members of the Dalai Lama's staff oversaw the transfer of the gold from Sikkim to Calcutta: Gadrang Lobsang Rigzin, Tibet's ranking monk official and the Dalai Lama's chief of staff, Khenchung Lobsang Gyaltsen, who had been in charge of overseeing the bullion from Kalimpong, the Dalai Lama's Simpon Khenpo (master of the robes), and me. We accompanied the bullion as it was taken by truck from Sikkim to the Bagdogra Airport and from there by a chartered Indian Airlines plane to Calcutta. In Calcutta, the bullion was transferred to a bank.

We needed a respected businessman to handle the actual sale of the bullion and considered George Tsarong and Pandatsang, the heads of Tibet's two largest trading companies and the two richest men in the country, as the best candidates. We chose Tsarong. He was a fourth rank Tibetan official, had been educated in Darjeeling at St. Joseph's North Point, and, unlike Pandatsang, spoke excellent English. We had no reason not to trust Tsarong. His own personal wealth, his experience as a trader, and his excellent command of English seemed to make him the ideal choice.

We knew that Tsarong would need the help of a number of people to handle the financial transactions related to the sale. We made an agreement before handing over the bullion that he would not advance more than 500,000 rupees to any single person. We warned him to beware of his friends and to be careful of his Indian go-betweens. We knew that people would be after the money like snake charmers blowing their flutes to coax the cobra to dance.

The bullion was fully intact when we handed it over to Tsarong. But something went terribly wrong. Within just a few years, almost all the money was gone. Some of the money was apparently loaned to a group of Marwari businessmen. Most of that money was either lost or stolen. We still do not know. George Tsarong later claimed to have lost a suitcase filled with the certificates from the bonds the Indians claimed to have purchased on his behalf. He also used some of the money to invest in a pipe factory through a company called Gayday run by some Tibetan businessmen. He made me one of the trustees, but I never had anything to do with managing or overseeing the factory. That venture also failed because of mismanagement.

I think we made a big mistake in appointing Tsarong. We never suspected that he would deceive us. But we should never have appointed him. I have no real, concrete proof of what happened. I was too busy at the time with the CIA, the Indians, and the Americans to do my own thorough investigation of what went wrong. We could never disprove what Tsarong said, but I still have my suspicions.

Tsarong's father had been a thief, a big one. Tsarong the elder was originally named Dazang Dadul and had started out as a messenger boy in the Thirteenth Dalai Lama's court. The young boy was quick and intelligent, and the Thirteenth Dalai Lama took a liking to him. When the Thirteenth Dalai Lama escaped to Mongolia during the Younghusband expedition in 1903, he took the young messenger with him. Dazang Dadul served him well, even defending him militarily against the Chinese. When the Dalai Lama finally returned to Lhasa for good, he brought Dazang Dadul with him and arranged for the young man to marry into the aristocratic family of the Tsarongs. The family's only male heir had been executed for having been too pro-Chinese. The survival of the Tsarong line required a new heir to assume office in the Tibetan government. So this young, intelligent, and ambitious commoner married the daughter of an aristocrat, thus becoming an aristocrat by marriage and inheriting the family's vast estates. It was an unusual way to enter the aristocracy, but not at all unheard of. The new Tsarong continued to be one of the Dalai Lama's favorites, rising quickly in the ranks, first to become a cabinet minister and then to assume the position of commander-in-chief of the military.

As the new commander-in-chief, the elder Tsarong soon received an invitation from the British governor general of India to visit him in Calcutta. The Thirteenth Dalai Lama must have been suspicious of what the British governor general might want from the commander-in-chief of his military, so he sent Lukhangwa, then a cabinet secretary and later to become one of the prime ministers under the Fourteenth Dalai Lama, to accompany Tsarong to India. His instructions were to keep an eye on the commander-in-chief.[1]

Lukhangwa was a thoroughly honest person. He duly sent reports to the Dalai Lama in Lhasa. I think he concluded that the British were trying to dupe Tsarong into staging some sort of military coup. Such intrigues and conspiracies were still commonplace back then.

As Tsarong and his military entourage were returning to Lhasa, just after they had passed the Natula pass from Sikkim into Tibet before reaching Phari Dzong, a messenger from the Thirteenth Dalai Lama galloped up on horseback, dismounted, and knelt to read a message for Tsarong. The message declared that from that day forth Tsarong was relieved of his positions both on the Kashag and as commander-in-chief. Henceforth, he was to be nothing more than an ordinary official. From then until the death of the Thirteenth Dalai Lama, old Tsarong was never given another official appointment.

With the passing of the Thirteenth Dalai Lama, however, Reting Regent appointed Tsarong to become director of the Tibetan mint, responsible for overseeing the printing of the Tibetan currency. He held that position for many years, and was still director of the mint when my family reached Lhasa in 1939. I remember him as a jolly old man. Old Tsarong was rich. Very rich. Pandatsang was also very rich, but Tsarong was the richest man in Tibet.

The elder Tsarong stayed behind when the Dalai Lama fled in 1959, only to be captured by the Chinese. Two days later he was dead. No one knows why. Some say he was killed by the Chinese. Some say he swallowed poison himself. Many years later, the Mongolian monk Dawa Sangpo, who I learned later was really a Japanese spy named Hisao Kimura, told me that Tsarong had two printing presses, one in his house and one in the mint. He was printing his own money. I have no proof of that, of course. But it certainly is a good explanation for why the elder Tsarong was so fabulously rich. He had his own private printing machine. I think father and son were similar. They both found questionable ways of making huge amounts of money.

The government of Tibet must have done an investigation at the time of how the money disappeared under George Tsarong's care, but no one took any action against him. He was never accused of a crime. He continued his service to the Tibetan government in exile. I continued to interact with him as the occasion arose. Whatever portion of the money we were able to retrieve was put in the Dalai Lama's trust, set up and managed by Rinchen Sandutsang and another honest official. Such wanton financial mismanagement as occurred with Tsarong never occurred again. The financial management system of the Tibetan government in exile has been clean ever since. The money has been spent properly and the financial managers are accountable. The Dalai Lama's trust continues to accumulate with money he receives from prizes and awards.

Some people blame me for having appointed Tsarong. Some even still suspect that I stole the money. In 2004, His Holiness's private secretary in Dharamsala sent me a copy of a letter addressed to him from George Tsarong saying that he had received a bill from a Calcutta safe deposit company for some 6,020 rupees (around 80 US dollars), that he had given me the key to the safety deposit box when he had left for medical treatment, and that I had not responded to two letters to me about the key. Tsaring was trying to implicate me in something, implying that the security deposit box contained money and that I had taken it. But I knew nothing about any safety deposit box and had no key. I taped a long deposition to the Dalai Lama's private office, detailing everything I knew about how the money had been handled and what may have happened to it. I never received a response.

The disappearance of all that money has been a terrible burden for me. The whole incident was a terrible disaster. During our most difficult period in exile, the Tibetan government had no money. If we had not given the bullion to Tsarong, if we had, for instance, invested it in the property market in New Delhi instead, imagine what a fortune we would have now. That loss has given me such pain that I sometimes wonder if there is any god or any justice in this world. I have wanted to believe that the truth will prevail, but for us Tibetans the truth can be hard to find.

I have not spoken about this incident for all these years, even as some have doubted me. I have tried to follow my father's dictum of not responding to those who have tried to besmirch me. But in the course of writing this book, I realized I was still holding back on certain things, including this. When I explained my problem to His Holiness, he encouraged me to open up fully, not to hold anything back. So I believe I have to tell the truth. I never touched a single rupee of that money. I had nothing to do with the way it disappeared.

DESPITE SUCH AN uncertain and troublesome start, a new order eventually began to emerge for the Tibetan government in exile. Shakabpa became the Dalai Lama's representative in New Delhi, and I moved there to join him and set up an office. We rented a small flat in the Muslim section of the city and hung up a sign outside identifying us as the Office of His Holiness the Dalai Lama. For months we played cat and mouse with the Indian authorities. They were reluctant to allow us to advertise ourselves as anything so seemingly official. We always graciously complied when they stopped by to demand that we take down our sign, only to hang it up again once they had left. After months of playing cat and mouse, the Indians got tired of instructing us to remove the sign, and our identification as the Office of His Holiness the Dalai Lama became permanent. Soon similar offices, called the Office of Tibet, were opened in New York, Katmandu, and Geneva. Later Tokyo, London, Paris, Brussels, Australia, and several Eastern European countries also established Offices of Tibet. They continue to this day.

One of our early successes in New Delhi was the setting up of a small museum and library of Tibetan cultural artifacts. While most Tibetans fled to India with only the clothes on their backs, others were able to take some of their most precious possessions—thangkas, statues, manuscripts, and scrolls. Many of these were artifacts from monasteries, carried by fleeing monks. Some were valuable antiques, and their owners, desperate for cash, began selling them to Nepalese antique dealers for sums well below their actual value. With such valuable representations of Tibetan culture disappearing so cheaply into private hands, we began exploring ways to purchase some of the artifacts ourselves and to open a small museum. Khenchung Lobsang Gyaltsen was put in charge of the endeavor, and the CIA agreed to give us about half a million rupees for the purchases. We were able to assemble close to three hundred paintings and thangkas, one hundred statues, and an even larger number of manuscripts and old Tibetan books, including biographies of famous lamas and ancient religious texts. Some were very rare. While most of the collection came to us by purchase, some of the most valuable pieces, particularly those from monasteries, were donated.

We rented a two-story house at 16 Jorbak Road to house the treasures and unofficially dubbed the building Tibet House. Our hope was for Tibet House to become an official library and museum where Tibetans in exile, interested Indians, and tourists could come to experience Tibetan culture. We wanted to hold lectures and trainings on Tibetan Buddhism and open a small shop for Tibetan handicrafts. We approached ministry of external affairs official M. G. Kaul about our plans. He was amazed when we showed him our collection. Every room in Tibet House was packed with treasures. Our request for official approval was soon granted. Two young and learned reincarnated lamas, Dromo Geshe Rinpoche (whose Tibetan monastery was relocated in Kalimpong) and Dragyab Rinpoche (who is now in Germany) were recruited to run the new operation. India's minister of education, M. C. Chagla, graced our inaugural opening with a speech. Tibet House was so successful that it later expanded into a new three-story building on Lodi Road. Another Tibet House was later set up in New York and is still in operation today.

Our efforts to reestablish ourselves in India began to bear fruit. The Indian government gave us some land, and several Tibetan settlements were set up. My sister Tsering Dolma established the Tibetan Children's Village School and later, when she died, my younger sister Jetsu Pema assumed leadership over it. The Indian government established a Tibetan School Society, with schools in Kalimpong, Darjeeling, Simla, and Mussoorie. The monks and lamas were resettled in scattered places in many parts of India—Kalimpong, Assam, Uttar Pradesh, and Ladakh among them. Their monasteries were rebuilt.

Some people reconstituted themselves as small-scale entrepreneurs. In the winter, when the weather turns cold, Tibetans can be seen selling sweaters on the streets of many Indian cities. We have become famous for selling our sweaters to the Indians in winter. In Dharamsala, some have set up Tibetan restaurants and small businesses selling jewelry, clothing, and religious articles.

My wife established the Tibetan Refugee Self-Help Center on a small plot of land rented from St. Joseph's North Point in Darjeeling, near the spot where the Thirteenth Dalai Lama once stayed for more than a year. She became known as Diki Dolkar because Tibetans could not pronounce her Chinese name. The center began in 1959 with some 3,000 rupees earned from selling tickets to a local football game and later received funding from the Indian and West Bengali governments, the Central Relief Committee of India, Catholic Charities, CARE, and several British aid organizations. Pope John Paul was a particularly generous supporter. The center set up training courses in weaving, Tibetan *thangka* painting, and other traditional handicrafts. Proceeds from the sales of the crafts helped support the center. Its carpets and sweaters have been particularly popular sale items. The center included a nursery for orphaned children, a primary and middle school, and a medical clinic. At any given time, the center was usually providing support for some five hundred Tibetan refugees. Its principle of self-help has been emulated in several other areas with Tibetan refugees. My wife was still working there when she died, and the center continues to operate today. A small museum on the grounds tells its history and honors my wife's work in establishing and running it. Her presence is still felt in the photographs of her that look down from the walls, as though she is still guiding its work.

So we Tibetans are not starving in India. In fact, we have done so well in the fifty plus years since we fled that it sometimes seems miraculous. God seems to be looking after us Tibetans after all. We have our freedom—freedom to move, freedom to think, and freedom to speak—freedoms that our people in Tibet are lacking. We must thank the people and government of India for this. Maybe, too, God has been pushing the Indians to help us. But above all, we have succeeded because we Tibetans are helping ourselves. The Chinese must be very surprised.

23

The War between China and India

In the fall of 1962, not long before the onset of winter, the danger we had been warning India about for almost a decade finally came to pass. The Chinese army attacked Indian troops high in the mountains along the disputed borders of Aksai Chin and the North-East Frontier Agency (NEFA).[1] The war did not last long. The Indians were roundly defeated and badly humiliated. The Chinese troops quickly withdrew. Indian Defense Minister Krishna Menon was forced to resign, and the country's national defense forces began a thorough reorganization. Nehru's stalwart efforts to appease the Chinese, bending over backwards to please them, had come to naught. The Panchsheel Treaty was null and void, and the days of Chinese-Indian brotherhood were over. Nehru's rosy view of China had been an illusion. His policy of nonalignment had failed. The American strategy of provoking conflict between the two giants had worked.

India's shocking defeat changed Nehru's view of Tibet at the same time it opened up new opportunities in our struggle for freedom. Even before the gunpowder had dried, Indian foreign ministry official K. L. Mehta, who was in charge of the North-East Frontier Agency, invited me to meet him in his New Delhi office. Since 1959, I had been meeting with Indian intelligence chief B. N. Mullik and the chief of staff of the Indian army, encouraging them to set up a training center for Tibetan resistance fighters. The former resistance fighters who had escaped to India would have made perfect recruits. But my suggestions had always been dismissed with shrug of the shoulder and a wave of the hand. Now Mehta wondered how many people I could recruit for a top-secret military training center for Tibetan paratroopers. In case of another war with China, the paratroopers could be dropped in for reconnaissance, intelligence, and the Tibetan battle for freedom.

I was enthusiastic about Mehta's proposal but worried that the thousands of resistance fighters who had fled in 1959 had taken jobs as road workers and were scattered in Simla, Hamachel Pradesh, Sikkim, and Darjeeling. They had already settled into their jobs and might be difficult to reach. But I said that I could send out letters asking for volunteers and that I thought we could probably recruit about five thousand young trainees. The CIA was in favor of the plan, too, and wanted the training to be done by Indian intelligence rather than the military.

The call for a new batch of military recruits provided an opportunity for young men who had not been able to join the Mustang contingent. Within a month, six thousand young Tibetan men, mostly former soldiers from the Tibetan army, the Dalai Lama's bodyguards, and resistance fighters, had volunteered. The recruits were happy to be trained and eager to fight. The organization came to be known both as Establishment 22 and the Special Frontier Force and was an ultra-secret department within the Indian armed forces that continues to this day. Like the earlier Tibetan resistance fighters, the new recruits to Establishment 22 were true patriots who never thought of the consequences for themselves.

Also around this time in early winter 1964, Indian intelligence, the CIA, and the Tibetan exiles set up a joint intelligence office, known as the Combined Operations Center. The joint organization assumed overall direction of the ongoing Mustang operation in Nepal, which continued to carry out periodic ambushes of Chinese transport vehicles and to monitor telephones, telegrams, and broadcasts. The material the Mustang forces gathered was sent to offices in New Delhi and Nepal where dozens of people sifted through it for translation and analysis. The results were shared jointly between the Tibetans, Indian intelligence, and the CIA.

It was also around this time that Indian intelligence chief Mullik asked me to help him establish contact with representatives of the Chinese Nationalist government on Taiwan. Through the good offices of old friends in Taiwan, I paid a visit there so secret that it was never officially recorded. Nationalist officials met me on the tarmac at the Taipei airport and whisked me away without going through the formalities of immigration and customs. I paid a pleasant courtesy call on the Generalissimo and Madame Chiang, who were delighted to see me and happy to learn about the overture from India. Chiang Kai-shek was in his mid-seventies by then and still serving as president. But his son Chiang Ching-, kuo was taking on more political responsibilities, serving as head of the secret police and soon to become Taiwan's minister of defense. I presented the request from Indian intelligence to Chiang Ching-kuo and Taiwan's deputy foreign minister, who introduced me to the deputy director Wang of Taiwan's national security. Soon, Wang traveled to New Delhi, where I introduced him to B. N. Mullik, thus beginning a close relationship between the Indian and Taiwanese intelligence agencies. My role as an intermediary was over at that point, but collaboration between Taiwan and India continues today, even in the absence of formal diplomatic relations between the two countries.

I also used the occasion of my visit to Taiwan to urge the leadership there to make a public, internationally circulated statement in support of the Tibetan struggle for freedom and independence under the leadership of the Dalai Lama. In return for such a statement, the Dalai Lama would send his personal representative to open a real Office of Tibet in Taiwan. During a meeting in the president's home with Chiang Kai-shek, his son Chiang Ching-kuo, and the foreign minister Shen Chang-huan, I thought we had reached an agreement. The announcement was to be made within the fortnight.

But the announcement never came. I waited in vain to hear it. Chiang Kai-shek must have changed his mind. The Office of Tibet in Taiwan was never opened.

I DID NOT VISIT TAIWAN again for almost thirty years. In 1991, I finally went in my capacity as head of the Kashag in order to meet the recently elected president, Lee Teng-hui. By then, both Chiang Kai-shek and his son Chiang Ching-kuo were dead.

I had admired Lee for years, since his implementation of land reform on Taiwan shortly after the Nationalists' flight from the mainland, but this was our first meeting. President Lee was generally regarded as a supporter of Taiwanese independence, and once he assumed office, the claims that the Guomindang would soon retake the mainland stopped. We did not speak directly about his views on the question of Tibetan independence, but my assumption was that he supported it.

The president was full of apologies and sympathy for Tibet. The government of the Republic of China felt ashamed, he said, at how little it had been able to accomplish compared to the tremendous achievements of the Tibetan refugees. The Dalai Lama had arrived in India with only his bare hands—no army, no money, and no territory—Lee said, but he had achieved so much, singlehandedly establishing himself on the international stage, becoming a leading figure in India and the world. The accomplishments of the Nationalist government, even with its own territory, financial resources, and trained personnel, had been limited, he said. He felt ashamed, too, that the government of the Republic of China had never been able to help Tibet. He asked me to extend an invitation from him to the Dalai Lama to visit Taiwan.

The Dalai Lama made his first trip in 1993, spending a week visiting Buddhist temples and meeting with religious leaders and ranking government officials, including Lee Teng-hui. The visit was a huge success. The people of Taiwan mobbed the Dalai Lama wherever he went. Taiwan newspapers described the trip as an earthquake that shook Taiwan. At the end, President Lee Teng-hui made the most generous donation to the Dalai Lama and his secretariat that any national leader has ever given.

My admiration for Lee Teng-hui continued to grow. He had the courage and the wisdom to support the cause of the Dalai Lama and Tibet when so many other national leaders, including Chiang Kai-shek, had turned away. Our relations with Taiwan, especially with religious leaders and the Democratic Progressive Party (DPP), continue to be good. The Dalai Lama recently made his third visit to the island, at the invitation of the new DPP leader, Tsai Ing-wen. Today, the DPP openly supports the independence of both Taiwan and Tibet.

24

The CIA Stops Its Support

S ometime in 1967, I began to get quiet warnings that the CIA's support might be coming to an end. The Russians were the first to raise the possibility after the secretary of India's ministry of external affairs and former ambassador to the Soviet Union, T. N. Kaul, wondered why I was only dealing with the Americans and the Indians. He thought that I should be in contact with the Russians as well. The Soviet Union had representatives in New Delhi, he said. Mr. Markov, the head of the Russian news agency TASS, was the person to meet.

I met Markov at his residence. He expressed sympathy with the Tibetan cause and told me he would report our conversation to Moscow. He thought his government might send a special representative to meet me. The next meeting took place in the Soviet Embassy where two people newly arrived from Moscow joined Markov and me. The newcomers told me that the Americans and Chinese were meeting secretly in Warsaw and that the Americans were preparing to sell the Tibetans out. They thought I was naïve to think that the Americans had any real intention of helping the Tibetan cause. The Americans were just exploiting us, they said. More meetings followed, continuing sporadically for several years.

The Russians at first offered help that they claimed would bring real results, in contrast to what they called the useless help and empty promises that we were receiving from the United States. The Soviets proposed setting up a joint operation, headquartered in Tashkent, to train Tibetan soldiers to fight for independence. They could offer both training and financial help. It was an interesting proposition. But I had three big concerns.

The first was the logistical difficulty of getting the Tibetan trainees out of India and into Tashkent. That turned out to be the easy problem. The Soviet Union regularly flew arms into India through Palam Airport in New Delhi. The Tibetan recruits could be flown out in one of those planes. A truck could pick them up somewhere along the road to the airport. Or the Tibetans could apply for refugee status in one of the East European countries—East Germany or Poland, for instance. Once there, the Russians could send a plane to pick them up and take them to Tashkent.

My second concern was how to raise the issue with the Indian government. After all, eighty-five thousand Tibetan refugees were based in India, and we could not risk the Indian government's displeasure by taking military assistance from a country they did not approve. We could not make any move with the Soviets without first getting an agreement from India. The best arrangement would be for the Russians and Indians to join hands in the proposed endeavor. But the Soviets balked. They did not want India involved or informed. The Indians were useless, they said.

My third concern was China. The Communist Chinese were growing ever more vocally anti-Soviet. I was afraid that any Tibetan involvement with the Russians might complicate the possibility of later working out some sort of rapprochement with China. I took my dilemma to R. N. Kao, the founding father of the recently established Research and Analysis Wing of Indian intelligence. He was shocked. "Mr. Thondup, for heaven's sake, don't collaborate with the Russians," he exclaimed. "Don't listen to them. This is very dangerous."

The political divisions within the Indian government were suddenly glaringly obvious. On the one hand, the secretary of external affairs, T. N. Kaul, was putting me in contact with the head of TASS in India and encouraging us to cooperate with the Soviets. At the same time the head of Indian intelligence was viscerally horrified at the prospect of Tibetans joining hands with the Russians.

I tried to test the Russians' commitment by setting my own condition. I asked them to support the Tibetan cause in the United Nations. The Soviets were still siding with the Communist Chinese in UN discussions of Tibet. In order to convince my fellow Tibetans that the Soviet proposal was serious, I told the Russians they would have to come out publicly on our side. So long as the Soviet Union continued to support Communist China, the Tibetan people would never believe or accept the Soviets' offer of help. But the Soviets never agreed to my terms. They would not involve the Indians, and they were not going to support our cause in the United Nations. The talks continued off and on for several more years and then petered out. By then, our support from the CIA had also stopped.

When I reported to William Grimsley, the head of the CIA operation in New Delhi, about my discussions with the Russians and their assertion that support from the United States would soon come to an end, he was silent, listening. I was naïve to have told him. He must have been laughing inside. He knew all along.

Soon, even the CIA was warning me to prepare for the termination of American assistance. Frank Holober was a Washington-based CIA officer who made frequent trips to India to give us technical advice. He had genuine sympathy for the Tibetans, and we were friends. During my periodic trips to Washington, we used to drink beer together after hours, chatting unofficially and off the record. By 1968, he had begun urging me to ask the CIA for more money, enough for us to continue our operations if they withdrew their support. I was still naïve. I did not really believe that the CIA would pull out. And I did not think it right to ask for more money in case they did. Holober issued his warnings often, but always privately and unofficially.

He was right. The Russians were right. The United States did pull out.

William Grimsley, still the head of the CIA in Delhi, broke the news. It was in 1969. President Nixon was already in office, and Henry Kissinger was his national security advisor.[1] Neither of them knew anything about Tibet. Neither of them cared. Grimsley's message was simple. The United States and China had been in negotiations. The Chinese government had set two preconditions for détente with the United States: sever diplomatic relations with Taiwan and terminate all contact with and assistance to groups under the leadership of the Dalai Lama. The United States had agreed. Help to the Tibetans would have to stop.

Some of our men in Mustang thought I was lying when I broke the news. They could not believe that the Americans were pulling out. They thought I had stolen the money meant for them and was keeping it for myself. They felt stranded in Mustang without support. But our joint intelligence office with India continued, and the Indians soon took over support for much of the work that the CIA had been funding, including Mustang. The Mustang operation continued for several more years, until 1974, ending finally through a combination of internal dissent and withdrawal of external support.

In fact, the guerrilla activities of the Mustang fighters had already begun to wind down by the time we got word that the CIA would withdraw its support. As early as 1966, internal conflict was beginning to tear the Mustang operation apart. Baba Yeshi, the elderly leader of the Mustang guerrillas, was coming under criticism from the Combined Operations Center both for his increasingly ineffectual leadership and for accumulating some 20 million rupees of CIA-proferred money for himself while paying his soldiers a pittance. I sent my deputy, Lhamo Tsering, to investigate the situation. The Combined Operations Center eventually decided to appoint Wangdu Gyatotsang, the leader of the second team in the first group of CIA-trained recruits and considerably younger than Baba Yeshi, to replace him. The money being held by Baba Yeshi was supposed to be handed over to Wangdu, too. Baba Yeshi and several of the older resistance fighters were offered office positions in Delhi and Dharamsala. Wangdu was something of a hero to the Tibetans then, respected both for his military skills and his ability to train and lead the soldiers. But Baba Yeshe never fully accepted the decision that he step down, and tensions between the two camps continued.

Tensions only heightened after the CIA's decision to stop funding. The terms of suspension included a three-year period for resettlement and reemployment of the Mustang soldiers. But some of the Mustang fighters continued to oppose the closure of the operation and even those who agreed on the closure could not agree how to do it. In early 1974, the Nepalese government summoned Wangdu to Kathmandu and demanded that the Tibetan resistance fighters leave Mustang and surrender their weapons first. The Chinese were probably behind that order. When Mao Zedong met the new Nepali King Birendra[2] in Beijing in 1973, the Chinese leader apparently asked him to close the Mustang base. The Tibetan guerrillas were much better trained and adept at fighting than the Nepalese army. Just as many of the resistance fighters wanted to keep their arms in fear of an ambush by the Nepalese, so the Nepalese wanted the Tibetans to surrender their weapons out of fear of a possible strike by the Tibetans. Again, Lhamo Tsering went to Mustang to help Wangdu and his men work out a solution and oversee the withdrawal. But the Nepalese arrested Lhamo Tsering as he was en route, following which six other Mustang fighters were also arrested. The issue was still unresolved.

Finally, in July 1974, the Dalai Lama sent a tape to the men in Mustang urging them in his own voice to lay down their arms and search for peaceful ways to obtain their objectives.[3] Several of Wangdu's men were so distraught over the message that they committed suicide rather than surrender. Wangdu and a small band of his followers still refused to lay down their arms and escaped secretly from Mustang through Tibet, only to be ambushed and killed in the dark of night by the Nepalese when they arrived at the Nepali-Indian border. Wangdu's loss was a terrible blow. He was one of our best, most able, and respected guerrilla fighters.

Lhamo Tsering in Darjeeling

Lhamo Tsering and the six resistance fighters spent five years in prison without being formally charged or tried. I did everything I could to get them released but to no avail. Lhamo Tsering's family was only able to visit him once a year. Finally in 1979, the Nepalese held a show trial. Six of the men, including Lhamo Tsering, were sentenced to life in prison. One was sentenced to death. Two years later, after the Dalai Lama wrote a letter to the Nepalese king appealing for their release, the king granted them amnesty, and they were at last released. Lhamo Tsering went on to become a member of the Kashag and a respected member of the Tibetan exile community, continuing to serve the Tibetan cause until his death in 1999. He was a modest and unassuming man, but he played a vital role in the resistance movement, doing much of the practical, behind the scenes work that allowed the movement to survive as long as it did. He deserves an important place in modern Tibetan history.

The Resistance Fighters in Lhokha

25

A New Life in Hong Kong

By the mid-1960s, I was spending much of my time in the British colony of Hong Kong. The city was in turmoil. China's Cultural Revolution was spilling over the border, and Hong Kong's workers, inspired by China's Red Guards, were taking to the streets in protest. A series of violent riots ensued. In August 1967, the Red Guards in Beijing burned down the British Embassy, and Xinhua, the Communist Party's official news organ, triumphantly declared that the evil rule of the British imperialists in Hong Kong would surely be smashed. The Chinese threatened to stop sending food to the British colony. The threat was serious. Half the food consumed by the people of Hong Kong came from China.

I bought a flat on Hong Kong Island at 26 Magazine Gap Road not long thereafter, using some of the money Chiang Kai-shek had given me when I left for the United States. People were fleeing the violence of Hong Kong in droves, and housing prices had plummeted. I told people I was doing business. In fact, I was just eating in Chinese restaurants and learning as much as I could about China, supporting myself with funds from my business in India and the money left over after buying the flat.[1]

I went to Hong Kong for the same reason I had gone to study in Nanjing. China and Tibet, for better or worse, were inseparable. Whatever the solution to the problems between the two, the answer still depended on China. The Americans and the Indians could pay lip service to helping Tibet, but there was little concretely they could do. I wanted to understand what had happened in China since the Communists took over—the numerous political campaigns such as the *sanfan* and *wufan* movements of the early 1950s, the Great Leap Forward and the people's communes at the end of the 1950s, and the Cultural Revolution that had started in 1966 and was in full swing when I bought my Hong Kong flat.

I needed to understand why those movements had occurred, what they were about, and what effect they had had on the Chinese people. I needed to understand how this Communist government operated—how the politburo functioned, the nature of the educational system, and how agricultural production was organized with all the twists and turns of land reform and collectivization. I needed to investigate the continuing tensions between China and Taiwan and to understand why Mao had started lobbing canons at Quemoy and Matsu in 1958. I wanted to learn more about China's relations with the United States and Japan and to understand the rationale behind the party's policies toward Tibet and other so-called national minority areas. I had to study the role of the Chinese military and to investigate both the northwest military command headquartered in Lanzhou that controlled Qinghai, Xinjiang, and Inner Mongolia and the Chengdu-based southwest military command that controlled Sichuan, Yunnan, and the Tibetan Autonomous Region.

Hong Kong was the best place outside of China to learn what I needed to know. The Chinese language press—publications such as the *People's Daily, Dagong Bao, Wenhui Bao,* and *Ming Bao*—spanned every possible point of view, from the Nationalists on Taiwan to the Communists on the mainland to Hong Kong under the British and every possible political viewpoint in between. They all reported on day-to-day events in mainland China. International publications were readily available, too, from the English-language *South China Morning Post* to *Time* and *Newsweek*. Radio and television also broadcast news about China. I monitored the radio broadcasts from China and listened to the BBC and the Voice of America. I met with people whose job it was to know what was happening in China, people such as the Hungarian Catholic priest Father Laszlo LaDany, and later John Dolfin, the American director of the Universities Service Centre where Western scholars spent long stretches of time doing what I was doing—researching China from just across the border. People visiting China often passed through Hong Kong on their way in and out, and they reported on what they heard and saw. So I read. I listened to broadcasts. I talked to people in the know.

A lot of what was touted as news in Hong Kong was nothing more than gossip, and some of it was just plain rubbish. But from the many sources of information available to me there, I could piece together a pretty good picture of what was going on.

I still spent much of my time in India. Most of my work was still there. I was called back often. Sometime in 1970, I received a call from my wife in Darjeeling urging me to return immediately. An Indian newspaper had just published a story reporting that the government of Bhutan was planning to extradite me for plotting the murder of the young king of Bhutan. The Dalai Lama's representative in Bhutan, a man named Lhading, and his assistant, George Taring, had been implicated as well. I was accused of being the person directing the plot. I returned immediately.

I had known the old Bhutanese king well. He used to come to my house in Darjeeling. We spent pleasant evenings chatting and dining together. He was a kind man and sympathetic to Tibetans. He had allowed a few thousand Tibetan refugees to take up residence in Bhutan, and he helped them find work, for which I had always been grateful. He had died rather suddenly, and his ten-year-old son, the crown prince who was in line to succeed him, had been duly installed as the new king. The allegations that led to my wife's phone call were that a group of Tibetans with me at the head were plotting to kill the young king and replace him with the illegitimate son of the old king's concubine, a Tibetan woman name Yangkyi.

Yangkyi had born the old king at least two sons and possibly several more. Her relationship with the king was well-known both to the Bhutanese and to the Tibetans in Darjeeling and Kalimpong. Yangkyi visited Darjeeling often, and some of the Tibetans there regarded her as a second queen. Lhading and his assistant George Taring knew Yangkyi well, too, and often went to their fellow Tibetan when they needed favors from the Bhutanese government. When Tharchin Babu's Tibetan newspaper in Darjeeling published an article about one of Yangkyi's visits there, referring to her as Bhutan's second queen and thus making her relationship to the king public, some members of the Bhutanese family took offense. The Bhutanese government protested to the Indian government, demanding to know why I had published a piece describing Yangkyi as the second queen of Bhutan. But I had nothing to do with the publication of the article. I had nothing to do with Yangkyi. I had never even met her. I had not read the newspaper article either.

With the death of the old king, the Bhutanese royal family had begun quarreling among themselves. Yangkyi had fled Bhutan when the accusations began, going first to Darjeeling where she linked up with some fellow Tibetans, and then fleeing with them to New Delhi, where she had close ties with Indian intelligence. The Bhutanese were even more suspicious when they heard that she had fled with a group of Tibetans. Now a whole group of Tibetan refugees were implicated in the plot.

Several Tibetan refugees in Bhutan, including Lhading, were arrested and viciously tortured. Their captors rolled sizzling hot iron rods across their skin in an attempt to make the prisoners confess. They buried the prisoners in mud up to their necks and interrogated them relentlessly. They denied them food. Several of the Tibetans died under the torture, and Lhading was badly crippled. He never recovered from his ordeal.

I wrote a letter to the young crown prince as soon as I arrived in India, saying how much I had respected his father and what good relations we had. "How could I do anything to harm you and your people," I asked. I assured him that the Tibetans he had captured were innocent, and I appealed to him to examine this matter carefully. We were not involved in this incident at all, I told him. The Tibetans are being used as scapegoats. "You are chasing a shadow," I said.

Ordinarily, I did not respond to false charges against me. I usually followed my father's admonition to suppress my anger when wronged and to remain silent even when falsely accused. But the Bhutanese situation was so serious that it had to be clarified. The charges were so outrageous and the consequences so dire, not just for me but for others as well, that I had to respond to the charges publicly. I and Phuntsog Thonden, His Holiness's representative in Delhi, decided to hold a press conference to clarify our position and make a public denial.

Officials from the division of the Indian foreign ministry handling Bhutan and Sikkim wanted me to hold my tongue. They asked me not to make a denial. I would not be extradited, they assured me. Nothing would happen to me. I told them to go to hell and said that I would not take their advice even if they expelled me from India. We were innocent, and I had to deny the charges. The governor of West Bengal, Mrs. Naidu, was a good friend of ours and asked my wife to convince me not to issue a denial and not to hold a press conference. Mrs. Naidu was in Delhi at the time, as a guest of Indian Prime Minister Indira Gandhi, staying in the prime minister's residence. The attempts to convince me to remain silent went all the way to the pinnacle of Indian politics.

In fact, the entire incident had been concocted by Indian intelligence. While the old king was still alive, Indian intelligence had begun plotting to have Yangkyi become queen, using her to destabilize the monarchy. They were trying to manipulate her and her children to influence the king and the political succession in Bhutan. But the king's sudden death had foiled the Indian scheme. Now they wanted to wipe their hands of their own mess and accuse the Tibetans instead.

I went directly to R. N. Kao, the head of Indian intelligence. He knew exactly what was going on. He and his office were behind the whole mess. I pointed my finger at him, and said, "Mr. Kao, you are immoral. Why are you playing this dirty game in Bhutan? Why are you doing this to the refugees?" Kao bowed his head and had no reply.

We held the press conference despite India's official objections. Phuntsog Thonden officially made the arrangements. Some twenty-five to thirty correspondents came, and everyone seemed convinced that we had not been involved in any plot against the crown prince. Only the BBC wanted to know more. Their reporter pointed out that I had said that the Bhutanese were chasing a shadow. He wanted to know who this shadow was. I told him that he could speculate, but that I, as a Tibetan refugee, did not have the capacity to speculate. I could not tell him that Indian intelligence was behind both the false accusations and the actual plot——Indian intelligence at the direction of the foreign ministry.

The Sikkimese royal family was probably laughing and jumping with joy over the Bhutanese scandal. But the Indians were plotting similar things against Sikkim as well. In 1975 India was successful in taking over Sikkim. India had stepped in where the British left off, instigating all sorts of complicated political intrigues and plots to overthrow one ruler or another. The CIA was doing the same thing in places like South Korea, the Philippines, and Vietnam, secretly working to overthrow their leaders.

26

My Return to China

I demurred when I was invited to meet some representatives from the Xinhua news agency in the fall of 1979. Xinhua was the Communist Party's official news organization, but in Hong Kong it was also the unofficial representative of the Chinese Communist government. I no longer had any official responsibilities with the Tibetan government in exile and did not think a meeting with Chinese government officials would be appropriate. In fact, I generally avoided anyone connected with the Chinese government. But friends finally convinced me to join Xinhua deputy director Li Jusheng and staff member Pan Desheng for an informal lunch at the Tong Xing Lou restaurant in Wanchai.

The two officials had a message for me. Deng Xiaoping had recently returned as China's paramount leader after twice being purged during the Cultural Revolution. He had invited me to meet him in Beijing.

I had to refuse. I told them that I was in Hong Kong on business, not politics. But the Xinhua officials urged me to go. Deng Xiaoping was anxious to meet me, they said. Mr. Li could arrange for me to catch a flight to Beijing in the early morning and be back in Hong Kong the same evening. Again I demurred. While I was no longer an official of the Tibetan government in exile, I was still the Dalai Lama's brother. I could not go to China without his permission. I asked them to convey my regrets to Mr. Deng.

Actually, it was a strategic delay. I did not want to seem overly enthusiastic about the invitation. I did not want Tibetans to be seen as dogs wagging their tails just to be rewarded with a little Chinese bone and a pat on the head. Soon the Chinese invited me to lunch again, this time at their Xinhua office. They reiterated Deng Xiaoping's invitation. My response was the same. I had no authority to meet Mr. Deng. If I were to go, I would have to ask permission of His Holiness.

They encouraged me to seek the Dalai Lama's permission. It was a request I could not refuse. I left almost immediately to discuss the invitation with my brother.

The Dalai Lama urged me to accept. The only proviso was that I had to make clear to Deng and other Chinese officials that I was visiting unofficially in my personal capacity and with the Dalai Lama's permission. My role was to listen.

Deng Xiaoping was not in Beijing when I arrived. China had invaded Vietnam only days before, on February 17, 1979, and he had left for Guangxi province just across the border from Vietnam to direct military operations from there. Some friends had urged me to postpone my trip when we learned of the invasion. They thought a visit to China in the midst of a war might be dangerous. But I had already made a commitment to both my brother and Deng. I had to go.

While I awaited Deng's return, my hosts put me up in the spacious villa where Peng Dehuai had once lived. Xinhua deputy director Li Jusheng, who accompanied me for the entire trip, was staying just across the hall. Among the villa's many large rooms was one set aside especially for mahjong, and the grounds included a swimming pool. Peng Dehuai had not lived there for years. Mao's onetime defense minister had been purged only months after having belatedly urged Tan Guansan not to move against the protesters in Lhasa. In that summer of 1959, with China facing the worst famine in its history, Peng had challenged Mao's policy of the Great Leap Forward that was bringing the country to disaster. Peng had initially been kept under house arrest in the villa, but during the Cultural Revolution, the attacks against him had intensified. He remained in prison from 1967 until his death in 1974.

Wulanfu, the former first party secretary of Inner Mongolia and then the head of the Communist Party's United Front Work Department that manages relations with non-Communist entities, both foreign and domestic, hosted me in Deng's absence. On my first evening in Beijing, I was his guest of honor at a lavish banquet in the Great Hall of the People, the cavernous, Soviet-style building overlooking Tiananmen Square and Chairman Mao's mausoleum. The Great Hall of the People is the site of the annual meetings of the Chinese Communist Party Central Committee and the National People's Congress and the place where foreign dignitaries are met and feted. The seventy or eighty officials attending the banquet all seemed to have been connected in one way or another to Tibet or Xinjiang. Many were military officers from the Southwest Military Command, headquartered in Chengdu, or the Northwest Military Command in Xian. Wulanfu welcomed me with a toast and a speech about how happy he was that I was returning to China. There was no political talk, just polite discussion about the situation of the Tibetan exiles in India. I assured them we were not doing badly in exile. We had set up rehabilitation centers, new monasteries, and educational institutions during our twenty years in India. Many people came to my table to toast me, inviting me to join them in the traditional *ganbei,* or "bottoms up." After so many toasts, many of the guests were quite tipsy. My escort Li Jusheng was so intoxicated he nearly fell under the table. I had always held my liquor well.

Wulanfu was a reasonable man. He never tried to deny or cover up the past. He was straightforward about China's mistakes in Tibet and sympathetic to our difficulties. He himself was Mongolian and had spent some seven years in jail during the Cultural Revolution. As first party secretary of the Inner Mongolia Autonomous Region, he had fought against the central government's decision to reduce its size by ceding administrative control to several of its adjacent provinces. Mongolia had already been split in two with the Communist revolution in Russia, and the newly established country of Mongolia became a puppet of the Soviet Union. Wulanfu did not want to see a further diminishment of Mongolia through transferring parts of Inner Mongolia to other provinces, even if they were still Chinese. He lost the battle in 1967, but in 1979, at the end of the Cultural Revolution, he won. The breakaway areas were returned to Inner Mongolia.

In reflecting on mistakes of the past, Wulanfu was unwilling to blame any single individual or group. He described the situation in Tibet as a legacy of history. *Lishi zaocheng de.* "Created by history." Wulanfu's view was different from Mao's and others in the Communist Party leadership. Mao blamed the problems in Tibet on the nonexistent Western imperialists and the feudal aristocratic class, who were in fact the Communists' closest collaborators. Wulanfu traced the problems further back to the expansionist policies of the Manchu dynasty that had successfully incorporated both Mongolia and large parts of the Tibetan provinces of Amdo and Kham into its empire. Wulanfu's perspective, couching the Tibetan problem in terms of the legacy of the Manchu expansionists, made sense to me. Mao and the Communists had inherited the Manchus' colonial mindset.

WHILE DENG XIAOPING was directing the military operations in Vietnam, I revisited some of the ancient sites that I had explored during my previous visit to Beijing in 1946—the Forbidden City, the great Buddhist temple of Yonghe Gong, the Reclining Buddha Temple, the Yellow monastery, the Hall of Ten Thousand Buddhas, and the underground tombs of the Ming emperors at Badaling. My first visit to the city had impressed me deeply. Beijing then was still *Da Ming Fu,* the Ming dynasty's grand imperial capital. Nothing can describe the shocking difference between what I saw in 1946 and what I saw in 1979. The grand old city had been destroyed. Mao Zedong had pulled everything down, starting with the great city walls and proceeding to the courtyard-style houses that had given old Beijing so much of its traditional flavor. The little that was left standing was dilapidated. Nothing had been properly maintained.

Many of the places I had visited in the past were under lock and key, no longer open to the public. They had been badly damaged during the violence of the Cultural Revolution and had yet to be repaired. But since I wanted to look, they allowed me to see.

The Imperial Palace was so damaged and decayed and deserted that it seemed haunted. Many of the windows had been smashed and were covered over with plywood. Wild grass was growing everywhere, even through the yellow-tiled roofs. It was a wretched, ugly place, pathetic to contemplate. I could not help but compare it to the grandeur of the Potala Palace.

The Yonghe Gong, once Beijing's great monastery of Tibetan Buddhism, was also deserted and neglected. Only a couple of old Mongolian monks seemed to be in residence, and they were surprised to see me. They did not know who I was, but they must have thought I was special, riding around in a big Hongqi limousine with my Chinese escorts. The monastery's buildings were in a state of near collapse. Only the magnificent four-story wooden Buddha, carved from a single gigantic tree and transported over ground to Beijing all the way from Yunnan in China's far southwest, was completely intact. It was an impressive sight.

The huge underground tunnel complex that the Chinese government had built in preparation for an attack by the Soviet Union was also part of my itinerary. The whole population of Beijing, government officials and ordinary citizens alike, was prepared to move underground in case of an attack. Several feet below the surface was another entire city with offices, conference halls, shops, and spaces for living, working, cooking, and eating. The underground complex was cold and uncomfortable, but the massive digging necessary to construct the tunnels had unearthed fantastic archaeological finds. Many of them were on display in the history museum in Tiananmen Square. I had never seen so many thrilling and wonderful artifacts, ancient relics from the Song, the Yuan, and the Ming. In fact, archaeological excavations were taking place all over China, and museums in many parts of the country were filling up with ancient relics. Shanghai and Nanjing had particularly striking collections.

Almost as striking as the ancient relics in the Beijing museum was the display at its entrance. Hanging on the wall as one walked in the door was a huge watercolor painting with an inscription in Mao's calligraphy. "The water of the Yellow River flows from heaven," read the first part of the inscription. "China has many national minorities," began the second. "If national minorities are oppressed, they will rebel." What great propaganda! Mao's words suggested that he was concerned about China's minorities when in fact he was intent on oppressing them. I pointed out the incongruity of the inscription to my hosts. The next time I visited, it was no longer there.

As my wait for Deng Xiaoping dragged on, the United Front Work Department invited me to occasional dinners on the top floor of the Minzu (Nationalities) Palace. Built in 1954 under Mao's instructions, the palace was meant to house the Dalai Lama, the Panchen Lama, and other special national minority guests. But the place was a graveyard. The curtains in the special penthouse where my dinners took place were torn and dirty. Nothing had been cleaned for at least twenty years.

Why did they get rid of so much of old Beijing? Why didn't they preserve the original city and build another modern one adjacent to it? What a terrible pity that so much was destroyed.

Something about the Chinese culture was lost, too. As a student in 1946, I received a gracious welcome everywhere I went. Shopkeepers would invite me to please come in, *qingzuo qingzuo*, please have a seat. They would offer me a cup of tea, a cigarette, some sweets. But people had forgotten their manners. Mao Zedong's Great Proletarian Cultural Revolution had been a revolution against traditional Chinese culture. One of the slogans called upon the young rebels to smash the four olds—old ideas, old culture, old customs, and old habits. Mao had done a good job at wiping out China's traditional culture. My backward, conservative mind felt strongly that too much had been destroyed.

I felt sad for China. But I was not surprised. I had learned much about the destruction in China from my study and research in Hong Kong. When I told one of my Hong Kong friends that I would soon be going to China, he lamented that there would be nothing to do there, and cautioned me to take my own toilet paper. He was practically shouting in outrage as he decried China's lack of toilet paper. I was shocked to think that China did not even have enough toilet paper for its guests. It seemed so ugly and odd.

In a later visit to China in 1980, I spent two months visiting the three northeastern provinces of Manchuria (Jilin, Liaoning, and Heilongjiang), as well as Shaanxi, Sichuan, Yunnan, Shanghai, Zhejiang, Jiangsu, Guangxi, Guangdong, Tianjin, and, of course, Beijing. Again I was treated like a king, staying in government guesthouses inside large walled compounds with spacious accommodations and lovely, lush gardens. I was escorted everywhere by car and always greeted by delegations of local officials. But most of what I saw outside the compound walls was just as dismal as what I had seen in Beijing.

When I returned to the Chinese capital following my second visit, Wulanfu wanted to hear my impressions. I asked if I was allowed to speak the truth. "Yes," he insisted, "of course, of course."

So I spoke the truth. I pointed out that the five most ubiquitous words in China were *wei ren min fu wu,* meaning "serve the people." The slogan called out from countless billboards everywhere we visited. But nowhere did the government seem in fact to be actually serving the people. In the Hulunbei'er grasslands of Inner Mongolia, where the local government organized a lavish lunch on my behalf and we feasted on a freshly slaughtered sheep inside a warm nomadic tent, the clothes of the local Mongolian people were thin and tattered. They were shivering when I stopped to talk to them, and their hands were red and swollen from hard work and the cold. Nomads normally have plenty to eat. Their staples are butter, milk, yogurt, and meat. When I asked the local folk how they sold their milk and butter, they said that the Chinese took away their milk every morning and that they were not allowed to slaughter their animals for food.

The local government of Hulunbei'er had ten huge American John Deere harvesting machines, imported through Hong Kong at a cost of $45,000 each. One machine could do the work of hundreds of people. But only five of the machines were working. The others were broken. They could not be repaired, the nomads told me, because the technicians trained to repair them had been sent long ago to labor reform camps and had yet to return.

In northeast China, in the industrial cities of Shenyang and Changchun, I saw much the same situation in steel and truck factories. The huge machines inside the factories had been imported from East Germany and were of excellent quality. But many of them had broken down, and the technicians able to fix them were away in prison or labor reform camps. All the professional leadership in the factory had been sent away to some kind of labor reform. The uneducated, unskilled Communist Party members in charge had no idea how to repair the machines. The factories were functioning at a fraction of their capacity.

When we chatted with the local farmers at the Dazhai people's commune in Xiyang, Shanxi, they told us how difficult it was to send their children to school. Permission to attend required "going through the back door," using connections, which ordinary farmers did not have. Their children were not going to school. Dazhai had been a nationwide model commune during the Cultural Revolution. Everyone knew the slogan "in agriculture, learn from Dazhai." But even in this nationwide model, children could not get an education without using connections.

Even in cities like Chengdu in Sichuan, ordinary people were in difficult straits, still living in mud houses with dirt floors. It was painful to see. If Tibetans had been forced to live in such difficult circumstances, they would surely rebel. But the Chinese people were patient. They persevered. They did not dare rise up.

So I told Wulanfu that the ubiquitous slogan of "serve the people" should be removed. "Mr. Thondup," he replied, "you are absolutely correct." He told me that during the past decade, professionals everywhere in China had been purged—schoolteachers, technicians, educated people from all walks of life. The party members who were running things then were uneducated. Some were barely literate. China was in the process of bringing the exiled professionals back to resume their previous positions, he said. Once the technicians had returned, the country could return to normal. The economic situation would improve.

27

The Tenth Panchen Lama

In fact, the process of rehabilitating people who had been purged during the Cultural Revolution was already well under way. In Beijing, many who had been imprisoned or exiled had already been allowed to return home. The Panchen Lama was one of them.

I had met the Tenth Panchen Lama only once before, in 1952, not long after he had arrived in Lhasa under Chinese escort. He was only thirteen or fourteen years old at the time and had gone to the Potala Palace to pay his respects to the Dalai Lama. I then paid a courtesy call on him. He was still so young and untutored that we had nothing of substance to say. Che Jigme, who had participated in the selection of the Tenth Panchen Lama and then had become his behind the scenes political advisor, was the man I really wanted to see.

Che Jigme and I had become friends when I was a student in Nanjing and he was the head of the previous Panchen Lama's office there. By 1952, he was the new Panchen Lama's major spokesman, practically serving as the Panchen Lama's oracle. And he had fallen into the Communists' arms. The Chinese in Lhasa were already trying to groom the new Panchen Lama to serve as their tool. They wanted to elevate him as an equal to the Dalai Lama and then to promote rivalry between them. The Chinese were intent on creating enmity, and Che Jigme was playing the Chinese game. As his friend, I thought I should caution him against becoming too close to the Communists. I hoped at least to persuade him to put a brake on his collaboration.

I encouraged Che Jigme to develop a good relationship with the Dalai Lama and the government of Tibet and pointed out that the Communists were trying to create divisions both within the Tibetan government and between the Panchen Lama and the Dalai Lama. If he were not careful, he could easily be used.

But Che Jigme was already their tool. Otherwise the Communists would not have brought him and the Panchen Lama to Lhasa. Che Jigme was a Tibetan official who had been brought up in China and knew the Chinese well. But he never understood power. He did not understand that once you allow yourself to be manipulated, you fall under the manipulator's control. You lose your conscience. Che Jigme thought he would have more power if he supported the Chinese, so he turned against the Tibetan government and allowed himself to be used. I was naïve to think that I could stop him. He no longer had a conscience.

Che Jigme and others in the Panchen Lama's orbit collaborated with the Chinese for years, and the Panchen Lama's star continued to rise. After the Dalai Lama fled to India, the Communists made the Panchen Lama the new head of the Preparatory Committee for the Autonomous Region of Tibet (PCART). They expected him to remain their accomplice, and at first he seemed to be. The Panchen Lama was cooperating fully with the Chinese. It was painful for Tibetans to see.

I NEVER HAD much respect for the Panchen Lama. I saw him as a blind follower of the Chinese Communists. But I also understood that the course he had taken was not his own. The young Panchen Lama was at the mercy of the men who were bringing him up. He had never received the rigorous training in the sacred Buddhist teachings that reincarnated lamas needed to assume their religious roles. He had never become a learned man, never developed that spiritual quality that even a layman like me can sense in the presence of a deeply religious lama. In that sense he was very different from my brother. He was just an ordinary man.

But then, suddenly, he changed. In 1962, the twenty-four-year-old Panchen Lama wrote what came to be known as the "Seventy Thousand Character Petition," a detailed and damning critique of China's policies in Tibet.[1] He submitted it for review to Premier Zhou Enlai. The secret letter was a scathing indictment of the Chinese government's mismanagement of Tibet—their violent suppression of the uprising following the Dalai Lama's flight; the large number of innocent people jailed, tortured, and killed; the attacks against Tibetan Buddhism, the monasteries, and the monks; and the inappropriate implementation of land reform. The people's standard of living had declined under Chinese rule, he pointed out. The Panchen Lama appealed to Mao and the Chinese government to correct their mistakes. He believed that the survival of the Tibetans as a people and Tibetan Buddhism as a religion were at stake. The petition was an act of bravery. The Panchen Lama had broken free.

Mao Zedong must have been angry. He labeled the document a "poisonous arrow" shot at the Party by reactionary overlords. In 1964, two years before the start of the Cultural Revolution, the Panchen Lama was dismissed from his position as head of PCART, put into prison, labeled a reactionary, and accused of wide-ranging crimes, from plotting a revolt against the party to splitting the motherland. He was put on public trial and physically attacked when he tried to defend himself. Later, he was repeatedly tortured. The Red Guards stuffed dirt down his throat, and forced him to eat his own feces. Several times he was almost killed. But somehow he survived.

He was in jail for fourteen years. Then, not long before my own arrival in Beijing, the Chinese government suddenly released him. He was given simple living quarters—a small courtyard for himself and another for his parents and brother. I paid him a visit. The Panchen Lama was still not officially rehabilitated. A soldier stood guard at his door. He still seemed desperate. His situation was difficult. He had no work. He wanted to be reinstalled to his previous position in Tibet. He wanted the return of his properties. He wanted justice.

He urged me to raise his case with Deng Xiaoping and the Chinese government. I promised that I would. He continued to call me after that, wondering whether Deng had returned and when I would be meeting him, reminding me again to plead his case.

28

Meeting Deng Xiaoping

Deng Xiaoping met me in the Great Hall of the People, in one of the smaller rooms reserved for greeting foreign dignitaries. He was already there when I entered and immediately stepped forward to greet me, smiling, his hand extended in welcome. He motioned me to sit down and began talking even before I opened my mouth. "How is the Dalai Lama's health?" he wanted to know.

I assured him that the Dalai Lama was in very good health and both thanked him for inviting me and expressed my apologies for not being able to come sooner. I first had to get permission from the Dalai Lama, I explained.

Deng spoke with a thick Sichuan accent that was sometimes difficult to follow, but the translator, Xiong Xianghui, a deputy minister in the United Front Work Department who was also fluent in English, could help with the words I did not understand.

Deng Xiaoping wondered how many years had passed since my last visit to China and whether I was surprised by what I was seeing. I told him that I had left thirty years before, in 1949, and this was my first visit since. But I had spent so much time in Hong Kong, studying China from the outside looking in, that I knew a great deal about what had happened over the years, including the violence and chaos during the Cultural Revolution. I had suspected that the conditions would be something like what I had seen. I was not so surprised.

Deng was pleased with my reply. Many Chinese returning after twenty-five or thirty years were shocked by the devastation and decay, he said.

Among China's top leaders, Deng was one of the most knowledgeable about Tibet. He had served under Liu Bocheng in the Southwest Military Command, in the Eighteenth Army. He was on the party committee that had ordered and directed the army's attack on Chamdo in 1950 and later had pushed for the early introduction of so-called "democratic reforms" in Amdo and Kham. He described Tibet as a basket of jewels, rich in every kind of mineral deposit on earth, including gold, uranium, lithium, magnesium, and copper. But it was a difficult place to reach. Chinese engineers were still trying to figure out how to build a rail line into Tibet. He wondered how well I really knew my own homeland.

He urged me not to look back. There was no point dwelling on the past, he said. Whatever happened had already happened. What was important now was to think about how to move forward. He knew that the Tibetan people had suffered greatly in recent years, but the Chinese had also suffered. He himself had suffered immensely. So had United Front minister Wulanfu, who was with us at the meeting. Deng asked Wulanfu how many years he had suffered, how many years he had been in jail. I already knew that Wulanfu had spent seven years in jail.

He turned to the issue that was his reason for inviting me, the question of Tibet. His starting point was clear. The complete independence of Tibet from China was not negotiable, he said. No future leader would ever be able to negotiate an independent Tibet. *"But except for independence, everything is negotiable. Everything can be discussed,"* he said.[1] "This is what I want to raise with you today," he said. "This is what I want to discuss with you."

Deng Xiaoping wanted the Dalai Lama to return to China. All his positions would be restored, he said, and the Tibetans who had

From right, Deng Xiaoping, Gyalo Thondup,
Wulanfu, and Yang Jingren

accompanied him into exile, officials and ordinary people alike, would also be welcome to return. The government of China would take care of them.

Deng Xiaoping asked what issues I wanted to raise.

I reminded him that I had no authority to negotiate. I had come in my personal capacity as His Holiness directed me, I said. I had come to listen. His Holiness wanted me to listen to what he had to say and to report to him when I returned. Deng Xiaoping asked whether, in my personal capacity, I had anything to raise.

I did.

First, I told Deng that in the twenty years since the government of China had sealed the border between Tibet and India, Tibetans living in India and Nepal had had no way to communicate with their relatives and friends on the other side of the border. We had been completely cut off. We knew nothing of our families, our brothers and sisters, or the wife who was left behind when her husband escaped. We did not know whether they were dead or alive. I asked Mr. Deng to open the border so people could visit their families. Some might even want to move back permanently, I suggested.

Deng Xiaoping agreed. He said that he would give the order to open up the border immediately. Tibetans would be free to go to Tibet to find their families. They would be welcome to return permanently if they wanted, and the Chinese government would look after them well.

My second point was about the Panchen Lama. I told Deng Xiaoping that I had visited the Panchen Lama while awaiting his return to Beijing. I blamed the Chinese government for the Panchen Lama's mistreatment. I told him that now the Chinese government had the responsibility to look after him and treat him well.

Again Deng Xiaoping agreed, both that the Panchen Lama had been badly treated and that the Chinese government would now look after him well. Deng was going to make the Panchen Lama a vice chairman of the Chinese People's Political Consultative Conference, he said.

My third point was a request that the Chinese government allow us to send a few Tibetan-language teachers to teach in Tibetan areas. We had heard that in the past twenty years, many Chinese had been sent to serve as teachers in Tibet. They had no facility with the Tibetan language. Young Tibetan students were largely being taught in Chinese. Schools had neglected the teaching of Tibetan. Some people feared that the Tibetan language could be lost in their Tibetan homeland. During our years in India, with the help of the Indian government, we had trained a large number of professional teachers of Tibetan. I wanted to send some of them to teach in Tibetan schools.

Deng Xiaoping was amenable to this suggestion, too, and wondered how many teachers I might be able to send. He thought my proposal of twenty to thirty teachers a year was too low. He hoped I could send one thousand teachers a year. Tibet was not the only place that needed Tibetan teachers, he said. The Central Institute of Nationalities in Beijing and national minority schools and colleges in other places needed them, too. I told him that one thousand would be too many to send immediately, but the number could increase over time.

He asked whether I had seen all the wall posters on display around Beijing. The Democracy Wall Movement was still in full swing. Protest posters had gone up all over the city, many of them concentrated around a wall in the Xidan area of Beijing along Changan Avenue.

Gyalo Thondup and Deng Xiaoping.
Wulanfu is walking behind them.

Thousands of people were congregating to read and discuss the posters. Most of them criticized corruption within the Communist Party
and the high-handed manner in which the people in power treated
ordinary citizens. Some of the posters were critical of the Cultural
Revolution, and some called for more democracy and human rights.
The poster that would become the most famous in the West was one
that had been written by a young man named Wei Jingsheng called

"The Fifth Modernization." Upon his return to power, Deng had promised an end to the era of class struggle that the country had suffered under Mao. Henceforth, China would pursue the goal of the "four modernizations"—the modernization of agriculture, industry, science and technology, and the military. Wei Jingsheng wanted a fifth modernization, too—democracy. But most of the posters were less about democracy than about accountability. People wanted their government to be held accountable for their actions. Deng told me that if we sent some Tibetan teachers to Beijing, they could put up big character posters, too.

My final point to raise with Deng Xiaoping was the possibility of the Dalai Lama and the Tibetan exiles opening an Office of Tibet in Beijing in order to coordinate with the Chinese government. Maybe from time to time, we could visit Tibetan areas. Deng agreed to this proposal as well. In fact, he enthusiastically agreed to everything I proposed.

Deng also had a favor to ask. When I returned to Hong Kong, he wanted me to go to Taiwan to pass on a message from him to Chiang Kai-shek's son, Chiang Ching-kuo. Chiang Kai-shek had died in 1975, and Deng wanted Chiang Ching-kuo to send his father's coffin back to China to be buried in his native place of Fenghua in Zhejiang province. When I returned to Hong Kong, I contacted Chiang Ching-kuo's aide and conveyed the message to him. The reply was quick. Chiang Ching-kuo did not want me to go to Taiwan. He was frightened. The government in Taiwan still had no contact with the mainland, and they did not want to start then. I conveyed this to the Xinhua people in Hong Kong, who passed my message back to Deng.

Not long after I left Beijing, Deng cracked down on the protests that had been going on there for a number of weeks. He himself had become a target of criticism. He could not allow the movement to continue. His governing style was to let things go just so far and then call a halt and order a crackdown. Wei Jingsheng was arrested and sentenced to fifteen years in jail. Many others who had participated in the movement were also jailed, though most received lesser sentences.

29

Return to Tibet

M y visit with Deng Xiaoping opened a whole new chapter in our relations with both China and Tibet. The single most important sentence in my conversation with Deng was that except for independence, everything could be discussed. Deng Xiaoping was committed to that principle. Returning to India, I urged the Dalai Lama to use this opening to move forward step by step, feeling our way as we went. I felt that we should not try to do everything at once.

The most important first step was for us to let some of the exiles return home. Visits could serve a dual purpose of gathering information about what had happened and how our fellow Tibetans had fared in the past twenty years and of allowing the exiles to locate and be reunited with their families. That way, we Tibetans could begin re-rooting ourselves on our native soil.

Between August 1979 and June 1980, the Dalai Lama was able to send a series of three fact-finding delegations to visit Tibet.[1] My younger brother Lobsang Samten was a member of the first delegation that was headed by senior cabinet minister Juchen Thupten and arrived in China in August 1979. They spent five months visiting eastern China and Tibet. After flying from Beijing west to Lanzhou, the delegation traveled mostly by car, visiting Amdo, Kham, and Lhasa, accompanied by a handful of United Front Work Department officials from Beijing. I had worked with Xinhua in Hong Kong to make the travel arrangements, and I briefed the delegation before their departure, giving them strict instructions not to talk politics. I asked them to deliver two messages from the His Holiness the Dalai Lama to the people of Tibet: one, that His Holiness was deeply concerned about their well-being and livelihood, and two, that the Dalai Lama sent them his best wishes. And I asked the delegation to listen, to learn what the Tibetan people were saying and thinking.

The delegation was both happy to be returning home after so many years but apprehensive about what they would find. They did not know what the economic conditions would be, whether they would be able to find their relatives, or who would still be alive. In Tibet, they spent one month in each of the provinces of Amdo, Kham, and Central Tibet,[2] their itinerary planned in advance in Hong Kong and Beijing, based on the delegation's requests. The Chinese officials in Beijing had little concrete knowledge of the situation in Tibet, little understanding of the devastation of the past twenty years. The itinerary included virtually all of the delegation's requests.

Wherever they went, delegation members explained that they had been sent to understand the conditions in Tibet and to let the Tibetan people know that the Dalai Lama was doing well and wished them well, too. Everyone wanted to know how the Dalai Lama was and what he was doing. Everyone had questions.

The delegation traveled mostly by jeep and thus discovered that the roads were still awful, mostly unpaved and always bumpy, but nonetheless an improvement over the roads of the past. The number of motorized vehicles had grown, though the number was still very small. In 1959, only the city of Lhasa had electricity. Now other cities and large towns had some electricity, too. The economic situation in the cities was still dismal, but better than in any of the rural areas. Most rural areas the delegation visited were worse off than they had been in 1959. The depth of rural poverty was distressing. The situation in Amdo was a bit better than in Kham or Central Tibet. More of the cadres in Amdo were Tibetan. In Kham and Central Tibet, most were Chinese.

Most shocking and tragic was what had happened to the monasteries. All of Tibet's leading monasteries were on the delegation's itinerary, and not a single one was intact. The great red, white, and gold Ganden monastery some thirty miles outside of Lhasa had been totally destroyed. Local people were working together to reconstruct it bit by bit, and monks who had been persecuted and imprisoned in the previous decades were slowly returning to hold religious prayer ceremonies in tents. Some prayed for a free Tibet. Sera, too, was in ruins, and so was much of Drepung, though the damage there had been less extensive. Only a few monks remained in Sera and Drepung, though some may simply have been making themselves inconspicuous by dressing in civilian clothes. Some parts of the Kumbum monastery in Amdo that had been so important to my family were still standing, but much of it lay in ruins, too. Everywhere, monks had been forced back to the life of the layman. Many had been imprisoned, and some had died from their suffering. The delegation's requests to visit those still in prison were refused.

The Tibetans' response to the delegation was a vast outpouring of emotion, a mixture of joy that people representing the Dalai Lama had come to meet them and grief as they recounted the tragedy of their lives over the past twenty years. The delegation was mobbed everywhere they went, confronted with throngs of ordinary Tibetans weeping and crying and wanting to touch them. So many people wanted to touch my brother Lobsang Samten that his clothes were ripped to shreds. Because their Chinese minders were always nearby, people sought the delegation members secretly in restrooms or late at night in their hotels as their Chinese overseers were sleeping. Some delegation members were regularly staying up all night as fellow Tibetans came to their hotel room to pour out their tales of woe.

People passed written messages surreptitiously through a handshake, and the delegation members hid the slips of paper inside their clothes. Some messages were addressed to His Holiness the Dalai

Lama, others to members of the Tibetan parliament, some directly to members of the delegation, and many to their family members in exile. Some had scrawled the names of people who had died or had been tortured or imprisoned on scraps of paper. Everyone on the delegation received letters and petitions describing what Tibetans had suffered under the Chinese occupation. The delegation returned to Hong Kong with at least seven thousand letters to their relatives and the Dalai Lama. Some are still in the archives in Dharamsala. The descriptions are frightening. I wept when I read them.[3]

Others shouted out their grievances in public, in front of the Chinese, lamenting their suffering and the pressures they were still enduring, and warning the delegation to be wary of their Chinese hosts. In some instances, the gathered crowds dared to raise their clenched fists and shout slogans for the independence of Tibet. Some who spoke too openly were arrested after the delegation departed.

The Chinese had an explanation for what the delegation was seeing. The Tibetans had not been the only ones to suffer. The Chinese had suffered, too, including many representatives of the United Front who were hosting their trip. Wulanfu and Yang Jingren, two ranking members of the United Front, had both been jailed. The problems were the fault of the Gang of Four, the radical group, including Mao Zedong's own wife Jiang Qing, that had once been closely associated with Mao. The Gang of Four was behind the chaos and destruction of the Cultural Revolution, the officials explained, and they had been arrested only weeks after Mao's death in September 1976. Li Xiannian, who had greeted the first delegation in Beijing and was soon to assume the presidency of China, had been instrumental in bringing about their arrest. Things had been getting better since. Everything was returning to normal. Deng Xiaoping was implementing the four modernizations, which would lift millions out of poverty and bring benefit to all. Now, everyone had high hopes for the future.

When Xinhua chief Li Jusheng asked me to report on what that first delegation had learned, I spent two hours describing the difficulties the Tibetans had endured for the past twenty years. I asked him to deliver a message from me to his government. I had read about the atrocities committed by the Germans during the Second World War, but I thought that the Chinese Communist Party in the last twenty years was worse than Hitler. The Chinese never built gas chambers, but they deliberately set out to kill as many Tibetans as they could through execution, starvation, torture, hard work, and by driving people to suicide. This was deliberate. I do not know the exact number of people who died and would not want to guess. These numbers, unfortunately, have often been exaggerated. But as a percentage of the Tibetan population, the number of deaths in Tibet during those years was very high. Every family suffered. Everyone had someone who was killed, or who died of starvation, or who committed suicide in anguish, or who was tried and convicted and imprisoned and sometimes sentenced to death.

The communist government of Deng Xiaoping was shocked at the Tibetans' response to our delegations. They had believed their own propaganda. They thought they had won the hearts and minds of the Tibetan people. They had been afraid that the Tibetan serfs would rise up in protest against the delegations of Tibetan reactionaries. The reaction was exactly the opposite. The delegations were repeatedly swamped by Tibetan people who loved the Dalai Lama and wanted him back. The delegations forced Deng Xiaoping and his government to face the reality that Tibetans had merely been paying lip service to the Communists. The souls of the Tibetan people were still with His Holiness the Dalai Lama. Deng must also have sensed how dangerous the situation could be if they did not handle the Tibetans carefully.

With each succeeding delegation, tensions between the Chinese and Tibetans grew stronger. The second delegation, headed by director of the New York Office of Tibet Tenzin Tethong, was younger and more outspoken than the first and soon locked horns with their Chinese hosts. The delegation arrived in Lhasa at the end of July 1980, staying in the same hotel as a group of foreign journalists. The journalists unwittingly arrived at the hotel just as a huge crowd of Tibetans was surrounding the delegation chanting "Long Live His

Holiness the Dalai Lama." The Chinese abruptly cancelled the Tibetans' trip and sent them back to Hong Kong.

The third delegation, headed by my sister Jetsun Pema and composed of teachers and school administrators, was already in Tibet at the time and continued its itinerary despite growing tensions over the Chinese refusal to let the delegation interact with their follow Tibetans or have any substantive meetings with Tibetan teachers and students. A fourth delegation planned for August 1980 was delayed until April 1982. The three-person group never left Beijing.

I RETURNED TO BEIJING in 1981 and met with Hu Yaobang, the general secretary of the Chinese Communist Party. Hu was from a younger generation than Mao Zedong or Deng Xiaoping and was more straightforward and less complex. He had visited Tibet with Wan Li in May 1980 as part of a Central Committee Work Group, and had been shocked by what he found. He accused the Chinese cadres in Tibet of wasting millions of yuan from the central government. The money that was meant to improve conditions for the people of Tibet might as well have been thrown in the river for all the good it did, he said. The lives of the people of Tibet had not greatly improved in the past twenty years, and in some cases their situation had become worse. Hu placed much of the blame on the Chinese cadres in Tibet and proposed sending many of them home. He called for real autonomy—the right to decide for oneself.[4]

I told Hu Yaobang that I thought the people of Tibetan nationality should be unified under a single administration. The Tibetans were a single nationality who became divided only because of the colonialist tactics of the Manchus, I explained. Under the Manchus, parts of Kham and Amdo were split off from Tibet and incorporated into the Chinese provinces of Qinghai and Sichuan. I compared Tibet to the human body. If you cut off the arms and legs of a human being, the human being is incomplete. With Kham and Amdo cut off from Tibet, Tibet was not complete, either. It was deformed. I said that the current Communist government of the People's Republic of China was supposed to be a progressive, liberal government,

concerned about ordinary people. It should adopt a more enlight-
ened policy toward Tibet. I hoped that the Chinese government
would take a less colonialist, more progressive view and reinstitute
a unified Tibet under a single Tibetan administration. I did not talk
about greater Tibet (*da zangchu*). I was not requesting independence. I was requesting the unification of the Tibetan nationality
into a single, unified, self-governing entity.

Hu Yaobang was hearing the argument for bringing Tibetans together under a single, unified administration for the first time. I
told him that the people of Tibet were still asleep. But when they
awoke, they would demand unification. Hu Yaobang did not dismiss my ideas. He said there would be plenty of time to discuss
them later.

Hu Yaobang also had something for me—a written statement
of China's five conditions for the Dalai Lama's return to China.[5]
First, the Chinese government wanted the Dalai Lama to return to
China. Second, if the Dalai Lama did return, the Chinese government wanted to know where he would be entering. They wanted to
send a delegation there to receive him. Third, upon his return, the
Dalai Lama would resume his former position as vice chairman of
the National People's Congress. Fourth, if the Dalai Lama returned
and resumed his position as vice chairman, the Chinese government
suggested that he live in Beijing with occasional visits to Lhasa and
other Tibetan areas. Fifth, not only the Dalai Lama but all the Tibetan officials and Tibetan people in exile were welcome to return.
The Chinese government would look after them.

The Dalai Lama and the Kashag were surprised by Hu Yaobang's
five points. They were especially concerned about the fourth one,
suggesting that the Dalai Lama remain in Beijing and only occasionally travel to Tibet. The Chinese rationale was that since the Dalai
Lama would be a national leader, he should therefore be based in
the nation's capital. Tibetans, though, were reminded of Tan Guansan's March 1959 invitation asking the Dalai Lama to attend the military's cultural show. Everyone then was afraid that the Dalai Lama
was about to be kidnapped. Now they feared that if the Dalai Lama

returned to China, he would be held hostage in Beijing, set up to be China's rubber stamp, powerless to act on his own.

I suggested to His Holiness that we not make the fourth point public. If we made it public, Tibetans would again think that the Chinese were going to hold the Dalai Lama hostage. If people suspected that he could be held hostage, or thought that the Chinese intended for His Holiness to become nothing more than a rubber stamp, their anger and suspicion of the Chinese government could fester and grow. People might protest. This, in turn, could undermine the dialogue we were beginning with the Chinese. I thought that continuing the dialogue was too important to risk.

Looking back, I think I made a mistake in meeting with Hu Yaobang. I should have had another meeting with Deng Xiaoping. When I arrived in Beijing that year, my hosts at the United Front asked whether I would prefer to meet again with Deng or Party General Secretary Hu Yaobang. Since I had already met with Deng and knew little about General Secretary Hu, I asked to meet with him. Later, people from the United Front told me that Hu had a reputation for impulsiveness. Many had been shocked when Hu, unexpectedly and without consulting anyone first, had invited one thousand young Japanese students to visit China at the Chinese government's expense. The five-point document Hu Yaobang gave me had to have been approved by Deng. If I had met with Deng, he would have been the one to present it to me, and I could have discussed the contents with him. Deng Xiaoping may have been disappointed with me for meeting with Hu.

I never considered Hu Yaobang a liberal. The speech he gave about Tibet was not based on any particular sympathy for the Tibetans. He knew little about Tibet. He was angry with the Han Chinese cadres for making such a mess of things, for spending so much of the central government's money on their own salaries rather than improving the Tibetan economy. And I thought his five points were ridiculous. Either the Chinese were fools for thinking that the Tibetans might go along with their conditions or the Chinese thought the Tibetans were fools—foolish enough to accept the condition that the Dalai Lama could return to China and remain in Beijing with only occasional visits to Tibet.

Gradually the door that had been opened to Tibet following my visit with Deng Xiaoping began to close. The Chinese were alarmed by the outpouring of welcome engendered by our visits, and by what happened when Tibetans began to recount their stories of atrocity and abuse. The Chinese began limiting the number of Tibetan exiles allowed to visit Tibetan-speaking areas. The promises Deng Xiaoping had made on my first visit never materialized. We never opened an office in Beijing or sent teachers to teach Tibetan. We continued to talk about the return of the Dalai Lama but never came up with a concrete plan. The Chinese still said they wanted him to return, but the talks were not moving forward.

Both sides were playing a complicated game, like some strange Chinese shadow boxing. Behind my back, the Chinese were saying that I was a political game master, and Hu Yaobang once directly told me to stop playing hide and go seek. Sometimes I wonder how I managed all those years. I think it was my patience. An Indian friend once taught me a proverb: "He who loses patience is a loser. He who gives in loses." That saying has stuck with me. I have never lost patience. I have never given in. Nor has the Dalai Lama.

But by 1983, my role as a messenger, going back and forth between Dharamsala and China, had begun to take its toll, both mentally and physically. I was tired of being a go-between. The responsibility was too heavy a burden for me alone to bear. I thought the Chinese should have direct dealings with Dalai Lama's own ministers. The Chinese were surprised when I told them that I wanted to resign. I could communicate with them directly in Chinese, and they thought I was serving a useful function. They wanted me to continue. But when I returned to Dharamsala and asked the Dalai Lama to release me from my duties, he raised the issue with the Kashag. They agreed that I could step down.

I relinquished my responsibilities. Juchen Tubten, the Tibetan prime minister and head of the Kashag began leading the delegations to China on behalf of the Dalai Lama, accompanied by cabinet minister Alak Jigme Rinpoche, Lodi Gyari, and my brother-in-law Phuntsog Tashi Takla. They met and held talks with the Chinese United Front Work Department several times between 1983 and 1986. But the talks did not progress.

Then, in 1986, their talks broke down. Prime Ministers Lodi Gyari and Juchen Tubten invited me to Dharmasala to talk about what had happened. When I refused to go, the negotiating team—Juchen Tubten, Alak Jigme, and Phuntsog Tashi—visited me in my Delhi apartment. The Chinese government had accused them of being useless and told them not to come back. The Tibetan officials did not understand why. They wanted me to return to China to reopen the dialogue.

I was reluctant. I did not know what kind of blunder the Tibetan team had committed to make the Chinese so angry. I had not visited China in three years—1984, 1985, 1986. I had had no contact with the United Front. Now they wanted me to rebuild connections. Maybe the Chinese would refuse to meet me. How could I go?

They insisted. These are instructions from His Holiness the Dalai Lama, they told me. Finally I agreed, but only on the condition that I would not go alone. Two Kashag members would have to accompany me. And I would have to inform the Chinese ambassador to India and get permission from China for the visit.

The Chinese were quick to reply. They had sent a message to Deng Xiaoping. I was an old friend, they said. My family and I were welcome to visit China. But members of the Kashag were not. In the end, I went to China alone, with neither my family nor any Tibetan officials. I arrived in Beijing to meet with Mao Zedong's onetime Russian translator and then the new director of the United Front Work Department, Yan Mingfu, in September 1987.[6] Unbeknownst to me, the worst riots since the rebellion of 1959 had broken out in Lhasa while I was en route.

30

Our Negotiations Fail

By the 1980s, the face of the Dalai Lama was recognized around the world. He was a man of international stature. His message of compassion and tolerance was widely known and respected. The story of the Tibetans' plight had reached a worldwide audience. The cause of justice for Tibet had champions far and wide.

The Dalai Lama was searching for ways to move our conversations with the Chinese forward. In 1959, the Dalai Lama had told the world that Tibet was and always had been an independent country and that the Seventeen Point Agreement had been signed under duress rather than of our own free will. He said that the Chinese had illegally invaded Tibet and violated the human rights of the Tibetan people. For the twenty-year period between 1959 and 1979, the Dalai Lama continued to reiterate that message. He never said that we were giving up our demand for independence. But by the 1980s, he was searching for ways to compromise. He began talking about a "middle path."

In September 1987, at a meeting of the US Congressional Human Rights Caucus, the Dalai Lama outlined a five-point peace plan for Tibet and the rest of Asia. Its content was carried by media around the world. The plan called first for the transformation of Tibet into a zone of peace from which all troops would be withdrawn. Tibet would serve as a buffer zone between India and China, thus permitting both countries to withdraw their troops from the border. The second point proposed an end to the large-scale transfer of Chinese into Tibetan areas, which was leading to the possibility of Tibetans becoming a minority in their own country. Third, the plan called for respect for the human rights of the people of Tibet and for the freedom of Tibetan people to develop culturally, intellectually, economically, and spiritually in their own way. Fourth, the statement asked for an end to nuclear testing and the dumping of nuclear waste and the initiation of serious efforts to restore Tibet's natural environment. Finally, the Dalai Lama asked that negotiations on the future status of Tibet and on the relationship between the Tibetan and Chinese peoples begin in earnest.

Days later, on September 27, a group of monks from Drepung monastery in Lhasa, carrying a Tibetan flag and shouting slogans in support of the Dalai Lama and Tibetan independence, marched to the Jokhang and then on to offices of the Chinese government. Some of the monks were arrested, though some were almost immediately released. On October 1, the day the Chinese celebrate the establishment in 1949 of the People's Republic of China, both monks and lay people in still larger numbers took to the streets in protest. When a number of the demonstrators were arrested and incarcerated in the city jail, the crowd, then in the thousands, set fire to the police station. Most of the prisoners escaped. In the ensuing melee, several people were killed, many were wounded, and more arrests were made. The protests and riots continued for another two weeks.[1]

When I landed in Beijing on September 27 to meet with Yan Mingfu, I knew nothing about the protests. He was furious about the demonstrations, accusing the Tibetan government in exile of having instigated the riots. He even claimed to have evidence to prove it. One piece of evidence was that guns destined for Tibet had recently been unloaded from Taiwanese or Japanese cargo ships docked in Calcutta. The second was that foreign visitors carrying pictures of the Dalai Lama and recorded messages in his voice had arrived in Lhasa just before the riots. He was convinced that we had instigated the demonstrations.

I assured Yan Mingfu that these accusations could not be true and told him that I would take his complaints to the Kashag upon my return. We would investigate the question of the shipment of arms and the recorded messages and photos and determine whether anyone associated with the Dalai Lama had sent someone to Lhasa to do this work.

When I looked into the allegation that Tibetans had received a shipment of guns through Calcutta, I discovered that a shipment for the government in exile in Dharamsala had indeed recently arrived in Calcutta. But the crates did not contain guns. They held a couple of secondhand Toyotas. Cabinet minister Alak Jigme had recently been in Japan and persuaded one of the organizations there to donate the cars.

I began looking into the question of the Dalai Lama's pictures and the recorded messages. One of my friends in Hong Kong told me that before the demonstrations he had met with some foreigners who were taking a film crew to Lhasa because they were expecting a riot there. They knew about the deomonstrations before they started.

I was suspicious. When I returned to Dharamsala and checked with security officers there, I learned that yes, some foreigners had been carrying pictures of themselves with His Holiness and had recorded messages of good wishes from him, too. Later, I asked some lamas who had escaped from Lhasa about the pictures. They also said foreigners had been coming to the monasteries and showing pictures of the Dalai Lama, encouraging them to demonstrations.

I returned to Beijing and reported my findings to Yan Mingfu— that there were no weapons but that foreigners en route to Tibet had apparently been expecting the riots before they happened. I insisted again that we had nothing to do with it. But I told him that I did believe that some international intelligence agency had financed foreigners to travel to Tibet to do a sophisticated job of instigating the riots. Their goal was to sabotage the dialogue between China and Tibet and to create dissension between the Tibetans inside Tibet and the Tibetans in exile.

We had a lot of problems that year. The Chinese killed and arrested many people, worsening our relations with China and undermining the possibility of talks. Eventually the Chinese must have also done their own investigation. Gradually, their anger subsided and I managed to persuade Yan Mingfu and his associates to continue the negotiations.

On June 15, 1988, the Dalai Lama made another major statement, this time to the European Parliament in Strasbourg, France. In his search for a peaceful way forward with the Chinese, the Dalai Lama had been soliciting suggestions from a variety of people, including his longtime advisor Michael van Walt van Praag. The Strasbourg Statement reiterated his hope for early negotiations with the Chinese and presented several points of compromise. He was willing for China to retain responsibility for Tibet's foreign policy, so long as the government of Tibet could maintain its own foreign affairs bureau for matters of commerce, education, culture, religion, tourism, science, sports, and other nonpolitical activities. He mapped out his vision for a democratic Tibetan government based on a constitution providing for economic equality, social justice, and protection of the environment, and he called for a regional peace conference to ensure that "Tibet becomes a genuine sanctuary of peace through demilitarization." He said that he was ready to present a proposal to the government of the People's Republic of China based on his thoughts as outlined in Strasbourg. A negotiating team had already been selected. "We are prepared to meet with the Chinese to discuss details of such a proposal aimed at achieving an equitable solution," he said.

At the end of 1988, Yan Mingfu and the Chinese government agreed to reopen negotiations with the Dalai Lama's representatives. Yan Mingfu did not agree with all the points the Dalai Lama had outlined in his Strasbourg Statement, but he thought the statement could serve as a basis for new discussions. He even agreed that the

Dalai Lama could choose both the venue for the meetings and the negotiators on the Tibetan side. Yan asked me to convey this decision to the Dalai Lama.

I was encouraged. Yan Mingfu's suggestions seemed reasonable. I carried the message to the Dalai Lama, asking him to choose the venue and decide who would represent his government. The Chinese would respect his decision. I spoke to members of the Kashag, too, emphasizing how important this new opening was and what a big step forward the meeting would be.

The Research and Analysis Wing of Indian intelligence somehow got wind of this new turn in our negotiations. Mr. Nair, the head of the research division there asked me to meet him in Delhi. I took Tashi Wangdu, the Dalai Lama's representative in Delhi, and Kashag member Lodi Gyari with me. I needed them as third-party witnesses to what the Indians might say. When I reported on my meetings with the Chinese government and told them that the Chinese had asked the Dalai Lama to choose the venue and the Tibetan representatives, Mr. Nair's deputy, Ranga Natam, protested immediately. Almost before I stopped speaking, he declared that the Chinese could not be believed and urged us not to participate in such negotiations. He thought Tibetans should fight for their independence. He almost jumped out of his chair as he said this, the words bursting from his mouth.

My response was a sarcastic retort that the Indians wanted to hide in the bushes while we Tibetans fought the Chinese. Both men, Mr. Nair especially, were embarrassed. Nair apparently had not meant to be so blunt about his view that the Chinese could not be believed. At least Tashi Wangdu, Lodi Gyari, and I now understood that the Indian intelligence did not want us to negotiate. They wanted an independent Tibet—and for us to fight for it.

I had already returned to Hong Kong when I saw the news that Tashi Wangdu had just made a public announcement asking the Chinese to meet the Dalai Lama's representatives in Geneva on January 15, 1989. I knew immediately that this was an unacceptable breach of protocol. He had not informed the Chinese first.

Before I could even think about what to do, Yan Mingfu called me, demanding that I come to Beijing immediately. I did not even speak to Dharamsala before flying to meet him.

Yan Mingfu was furious. He wanted to know why the Dalai Lama had made a public, unilateral statement without first informing or consulting China. He said that this breach of protocol demonstrated that the Dalai Lama was not sincere, that he was not taking the negotiations seriously, that he was engaging in cheap propaganda. Yan pointed out that there were international procedures to be followed when setting up negotiations, that we must have joint consultations. The Chinese had asked the Tibetan side to choose the venue and composition of their delegation out of respect for the Dalai Lama. The announcement should have been made only after the Chinese side had been informed and the two sides had agreed. After reaching mutual agreement, each side could make an announcement, jointly or separately. That was the procedure.

I left Beijing and went straight to Dharamsala to complain to the Kashag. When I later pressed Tashi Wangdu on why he had made the announcement without consulting the Chinese first, he said that Indian officials had advised him to. Indian officials had told him that the Tibetans had the right to make this unilateral announcement. He never said which Indian officials, and I still do not know.

Oh, the Tibetans! The Indians were playing with us, exploiting us. The Tibetans were so naïve. No one seemed to know what they were doing. They had no idea what the consequences of their premature announcement would be. The decision was incompetent. I was frustrated and sad. I am still frustrated and sad. The Indians had deliberately sabotaged our negotiations. And the Tibetans had destroyed the best opportunity we had had since 1959. When the Dalai Lama and his officials realized that they had made a mistake, I was dispatched to China to apologize on their behalf. The Chinese were still upset. The negotiations were put on hold.

31

Another Opportunity Lost

But Deng Xiaoping gave us another chance. The occasion was the death of the Tenth Panchen Lama.

I had continued to meet the Panchen Lama whenever I visited Beijing. He had been grateful to me for pleading his case to Deng, and we often discussed the issue of the Dalai Lama's return. He always urged caution. Without a clear understanding with the Chinese, he thought it unwise for the Dalai Lama to come back. He worried about the Dalai Lama's safety.

The Panchen Lama was visiting Tashilunpo, his monastery in Shigatse, in January 1989, when he suffered a sudden heart attack. United Front Work Department Director Yan Mingfu immediately sent a medical team from Beijing to treat him. Wen Jiabao, then an official with the United Front Work Department and later to become China's premier, flew with the team, first to Lhasa by plane and then to Tashilunpo by helicopter. They were delayed by bad weather, and by the time they arrived in Shigatse it was already too late. The Panchen Lama had slipped into a coma. He died on January 28 before the doctors could help.

The Panchen Lama was only fifty-one years old. Rumors that he had been poisoned began circulating immediately and still persist to this day. The Panchen Lama had continued to be critical of the Chinese government's behavior in Tibet, even after suffering all those years in jail for having spoken out in 1962. In March of 1987, he had again spoken out strongly in criticism of China's behavior in Tibet. He argued that Tibetans were the only legitimate masters of Tibet, and he decried the amount of money being spent to keep Chinese cadres there, pointing out that the cost of keeping one Chinese in Tibet was equal to keeping four in China. He criticized the quality of schools and the inappropriate content of education for Tibetan children who were being taught nothing of their own history. He did not approve of the practice of sending Tibetan students to other provinces to study. He was scathing in his criticisms of the unjust and excessive punishments meted out to innocent Tibetans with the quashing of the rebellion in 1959 and later with the implementation of so-called democratic reforms. He returned to some of the questions he had raised in 1962, especially the very high number of innocent villagers jailed after the Dalai Lama's escape and figures suggesting that almost half of all those prisoners had died in jail. The Tibetans were subjected to untold suffering, he said. They would never forget their suffering.[1]

On January 17, 1989, just a few days before his death, he reiterated some of his criticisms, concluding that the price of development under the Communist Party in China had been greater than the gains.

Many people believe that because the Panchen Lama had spoken out so strongly, some people wanted him gone. And his death had happened so suddenly, without warning. The doctors who were dispatched to treat him were not the Panchen Lama's regular doctors. Why did they get there so late?

But the Panchen Lama was a big, heavy man. He weighed close to 250 pounds. He was so heavy that he had to be physically helped up after making his prostrations. He had diabetes and high blood pressure. And he had been working hard. During the Cultural Revolution, the tombs of the previous Panchen Lamas housed inside Tashilunpo had been badly damaged, and he was responsible for overseeing their restoration. Many people wanted to meet him, and he was receiving many visitors. He had spent fifteen years in prison, in miserable conditions. He was not a well man. I do not believe the rumors that he was poisoned. I believe that Yan Mingfu, Wen Jiabao, and the doctors did all they could to save him.

After the Panchen Lama's death, Deng Xiaoping wanted the Dalai Lama himself to conduct the memorial service. This would bring the Dalai Lama to China and give him the opportunity to meet with key Chinese religious and government officials. Many of the old revolutionaries were still alive—Chen Yun, Li Xiannian, Bo Yibo, and Ye Jianying. The Dalai Lama had met most of them during his visit to China in 1954. He could meet them all again. Yan Mingfu arranged for the invitation to come from the chairman of the Chinese Buddhist Society, Dr. Zhao Puzu. Zhao was a not a lama. He was a well-known, internationally respected scholar of Buddhism. He wrote the invitation in his own handwriting, and I delivered it to the Dalai Lama in Dharamsala. I, too, thought that the commemorative service would be a good opportunity for the Dalai Lama to meet the Chinese leaders—not for negotiations or official discussions but simply to conduct the funeral service and to reestablish personal contact with leaders in China. The meetings would be an opportunity to begin building trust.

But the Kashag persuaded him not to go. Their excuse was that there was not enough time to make the arrangements, but really they were still afraid that he might be kidnapped. The Chinese were not happy with this decision. In fact, they were quite upset. Deng Xiaoping's intentions were sincere. He wanted the Dalai Lama to go to Beijing to build a little trust and pave the way for more serious, concrete discussions in the future. I, too, was disappointed.

I still wanted to pay my personal respects to the Panchen Lama's family. The Panchen Lama had married and had a child not long after his release from prison, sometime after my first visit with him in 1979. His wife, mother, and daughter continued to live in Beijing, even after he began spending more time at Tashilunpo. When I arrived at their Beijing home to pay my respects, Zhu Xiaoming from the United Front Work Department was already there, guarding the door, refusing to let me in. I had informed the United Front that I would be visiting the family. They had simply taken note of it, not saying yes or no. But there was Zhu Xiaoming in front of the door, physically blocking my way.

I pushed him aside just as someone inside the house was opening the door. As I went in, the Panchen Lama's wife and daughter came rushing out, soon to be joined by his mother. The Panchen Lama's daughter must have been around seven or eight years old then and looked exactly like her father. His wife was agitated and distraught. Aside from grieving over the death of her husband, she was also upset about what she called the Chinese government's deprivation of her human rights. The government was claiming all of the Panchen Lama's possessions, leaving nothing for the family. Boxes stamped with the official government seal were sitting in the hallway. She wanted me to help.

Yan Mingfu was not happy when I raised the issue with him. I told him that whether he appreciated my intervention or not, the family was being mistreated. Yes, some of the property surely belonged to the Tashilunpo monastery, but some of it also belonged to the family. The government had no right to claim everything. Yan Mingfu assured me that he would do what he could.

THE STUDENT DEMONSTRATIONS began in Beijing a few months later, following the death of Hu Yaobang on April 15, 1989. Hu had been purged as general secretary of the Communist Party in January 1987 for his overly "bourgeois liberal" views, and the students took the occasion of his death to call for an end to corruption and demand the institution of new democratic reforms. Their call struck a vibrant chord as students by the hundreds of thousands, and then the ordinary citizens of Beijing took to the streets. At the height of these demonstrations, more than a million people were said to have joined the protests.

In Hong Kong, too, the movement and its goals won widespread support. As the protests intensified and the Chinese government failed to respond, many in Hong Kong were predicting the imminent demise of Deng Xiaoping and his government. They thought that Deng would be forced to resign.

People began urging the Dalai Lama to make a statement in support of the students. Kashag members were calling me every day to ask for my advice. I must have been the only person around the Dalai Lama who opposed the idea of his speaking out at such a time. I never saw any hint that Deng Xiaoping was about to resign or that democracy was suddenly going to descend on China. I did not think that this was an issue in which we should be involved. I thought we should stay quiet and wait. But the Dalai Lama did finally speak out in support of the students' democratic goals.

Instead of resigning, Deng Xiaoping brought in the army. On the night of June 3, 1989, thousands of soldiers marched into Beijing to quell the disturbances. Many people, students and ordinary Beijing citizens alike, were killed, injured, and arrested. Yan Mingfu had been one of the lead negotiators with the student demonstrators. He became a prominent victim in the purges that followed, removed from his position as chairman of the United Front.

Shortly afterward, I met with United Front deputy director Song Yingying and his staff in Shenzhen, just across the border from Hong Kong. They showed me hours of tapes of the violence that had occurred the night the army came in, the burning cars and trains, the angry mob turning violently against the troops, the soldier with his stomach cut open. Even at this point the Chinese were still talking about having a dialogue with the Dalai Lama. After the dust had settled on this Tiananmen incident and the situation returned to normal, discussions about negotiations could resume.

But soon some of the Dalai Lama's officials made statements that the Chinese did not like. The Dalai Lama won the 1989 Nobel Peace Prize. In 1990, he traveled to the United States and made a remark in front of Chinese visitors that within two years, the Chinese government would collapse. The Chinese never followed up on the question of negotiations. Our side never followed up, either. Negotiations were dead in the water.

32

Opportunity Lost Again

In 1994, during a visit to Beijing, I received a visit from several representatives of China's State Council and members of the search party for the next Panchen Lama. The search party had some gifts for the Dalai Lama and a letter from Chadrel Rinpoche from the Panchen Lama's own Tashilunpo monastery saying that he was praying for the Dalai Lama's prayers for the early discovery of the next Panchen Lama. The search committee wanted His Holiness's guidance on the selection. I promised to deliver the letter and gifts in person.

I was pleased to learn that the head of the search party was Chadrel Rinpoche and heartened that correct procedures were being followed in the search for the next Panchen Lama. The visit of the search committee was an indication that they were performing their proper function, including seeking contact with and blessings from the Dalai Lama. And since these discussions took place in the presence of State Council officials in charge of religious affairs, the requests were clearly being made with official permission from the Chinese government.

When I presented the letter and gifts to the Dalai Lama, he responded with a letter to Chadrel Rinpoche inviting him to come to India to discuss the search. He asked me make sure that Chadrel Rinpoche received it.

I could have returned to China to deliver the letter myself, but I chose instead to give it to the Chinese ambassador in Delhi, explaining the situation and asking him to send the letter on. Working through the Chinese embassy would be faster, and since Chadrel Rinpoche was under Chinese control, he would need official permission for his visit to the Dalai Lama. Using official channels seemed the wisest and most effective way to communicate.

I still do not know whether Chadrel Rinpoche received the letter. Perhaps he did not. The Chinese can be high-handed about Tibet whether official procedures are followed or not. But the Dalai Lama never received a response to his invitation, not from the rinpoche himself nor from the Chinese government. Chadrel Rinpoche never visited India.

But Chadrel Rinpoche did begin sending letters by courier across the border from Tibet into India, informing the Dalai Lama about the search party's arrangements, giving him the names of the contending candidates, and letting him know when the search party had narrowed the choice to two young boys. Finally, the time for the final decision arrived. The parties inside China, including Chadrel Rinpoche, had agreed on the final choice. All that was left was for the Dalai Lama to have his final say and to announce who the next Panchen Lama would be. Chadrel Rinpoche sent a letter to the Dalai Lama informing him of the conclusions of the search committee and asking him to make the announcement. That was the protocol. I never saw the letter, but I presume that Chadrel Rinpoche requested the Dalai Lama to accept the choice of the search committee. The Dalai Lama knew who that choice was and that it was Chadrel's choice.

I was surprised when the Dalai Lama's chief secretary, Khenchung Tara, called me in Hong Kong from Dharamsala asking me to inform the Chinese government that the Dalai Lama would be making the announcement about his choice of Panchen Lama the following morning. I wondered why Khenchung Tara did not first inform the Chinese of the Dalai Lama's choice. They should have let the Chinese know much earlier, I insisted. They were making the same mistake they had made in announcing their time and place for the meeting between the Dalai Lama's representatives and the Chinese negotiators at the United Front Work Department. I knew this would offend the Chinese. But Khenchung Tara said the decision had been made, the documents were in order, and the announcement would be made the next morning.

I had to warn the Chinese government. But it was five in the afternoon, the end of the business day in both Hong Kong and Beijing. The United Front offices were already closed. I called the Beijing operator requesting private home phone numbers for some of the United Front officials. The operator was cooperative, but phone numbers of Beijing officials were not easily available. Finally, at around nine in the evening and after many calls, the operator found the number of Zhu Xiaoming, the man who had physically tried to prevent me from visiting the Panchen Lama's family.

Zhu was outraged at the news of the Dalai Lama's impending announcement, accusing the Dalai Lama of having torn off his mask and of openly fighting against the Chinese government. I tried to calm him down, pointing out that rightly or wrongly, the Dalai Lama had made the decision and would make the announcement the next morning. Zhu had to inform the proper authorities.

The Dalai Lama may never have suspected that the Chinese would be angry with him for making the announcement. Overseeing the choice of the Panchen Lama's reincarnation was one of his functions as the Dalai Lama. But the Chinese did resent it. Within days of the announcement, Radio Beijing began publicly attacking the Dalai Lama, accusing him of ignoring the Chinese government's authority. The Chinese repudiated the Dalai Lama's choice and later announced that the second young contender was the new Panchen Lama. The Dalai Lama's choice, Choekyi Nyima from Nagchu, disappeared and has never been heard from again. Chadrel Rinpoche had been on his way back to Tibet, halfway there, when the announcement was made. He was arrested in Chengdu and later accused of "plotting to split the country" and "leaking State secrets" and sentenced to six years in jail. He was released in 2002 but remained under house arrest. His current whereabouts are still unknown.

The Chinese denunciations of the Dalai Lama went on for a month. Then Taiwan president Lee Teng-hui went to the United States and made a speech at Cornell University, his alma mater. The Chinese government stopped its verbal bombardments of the Dalai Lama and began attacking Lee Teng-hui instead. Eight years passed before our negotiations with the United Front resumed.

So who is to blame for this situation? The Dalai Lama or the Chinese? I think that our side made mistakes. We should have consulted the Chinese first. We created unnecessary conflict and acrimony. I think we Tibetans need to make more of an effort to understand the Chinese mentality. If we do not, we are always going to have trouble. The Chinese are always suspicious that someone is plotting behind their backs. If you pat the Chinese in one direction, everything is fine. If you pat them in the opposite direction, they get upset. Whenever we say what we think, we say it without thinking about what they will think. We need to think of what China's reaction will be. We get ourselves in unnecessary trouble by doing things our way without regard for the other side. Eventually, the suspicion with which the Chinese view the world may destroy them. But we Tibetans may destroy ourselves, too. We are just the opposite—endlessly hopeful, believing that tomorrow will be better. The better tomorrow never comes. We may kill ourselves with empty hope. We even have a proverb about this: Tibetans are ruined by hope, Chinese are ruined by suspicion.

33

Return to Tibet

For all the times that I went back and forth between India, Hong Kong, and China after that first meeting with Deng Xiaoping, despite the several delegations I arranged to visit Tibet and despite my own travels to many parts of China, I had never returned to Tibet myself. The Chinese at the United Front Work Department often offered to make the arrangements and wondered why I refused to go. I had come to think of my native Tibet as a land of blood and tears. I did not want to visit such a tragic place. Seeing my homeland in such a dismal state would be too painful. I told the Chinese I wanted to wait until conditions had improved.

By 1990, I thought perhaps the time had come. Xi Zhongxun, who had taken over Yan Mingfu's position at the United Front after the Tiananmen incident, was in charge of making the arrangements. Xi was one of the old first generation Chinese revolutionaries and had served under Peng Dehuai in the Northwest military region. His son, Xi Jinping, later became president of the People's Republic of China and general secretary of the Communist Party.

Xi Zhongxun and I soon clashed. When I arrived in Beijing ready to set out on my journey, Xi told me that my visit would have to be confined to my native place of Amdo. He did not want me to go to other parts of Tibet, citing tensions along the Indian border as grounds for refusing my request. He said that the Indians might make trouble for me if they discovered I had visited Central Tibet. I challenged his logic. I would not be visiting the border areas. Why should the Indians be upset? I told him that if I could not see all of Tibet, I was canceling my trip and returning home.

Xi first shook with fury and then turned profusely apologetic. He reversed himself and told me that I could go anywhere at all, anywhere I wanted. After another verbal jab at his lopsided logic, I told him I was returning home, packed my bags, and left.

Only in 2002, twelve years after walking out on Xi Zhongxun and fifty years after my escape from Lhasa, did I finally return to Tibet.

Everything had changed. Only the mountains and rivers were the same. I felt nothing. I was numb. My minders from the United Front never left my side. They hurried me from place to place and never let me talk to anyone. I was only allowed three hours in my native village, visiting my ancestral graveyard where my brother Norbu, the Taktser Rinpoche, had buried our father's ashes while I was still a student in Nanjing. I left immediately after a short lunch with my cousin's son who was then looking after my family's property. The communists, like the Manchus, had also torn down my family's house—after the Dalai Lama's escape to India. They rebuilt it again sometime later, before my visit, and then, a few years ago, tore it down and rebuilt it yet again. No one recognized me when I visited Kumbum monastery, where the Taktser Lama's labrang had long since been destroyed. Only as I was leaving did I tell the monks that I was the Taktser Rinpoche's brother.

In Lhasa, my visit to the Jokhang was also unannounced.

An elderly monk, sensing that I was a friend, whispered to me that everything inside was new. Everything but the two statues of Sakyamuni had been destroyed. After fifteen minutes inside the Potala Palace, the United Front officials hurried me off to a lunch somewhere outside of Lhasa. They refused to let me visit the three

Xi Zhongxun and Gyalo Thondup (Xinhua)

great monasteries of Sera, Ganden, and Drepung, taking me to Samye instead.

At Tashilunpo, the tombs of the panchen lamas that had been undergoing repair when the Tenth Panchen Lama died had all been fully restored, and the tomb for the Tenth himself had just been completed—a fabulously large and ornate stupa covered with gold and colorful jewels. The Chinese had wanted me to meet the new Panchen Lama, the one they had chosen after the Dalai Lama's office jumped the gun and announced the search committee's choice. I agreed to meet the Chinese choice of the Panchen Lama only on the condition that I also be allowed to meet with the young boy who had been chosen by the Dalai Lama. They told me that the Dalai Lama's choice was studying in Nanjing but refused to allow me to meet him. So I did not meet the Chinese Panchen Lama either. He was not in Tashilunpo when I visited. When I went to pay my respects before the tomb of the Tenth Panchen Lama, the United Front official beside me wondered why I did not prostrate myself before it, as the other visitors were doing. I told him that I only prostrate myself before people whom I consider my superior. I did not hold the Tenth Panchen Lama in particular esteem while he was alive, so I had no reason to prostrate myself before him in death.

34

Watching the World
from Kalimpong

By 1999, I had retired from my official duties and was ready for a different life. I decided to return to Kalimpong.

Kalimpong was the first Indian town had I visited on my journey to China in 1945 and was the place to which I returned with my new wife when we fled from China to India in the face of the civil war. Even when we settled in Darjeeling after my return from Tibet in 1952, we already had a dream of buying property and starting some kind of business in Kalimpong. I felt closer to home there. Kalimpong is just across the border from Tibet and was then still the center of Tibetan trade with India. I could meet my fellow countrymen every day. My wife and I wanted to make a living by doing something productive and useful, and we thought that with a plot of land, we could have a few cows and sell some milk and yogurt and maybe set up a noodle factory. The cost of land in Darjeeling was far beyond our means. A gentleman who ran a teashop there and worked with the wealthy Birla family told me that the Birlas had some land in Kalimpong that they were prepared to sell. My wife and I drove there in our jeep to take a look.

Mr. Birla's representative showed us ten plots of land in different parts of town, but all of it was much too expensive. Finally, he took us to a plot down the hill from the main town, and the price was right—about one hundred dollars for three acres of land. We began planting trees and growing some vegetables while the building was still going on. Then we bought a few cows and began selling milk and yogurt to St. Joseph's Convent and several of the local schools.

The noodle factory took longer to get started. It did not open until 1980. At that time, my wife was still deeply involved with her work at the refugee center in Darjeeling, and I was spending most of my time in New Delhi. We turned management of the factory over to a fellow countryman from Amdo and one of his friends. They ran it for almost twenty years. My wife came to visit every week to check the accounts and see how things were going. My visits were less frequent, only a couple days once every two or three months. In the mid 1970s, my mother moved into the main house, assisted by a kind, hardworking old nun who had accompanied her for years. Several personal attendants took care of her needs, and my mother spent most of her time in prayer. But she became lonely after a while and moved back to Dharamsala where the Dalai Lama and two of my younger brothers were living and she had more friends. She passed away there in 1981. My wife died five years later, in 1986.

When I moved back in 1999 to take over the noodle factory, I dismissed most of the work force and started afresh. We still have problems, even today. We never have sufficient capital. But our sales have improved and the business goes on. I am not rich, but I make a living. I do not have to go begging for money from other people. Noodle making is a profession that makes me feel proud. I am a productive person myself, and I give productive work to my neighbors. We supply thousands of people with noodles. We bring food to the tables of families in Kalimpong, Darjeeling, Siliguri and Bhutan.

And living in Kalimpong, running the noodle factory, gives me time to reflect. I have reflected so much in the past few years that I am mentally fatigued. As I look back over my life, I realize that the only time I have ever really been happy was as a child, first in Amdo and then later in Lhasa. My family was happy. When my great uncle, the Taktser Lama, returned from Mongolia, he was wealthy enough to buy back the land the Manchus had taken away and then to rebuild our family house in Amdo. My grandfather bought yaks, sheep, horses, and mules, and then my father inherited all that wealth. We hired servants. We got along well with our neighbors. We did not have to worry about where our food would come from or how we would pay our taxes to the local warlord Ma Bufang. We were a small family. My brothers all went to join the monastery when they were still small, leaving only four of us at home—my parents, my elder sister and me. And then my sister married and went to live with her husband. So we led a happy life in the village. My only worry was about school, and even in school I managed to spend most of my time playing.

When Kewtsang Rinpoche and the search party for the Fourteenth Dalai Lama came to Amdo and we traveled by caravan for almost three months across the Tibetan plateau to Lhasa, life was suddenly wonderful and thrilling. Those early days in Lhasa, the time I spent in school there, were the happiest days of my life, even happier than in Amdo. Everyone was so kind to my family and me, so warm and welcoming. I had no worries and no responsibilities. Everything we needed was provided by the Tibetan government.

From the time the decision was made to send me to school in China until now, I cannot say that my life has been happy. For the last sixty-five or seventy years, nothing has brought me particular happiness. The mission I chose of devoting my life to helping Tibet was a difficult job. Problems came one after another, and I tried to overcome them all, dealing with the Chinese Nationalists, the Americans, the Indians, the British, the Russians, and then the Chinese Communist government. The problems have never ended. Sitting here today in Kalimpong thinking back on those times, I wonder how I managed, how I was able to cope with all the responsibilities and all those problems. Looked at in another way, it was also thrilling—all that intrigue and plotting, the complexities and tough decisions. I will not say I managed well, but I tried to confront those difficulties head on, so in a way, yes, that was thrilling. Many people say that Gyalo Thondup is a hero, but I say no, I am one of you, trying to help, to serve the Tibetan people. I am no hero. I have no special ability. I have two hands, ten fingers, two eyes, nothing special. What I have done has been a matter of human effort, of never giving in or giving up, of going on and on and on, as I have for the last six-and-a-half decades.

In all my life, I have only one regret: my involvement with the CIA. Initially, I genuinely believed that the Americans wanted to help us fight for our independence. Eventually, I realized that was not true. It was misguided and wishful thinking on my part. The CIA's goal was never independence for Tibet. In fact, I do not think that the Americans ever really even wanted to help. They just wanted to stir up trouble, using the Tibetans to create misunderstandings and discord between China and India. Eventually they were successful in that. The 1962 Sino-Indian border war was one tragic result.

The Tibetans rose up in resistance in 1959 because they were being oppressed by the Chinese and because they resented the Chinese trying to destroy their traditional way of life. They fought out of anger and desperation, not because they really believed they could drive the Chinese out. They were not thinking of the consequences of their resistance, and many never really believed that they could win. But we were desperate for help in our struggle, and for a while we thought the CIA could give it.

What good was that support from the CIA? Not much. In reality, all the CIA did was to train a few people and drop them and a few arms into Tibet. The arms they sent were never even nearly enough. If the United States had really wanted to help, the least they could have done would have been to supply enough arms and equipment for the Tibetans to put up a good fight. But the resistance fighters did not even have enough weapons to do that. For this, I still resent the United States.

Our cooperation with the CIA provoked the Chinese, providing them the excuse they needed for launching massive reprisals against both the resistance fighters and the Tibetan people. Tens of thousands of Tibetans were killed as a result.

My role with the CIA still weighs heavily on my conscience. I have remained silent about this for decades, too. But now, I have to tell the truth. Our cooperation with the CIA was wrong. We should not have taken even the paltry support the CIA offered. If we had not collaborated with the CIA, if we had not taken the little bit of assistance the CIA was willing to give, the Chinese would not have had an excuse to kill so many Tibetans. Our collaboration led to the deaths of many, many innocent people. It was not only our people the Chinese killed. They tried to kill our culture, too. What I did by working with the CIA contributed to the complete destruction of the Tibetan culture. This reality causes me terrible pain. This is what has haunted me for so many years. This is what is on my conscience. I cannot get those events out of my mind. I feel guilty. This is my great regret.

And what have I accomplished? It is still too early to tell. Nothing yet. The situation in Tibet is still not settled. His Holiness the Dalai Lama has not yet returned home. There is still no relief. To even think of claiming any accomplishments now would be foolish.

This is a strange and complicated world. In 1945, with the end of the Second World War and the establishment of the United Nations, a wave of decolonization swept through Asia and Africa at the same time that Mao Zedong invaded and started to colonize Tibet and Xinjiang. And all those nations that had clamored for de-colonization and self-determination remained silent. None of them made any noise about the colonization of Tibet. But we Tibetans are completely different from the Chinese. We are a different people—our culture, our language, our religion, our customs, our system of political rule. Everything about us is different from the Chinese. The same is true for Xinjiang, too. And Mongolia. We have all been colonized, and the Chinese continue to rely on force to suppress us.

Watching the world from my hilltop perch in Kalimpong, I see the cold war continuing and fear that we are on the verge of a new era of international anarchy and conflict reminiscent of the three clashing kingdoms of Wei, Wu, and Shu as told in China's epic *Romance of the Three Kingdoms*. Russia, China, and the United States are the three clashing kingdoms of today. The cold war that began at the end of the Second World War continues, with Russia newly belligerent, China rising and increasingly aggressive, and the United States still struggling to redefine its international mission in the face of an increasingly chaotic and violent world. In the context of today's anarchic, war-torn world, the problems of Tibet are but a tiny, insignificant, almost infinitesimal speck.

Change for Tibet is not going to drop from the heavens. Change will come only through the work of many people working both independently and together. Among Tibetans, I look to the young generation to bring about change. On the one hand, many young Tibetans, particularly inside Tibet, have no knowledge of history, no understanding of what happed in the past. No one talks about the past there. People are afraid to talk. So many younger Tibetans remain ignorant of their own history.

On the other hand, this new generation of Tibetans is much smarter and better educated than members of my generation. We grew up ignorant and uneducated, stuck in the confines of a backward tradition, with no contact or understanding of the world beyond. Today, Tibetans both inside and in exile have much more opportunities to study and explore the world. Their education is so much better than mine. With the advent of television and the Internet, with the help of the Voice of America and Radio Free Asia, the people inside Tibet can learn what the Dalai Lama is doing and saying, where he is traveling, and who he is meeting.

The people of Tibet are united as never before. The divisions that once separated the people of Amdo, Kham, and Central Tibet have been transcended. If there are differences about how to solve our problems, there is unity that our problems are Tibetan problems. We are united as one in our commitment to the preservation of our unique culture, language, and religion—united, too, in our recognition of His Holiness the Dalai Lama as the revered spiritual leader of us all. If the Dalai Lama tells us that the tiger is an endangered species and Tibetans should stop wearing their traditional tiger skin coats, we stop wearing our tiger skin coats. The Dalai Lama has always exerted a powerful hold on Tibetans, even over those Tibetans from whom he is physically separated. That unity continues today, and is even easier now to maintain. There are so many new and different ways to communicate.

Each one of us Tibetans has a particular contribution to make to the preservation of our culture, and each of us must work to bring that about. We must continue to call for the recognition of our legitimate rights and speak out against our treatment as third-class citizens. But we Tibetans acting alone have little chance of bringing about the changes we seek. We need help. We must continue to cry out for help from the world's democratic powers. We still have much to learn from the United States. Even in exile, many of our young people have yet to become fully modern. They still need training in the whole range of skills that are necessary to become a part of the modern industrial and technological world. The United States could teach us.

And we must hope that China will change. The rise of China in the past several decades has been accompanied by massive corruption and abuse of power on the part of Chinese government officials. What we are witnessing in China today is ambition and greed unrestrained by conscience or principles. We Tibetans know that better than others. The morality of the Chinese leadership, and hence the legitimacy of the state, are in question.

More than a quarter century ago, some in the communist leadership began to recognize that force will not work. Yan Mingfu, when he was director of the United Front Work Department during the time of the 1989 demonstrations in Beijing, told me that he did not believe in force. "I do not think force will work," he said. "It is not useful." He thought that the minorities in China should be treated equally. But individuals like Yan Mingfu could not change China by themselves. Yan Mingfu lost his job, together with China's premier Zhao Ziyang and politburo member Hu Qili, because they disagreed with Deng Xiaoping about the use of force to suppress the demonstrators in Beijing. Deng Xiaoping in turn had been manipulated and misinformed by some of his closest associates, including Jiang Zemin, Zeng Qinghong, and his own son, Deng Pufang, about what was happening in Beijing. Deng was impulsive. I do not think he really understood what was happening.

Prospects for Tibet changed when Jiang Zemin took power and Deng Xiaoping died. Deng Xiaoping and Hu Yaobang had wanted a dialogue with the Dalai Lama. They were looking for a way to allow him to return to Tibet. But Jiang Zemin put up new obstacles. At a joint press conference between American President Bill Clinton and Chinese President Jiang Zemin during Clinton's 1998 visit to Beijing, Clinton publicly urged Jiang to meet with the Dalai Lama, saying that he had spent time with the Dalai Lama himself and believed him to be an honest man. He thought that if President Jiang and the Dalai Lama had a conversation together, they would like each other very much. But Jiang set two new conditions for the return of the Dalai Lama: The Dalai Lama would have to recognize that Tibet is an inalienable part of China and that Taiwan is a province of China.

These were new conditions. The international media seemed not to grasp their significance. Tibet has never been an inalienable part of China. For thousands of years Tibet has not been any part of China. It was conquered briefly during the Manchu period but that control soon ended. That was the major lesson I learned during my studies in Nanjing, from China's own written history. History is history. History cannot be changed. Tibetans can never agree that Tibet was part of China.

Sooner or later, China will have to change. It cannot continue to colonize Tibet, Xinjiang, and Mongolia. It cannot continue to subjugate its own citizens and rule by force forever. Rule by fear and oppression cannot work in the long run. The Chinese leadership knows this. The history of China teaches it. The ultimate power of history is the will and judgment of the people. That is the lesson of the classic *Romance of the Three Kingdoms*.

The fate of Tibet will be determined by how the problems of today's chaotic world are finally settled. It took eighty years of war before the three kings of Wei, Wu, and Shu finally found peace. Seventy years have passed since the Second World War ended and the new cold war began. Perhaps in the next decade the cold war between Russia, China, and the United States will finally be settled, too. We must hope that the United States comes out on top.

I have hope for the United States, and I have hope for Tibet. For so many thousands of years, Tibet has continued to exist on the Tibetan plateau, on the roof of the world. Tibetans have continued to survive until now, into the twenty-first century. I am convinced that Tibetans will continue to survive and that the Communist Party will one day realize that they have to treat the Tibetans as equals, not with suppression and guns. Things will change in the future. Of that I am quite sure.

We Tibetans have lost our land and our national independence. What we have never lost is our moral compass. Our belief in Tibetan Buddhism and His Holiness the Dalai Lama gives us a set of ethical values that is sorely lacking in China today. The Dalai Lama is still our deeply beloved moral guide. In this, we Tibetans have already won. China has much to learn from our values of tolerance and compassion and respect for human rights. Whatever happens, we Tibetans have begun our struggle for freedom and independence. That struggle will continue. The flame will not die. During a recent meeting with His Holiness the Dalai Lama, when I was feeling ill, he insisted that I could not die. "We have to return home together," he told me. I still believe that eventually the truth will prevail, that justice will be done, that Tibet will survive, and that we Tibetans will return home together.

AFTERWORD

Anne F. Thurston

The role of telling others' stories is not without its conundrums, and some of those conundrums deserve mention here. They generally fall into three categories: instances where, in my judgment, the evidence Gyalo Thondup presents does not warrant the conclusions he draws; instances when I would have drawn a different conclusion from the same evidence; and instances where Gyalo Thondup's account is so different from others that the differences need to be noted.

Most of my conundrums are related to questions of whether the evidence presented supports the conclusions drawn. Some are reasonably simple and straightforward. For instance, Gyalo Thondup believes that his father was murdered, poisoned by a family servant at the direction of a senior member of the Tibetan government. He is not alone in that belief. His mother and several other members of his family drew the same conclusion, and Lhasa at the time was surely filled with far more intrigue—and murder—than popular images of peaceful, idyllic Tibet might suggest.

But was the death of Gyalo Thundop's (and the Dalai Lama's) father really murder by poison? I am not fully convinced. Neither is the Dalai Lama.[1] Other possibilities seem equally reasonable. Some, for instance, have noted the high incidence of esophageal cancer among Tibetans and the similarity of the symptoms of such a cancer

303

to those of Gyalo Thondup's dying father. And one cannot help but wonder why poison should take forty-four days to kill.

Similarly, Gyalo Thondup attributes part of Dazang Dadul Tsarong's fabulous wealth to the presence of a mint he operated from his home (p. 217), in addition to the one he ran as an official of the Tibetan government. Tsarong is a colorful figure in Tibetan history, having first won and then lost the favor the Thirteenth Dalai Lama, becoming a member of the Tibetan aristocracy through marriage, and then taking several wives, including a mother and three of her daughters. He lived a life of remarkable luxury and as director of the mint was officially allowed to profit from the gold coins he produced. But was he really a thief? Did he really run a mint in his own home? Did his fabulous wealth really come from a mint he operated in his home, in addition to the one he ran as an official of the Tibetan government?

The statement of the Mongolian monk Dawa Sangpo, who was in fact the Japanese spy Hisao Kimura (and hence already well-versed in the art of deception), is hardly sufficient proof. The statement has the ring of humor rather than fact.

Gyalo Thondup also casts a considerable shadow on Dazang Dadul Tsarong's son George Tsarong (pp. 215–218), who was one of the men responsible for selling the gold bullion that the Tibetan government had deposited in Sikkim in the early 1950s. Was the also fabulously wealthy late George Tsarong guilty of theft or simply of very bad management when most of the proceeds from the sale of the Tibetan government's gold bullion seemed to vanish into thin air? This is a more difficult question. The allegations made by Gyalo Thondup will undoubtedly be controversial. George Tsarong was and remains for many a highly respected member of the Tibetan elite.

Gyalo Thondup believes that in the fall of 1981 some international intelligence agencies must have financed some foreigners to travel to Tibet to instigate the series of demonstrations that began in late September (pp. 275–276), and he suspects that the demonstrations in Beijing in the spring of 1989 were similarly inspired by outside elements. These are serious allegations.

Indeed, the Chinese government had also drawn similar conclusions about those popular protests before sufficient evidence could have been gathered. Immediately after the Lhasa demonstrations of 1987, the Chinese government declared the riots to be "solely a political incident created by a handful of separatists to coordinate with the Dalai Lama Cliques' activities abroad aimed at splitting China."[2] Similarly, the Chinese protests that began in Beijing in the spring of 1989 were seen by the Chinese government as "political turmoil incited by a very small number of political careerists after a few years of plotting and scheming . . . aimed at subverting the socialist People's Republic." Official blame for the political turmoil was directed at diverse individuals and organizations such as Communist Party General Secretary Zhao Ziyang and the Voice of America.[3]

In support of his conclusion that outsiders must have instigated the 1987 demonstrations in Lhasa, Gyalo Thondup cites a conversation with a Hong Kong friend who had met with several foreigners on their way to Lhasa not long before the demonstrations began and who appeared to have advance knowledge of the protests. And he cites United Front Minister Yan Mingfu's claim that foreigners carrying pictures of the Dalai Lama and recorded messages of his voice had arrived in Lhasa not long before the demonstrations began.

The Hong Kong friend remembers his conversation with Gyalo Thondup somewhat differently but does recalls that one of the foreigners was Steve Lehman. In 1998, Steve Lehman published a book called *The Tibetans: A Struggle to Survive*, filled with his own photographs of the 1987 demonstrations and including his own preface, an essay by Robbie Barnett (now the director of Modern Tibetan Studies at Columbia University), and a lengthy interview with Jampel Tsering, the Drepung monk who led the demonstration on September 27, 1987.[4] Jampel Tsering tells how he obtained tape cassettes of talks by the Dalai Lama from both visiting foreigners and Tibetans returning from India and the deep impression the Dalai Lama's words had on his own thoughts. He notes the importance to his own thinking of information he was receiving from outside, especially the report on the Dalai Lama's Five Point Peace Proposal presented to the US Congressional Human Rights Caucus on September 23, 1987. He describes the evolution of his own thinking about Tibetan independence and his decision to participate in his first political demonstration.[5]

Similarly, both Robbie Barnett and Steve Lehman, who first met on the back streets of Lhasa in the midst of those demonstrations, write of their own personal experiences as witness to the protests. Lehman tells of his instantaneous realization of his own personal obligation to document the demonstration through his photography.[6] Barnett writes of the disagreements that arose among the foreigners about what their role should be. "Should we witness these events silently from the sidelines," he asks, ". . . or should we stand in the middle of the crowd to show support and deter the soldiers from opening fire?" He notes, too, that the presence of foreigners in the crowd and the photographs they took have been cited by Chinese officials as evidence "that those protests were fueled by foreign provocateurs and not an expression of Tibetan belief."[7]

But the presence of sympathetic foreigners in Lhasa at the time and the fact that they carried both pictures of the Dalai Lama and taped cassettes of some of his talks is not sufficient evidence that foreigners actually instigated or were somehow "behind" the protests. Many foreigners visiting Tibet at the time knew that foreign tourists were often approached by Tibetans asking for pictures of the Dalai Lama and saw the giving of those pictures as a gesture of sympathy and good will. And they also had to have known that most Tibetans would surely have been thrilled to hear the voice of the Dalai Lama. Indeed, some well-informed Chinese specialists believe that the Chinese government itself later concluded that foreigners had not been involved in the Lhasa demonstrations of 1987, despite the presence of a number of foreigners in the city at the time.

The question of what led to these protests in both Tibet and Beijing deserves serious social science research. Identifying, understanding, and addressing the reasons otherwise apparently ordinary people are driven to violent acts of protest is surely one of the most vexing and important issues of our time. The questions are not new.

Social science research in the West, including some conducted in the United States, suggests that the factors leading to mass protest and violence are extraordinarily complex, requiring extensive case-by-case research to understand fully. Some of the best early social science research about violence in the United States was undertaken by commissions established following particularly troubling outbreaks of violence during the 1960s, bringing together scholars and experts from a variety of disciplines to study the problem from different perspectives.[8] None of these studies claimed to be definitive, but each contributed to our understanding of what happened and why. Each attempts to point the way to a more peaceful future. All agree that the causes of mass violence are complex.

Only serious social science studies of violence in Tibet and China similar to those conducted in the United States in the 1960s could give us the deeper, more nuanced, and comprehensive understanding of both the long-term and proximate causes of violence that might in turn help point the way to long term, reasonable means of redress. Until then, the conclusions drawn by Gyalo Thondup must remain very much an open question.

Gyalo Thondup's judgment of the Panchen Lama is the primary instance where I would draw different conclusions from the same evidence. Gyalo Thondup writes of the lack of respect he had for the Tenth Panchen Lama and his perception that the Panchen Lama had been groomed (admittedly without choice) to be a tool of the Chinese communists. When his Chinese hosts ask him why he refuses to prostrate himself before the late Panchen Lama's tomb, he replies that "I did not hold the Tenth Panchen Lama in particular esteem while he was alive, so I had no reason to prostrate myself before him in death" (p. 292). I hold the late Panchen Lama in considerably higher regard. Schooled under the Chinese to serve the government's goals, he nonetheless broke free from his reins as early as 1962 to speak out strongly, eloquently, and at length against the Chinese government's behavior in Tibet. His so-called Seventy Thousand Character Petition is a detailed, evidence-based account of Chinese misrule in Tibet, for which he spent some fourteen years in confinement, often

subjected to brutal criticism and torture. That he should write yet another scathing critique in 1987, after all he had endured in confinement, is to me an act of bravery that fills me with awe.

Finally, one important discrepancy between Gyalo Thondup's
story and the story as told by others must be noted. Early in our
encounters, when Gyalo Thondup occasionally could not remember a point or was not sure that he was remembering correctly, he
referred me to the memoirs of Lhamo Tsering, his longtime, trusted
deputy since his college days in Nanjing in the late 1940s. A good
part of Lhamo Tsering's memoirs has been translated into English,
including the period of Gyalo Thondup's return to Lhasa in 1952
and later escape the same year, the beginning of the CIA supported
underground resistance in the mid-1950s, and the Dalai Lama's own
escape in 1959. The differences between several stories as told to me
by Gyalo Thondup and the stories about Gyalo Thondup as told by
his closest associate are glaring and difficult to reconcile.

In explaining his decision to return to Lhasa in 1952, Gyalo
Thondup says (p. 129) that he returned because he thought he could
help, that he was optimistic about the future, that he wanted to help
introduce reforms and serve as an intermediary between the Chinese
and Tibetans. He saw the Chinese as allies. Lhamo Tsering, on the
other hand, says that Gyalo Thondup was convinced that the Tibetans' religious and spiritual convictions would prohibit them from
ever accepting Chinese rule, and that he returned to convince both
the secular and spiritual leaders of the Tibetan government that Tibetans should rise up and resist the Chinese Communists before they
could establish full control. Gyalo Thondup, his deputy says, was
prepared to carry out a resistance movement against Chinese rule
that would achieve complete independence for the Tibetan people.[9]

This description has some faint ring of truth. Gyalo Thondup
did meet with secular and religious leaders in Lhasa. But this was
a period of ostensible cooperation between the Tibetan government and their Chinese overseers in Lhasa, and Gyalo Thondup
wanted to encourage his brother the Dalai Lama to carry out sig-
nificant changes to the system of estates and ownership of land. For

Gyalo Thondup to have begun encouraging outright resistance in 1952 would have been suicidal and would have brought considerable difficulty to the very Dalai Lama he wanted to protect. Gyalo Thondup describes himself as feeling badly conflicted, wanting to help his brother and Tibet on the one hand but unable to challenge the Chinese directly on the other. In the end, he had no choice but to escape. Gyalo Thondup denies that he tried to convince anyone to rise up against the Communists or that he was planning then to carry out a movement to resist.

Similarly, Lhamo Tsering's memoirs quote in full a letter—written first in English, then translated into Tibetan, and then translated back into English—that Gyalo Thondup is said to have written to American Secretary of State Dean Acheson in November 1952 after he had escaped from Lhasa to India. The letter explains that Gyalo Thondup reported to the Dalai Lama on discussions he had had with Dean Acheson while in the United States and describes Thondup's plan to instigate a Tibetan revolt against the Chinese through force of arms. It calls upon the United States for military support.[10]

This letter, too, has something of a ring of truth. Gyalo Thondup does claim to have written a letter to American President Harry Truman when he arrived in India, and in that letter he did ask the United States to help. But Gyalo Thondup says he never met Dean Acheson let alone write to him about his meeting with the Dalai Lama or any plan to instigate violent revolt.

Finally, Lhamo Tsering describes two meetings between the Dalai Lama and Athar and Lhotse, both members of the first group of resistance fighters to be trained by the CIA, during the Dalai Lama's 1959 escape from Lhasa to India. Lhamo Tsering says that shortly before he crossed the border into India, the two freedom fighters "informed His Holiness the Dalai Lama of their activities from the beginning to the end." The Dalai Lama is reported to have praised the men for carrying out their secret duties successfully and urged them to persevere without losing courage. And he is said to have issued a message through them to all the other soldiers, urging them to continue with their struggle through to the end, saying that "all the lamas and *tulkus*, monks and ordinary people including the Dalai Lama himself would always pray for all those who sacrifice their lives for their country, its people and for the teachings of Buddha."[11]

If so, the Dalai Lama was far more thoroughly informed about the activities of the resistance and far more forthright in his support than Gyalo Thondup and most others who have written seriously about the subject have reported and believed. The Dalai Lama himself mentions his meeting with unnamed resisters in *My Land and My People*, saying that in spite of his beliefs, "I very much admired their courage and their determination to carry on the grim battle they had started for our freedom, culture, and religion. I thanked them for their strength and bravery, and also, more personally, for the protection they had given me. . . . By then, I could not in honesty advise them to avoid violence. In order to fight, they had sacrificed their homes and all the comforts and benefits of a peaceful life. Now they could see no alternative but to go on fighting and I had none to offer."[12]

What to make of the differences between Gyalo Thondup's personal account and those of his deputy Lhamo Tsering? Are these discrepancies a case of *Rashomon*? A failure of memory? A mistake? Misinterpretation? Deception? Many who knew Lhamo Tsering, Tibetans and Americans alike, describe him as a man of exceptional integrity, scrupulously meticulous and careful. They would believe what he has written. They suggest that perhaps someone has tampered with Lhamo Tsering's original manuscript. Some suggest Gyalo Thondup's memory is at fault. But I do not think so. Gyalo Thondup is prepared to believe that the differences are simply an instance of Lhamo Tsering both over-interpreting and not fully understanding what was happening at the time.

The question of Lhamo Tsering's manuscript is not insignificant. His memoirs provide detailed accounts of the relationship between the Tibetan resistance and the CIA, including the names of all the men who were trained by the CIA, the places and dates of their training, lists of when and where air drops of weapons and other materiel were made with an accounting of what was in each drop, and detailed descriptions of the activities of the several different groups of resistance fighters from the first batch of men sent to Saipan to the final denouement in Mustang which led to Lhamo Tsering's arrest and seven-year imprisonment. His memoirs may be the most exhaustive day-to-day record we have of the resistance. Hopefully someone will pick up the gauntlet, find the explanation for these discrepancies, and sort out what information within the memoirs is reliable and what is not, a task that is beyond the scope of this book. Generally, however, Lhamo Tsering's memoirs are most accurate when they focus on the specifics of the resistance fighters themselves, including their training, the battles they fought, and the weapons they were supplied and used.

Both the Tibetans and the editors who have read and commented on this book in manuscript form have pointed to instances where they see Gyalo Thondup as particularly controversial and provocative. These include statements about the Dalai Lama's views on Tibetan independence, Gyalo Thondup's judgment of the late Panchen Lama and the people around him (and Gyalo Thondup's own refusal to prostrate himself before a man he did not respect), allegations against both the elder Tsarong and his son George Tsarong, and criticisms of cabinet ministers Surkhang and Yuthok. I have reviewed each of these concerns with Gyalo Thondup.

Gyalo Thondup sticks to his guns. He knew from the beginning that his book would be provocative. At some point, well into the writing, he met with the Dalai Lama and told him that he felt he was holding back, that there were truths he was not telling. "You have served Tibet your entire life," the Dalai Lama replied. "You must open up."

Gyalo Thondup believes that he could not have opened up and told his truths without being controversial. "I am duty bound to tell what happened," he says. "If not, I would be dishonest." He knows that some of the harshest criticisms will come from his fellow Tibetans, and he welcomes the controversy. "I have been a daring fighter all my life," he says. "I am not afraid. I am not even afraid of the Chinese Communists." In fact, he asserts that in the case of George

Tsarong's mismanagement of the gold bullion, the Tibetan government should sue for its loss.

Hopefully, future historians and social scientists will continue exploring and weighing the competing and contradictory evidence to tell the tragedy of Tibet in all the complexity and nuance it deserves. I hope that this book will become part of the evidence. Reality is too complex for one account to set the record straight. But I hope I have allowed Gyalo Thondup to tell his story well. It surely will be found to contain mistakes that might have been avoided had I been a scholar of Tibet or able to be in greater contact with those who are. But the sensitivity of this undertaking, and the fear that engendered, limited the number of people who could be actively involved in this endeavor.

I want to thank them. Elsie Walker, who brought me into the project and stuck by me throughout, guiding me through the intricacies of India and Tibet, reading the manuscript in several of its iterations and making useful comments on all, taking me first to Kalimpong and later to Dharamsala, arranging a meeting with His Holiness the Dalai Lama, and sharing countless meals at Bistrot Lepic, receives the lion's share of my thanks and will forever remain a friend. Dr. Tanpa Thondup, Gyalo Thondup's Hong Kong–based younger son, was at my first meeting with his father and at many more meetings thereafter, in Washington, Hong Kong, Kalimpong, and Delhi. He has been both unwavering in his support, a major reason that his father's story is finally coming to light, and pretty much literally a lifesaver to me. Peter Bernstein and his wife Amy shepherded the book from the germ of an idea in Hong Kong through to a real proposal and on to the final book. Clive Priddle's editorial direction was invaluable in helping to steer the story in the right direction and shaping how it should be told. The editorial staff at Public Affairs was invariably professional, prompt, and responsive.

Very few people have read the manuscript, but I would like to thank them. Thubeten Samphel read both an early and later version and helped me correct Tibetan spellings and alerted me to places where the meaning is unclear and corrected a number of factual errors. Tseten Wangchuk and Tenzin Tethong read the next-to-final version and made a number of valuable editorial and substantive comments and alerted me to the potential pitfalls of some of its contents. I thank Warren Smith for providing me with his translation of Lhamo Tsering's memoirs. Of course, Gyalo Thondup and I are responsible for whatever mistakes surely remain and welcome the opportunity to correct them.

NOTES

INTRODUCTION

1. The monk's name was Jampa Tenzin, and he was from Jokhang Temple in Lhasa. In 1992, he was found strangled to death in his room at the temple. See Steve Lehman, *The Tibetans: A Struggle to Survive* (New York: Umbrage, 1998), 31.

2. *Testimony of Elliot Sperling Before the House Subcommittees on Asian and Pacific Affairs and Human Rights and the International Organizations on the Situation in Tibet* (Washington, DC: Asia Watch 1987).

3. Robert Barnett, *Report from Lhasa*, November 3, 1987 (Sent by Telex from Kathmandu, Nepal, November 19, 1987).

4. Jeremy Bernstein, "A Journey to Lhasa," *The New Yorker*, December 14, 1987, pp. 47–48.

5. See Anne F. Thurston, *Enemies of the People: The Ordeal of the Intellectuals in China's Great Cultural Revolution* (New York: Knopf, 1987).

6. The recent election of Narendra Modi as India's new prime minister has brought a new mood of political optimism that the Gorkha rebellion can eventually be resolved. But the well-known public enmity between new prime minister and the current elected chief minister of West Bengal, Mamata Banerjee, the first woman to be elected to the post, suggests the new benefits from the central government to West Bengal may await the election for a new chief minister that will take place in 2015.

7. See Akira Kurosawa, *Rashomon* (New York: Grove Press, 1969).

8. Chalmers Johnson, *Nemesis: The Last Days of the American Republic* (New York: Henry Holt, 2006).

9. See, most recently, *Frank Dikotter, The Tragedy of Liberation: A History of the Chinese Revolution 1945–1957* (New York: Bloomsbury Press, 2013), 83. For an early estimate of the number of deaths under the Chinese communists see, Committee

on the Judiciary, United States Senate, *The Human Cost of Communism in China* (Washington, DC: U.S. Government Printing Office, 1971). The report was prepared by Richard L. Walker.

10. Dalai Lama, *Freedom in Exile* (San Francisco: Harper, 1991) 129.

CHAPTER 1

1. See Alexander Norman, *Secret Lives of the Dalai Lama: The Untold Story of the Holy Men Who Shaped Tibet, from Pre-History to the Present Day* (New York: Doubleday Religion, 2008), 117.

2. The Kangxi emperor was born in 1654 and reigned from 1661 until his death in 1722.

3. See Norman, *Secret Lives,* 342.

CHAPTER 2

1. See also mother's account in Diki Tsering, *Dalai Lama, My Son: A Mother's Story* (New York: Compass Books, 2000). Mother's name was originally Diki Tsering (given to her by Taktser Rinpoche at the time of her wedding), but she was given the new name of Lhamotso after moving to Lhasa.

2. Diki Tsering has a long discussion of the cat ghost. See Diki Tsering, *Dalai Lama, My Son,* 49.

3. According to Diki Tsering she had a midwife only once. See Diki Tsering, *Dalai Lama, My Son,* 82.

4. Diki Tsering herself says she gave birth to sixteen children. See Diki Tsering, *Dalai Lama, My Son,* 87. Gyalo Thundup says that perhaps there were miscarriages that his mother never told him about. He is counting from his own knowledge.

CHAPTER 3

1. The Dalai Lama himself wrote that the objects were two black rosaries, two yellow rosaries, two drums, and two walking sticks. See Dalai Lama, *My Land and My People: Memoirs of the Dalai Lama of Tibet* (New York: Potala Corporation, New York, 1983), 23.

CHAPTER 4

1. Diki Tsering, *Dalai Lama, My Son,* 97.

2. At that time, Sera had about five thousand monks, Drepung had ten thousand, and Ganden had three thousand.

3. See also Charles Bell, *Portrait of a Dalai Lama: The Life and Times of the Great Thirteenth* (London: Wisdom Publications, 1987), 45, for this description.

4. See also Dalai Lama, *Freedom in Exile: The Autobiography of the Dalai Lama* (San Francisco: Harper, 1990), 11. According to the Dalai Lama, the regent saw the Tibetan letters *ah, ka,* and *ma,* followed by the image of a three-storied monastery with a turquoise and gold roof and a path running from it to a hill. Finally, a small house with strangely shaped guttering. *Ah* was Amdo. *Ka* was Kumbum.

CHAPTER 5

1. The Solpon Khenpo.

2. The Simpon Khenpo.

3. The Chopon Khenpo.

4. The Chikyab Khenpo. The three masters are in charge of the Dalai Lama's personal well-being. The chief of staff is in charge of all of the Dalai Lama's personal staff and serves as an intermediary with the government.

5. Donyer Chenmo.

6. See also, Dalai Lama, *Freedom in Exile,* 15–33.

CHAPTER 7

1. See, for example, Rinchen Dolma Taring, *Daughter of Tibet* (London: Wisdom Publications, 1970, 1986), 67–84. Rinchen Dolma Taring was the first female Tibetan to study at an English school in India. Her second husband, Jigme Sumtsen Wangpo Taring, was the first Tibetan male to study at an English school in India.

2. During a meeting with Lhalu in Lhasa in 2002.

3. Ma Baoxun served as the interpreter for both the Kashag and the regent, translating documents and interpreting for the regent in his dealings with Chinese officials and merchants.

4. The first Sixth Dalai Lama was reputedly poisoned by the Mongolian Lasang Khan, who then contrived to have his own son installed as the "true" incarnation. When the Tenth Dalai Lama died at the age of twenty-one just before his scheduled ascension to power, speculation about the cause of his death ranged from relatively bloodless poisoning to more violent, bloody murder. The Eleventh Dalai Lama died when he was just seventeen years old, eleven months after coming to power. Speculations about who killed him included the Manchu ambans and an earlier Reting Regent. The Twelfth Dalai Lama survived only two years after becoming head of state. His monk attendants were accused of orchestrating his demise. And

the life of the Great Thirteenth was threatened by the use of black magic shortly after he came formally to power.

CHAPTER 10

1. Hugh E. Richardson, *Tibet and Its History* (Boston, MA: Shambhala, 1984), 177, says that the decision was a complete surprise to him and the Indian mission.

2. See Tsering Shakya, *The Dragon in the Land of Snows* (New York: Penguin, 1999), 8, quoting an editorial from Xinhua news agency dated September 2, 1949.

CHAPTER 11

1. See Shakya, *Dragon in the Land*, 13–14, for military figures.

2. Based on a conversation between Gyalo Thondup and Ngabo Ngawang Jigme in Lhasa in 1952.

3. See Shakya, *Dragon in the Land,* 14.

4. See Robert Ford, *Wind between the Worlds* (Berkeley: Snow Lion Graphics, 1957), republished as *Captured in Tibet* (Hong Kong: Oxford University Press, 1990).

5. Regarding the decision to have the Dalai Lama assume full powers, appoint two prime ministers, and go to Dromo, see Dalai Lama, *My Land,* 82, and Dalai Lama, *Freedom in Exile,* 52–58.

6. Thubten Jigme Norbu and Heinrich Harrer, *Tibet Is My Country* (London: Wisdom Publications, 1960), 222.

7. Norbu and Harrer, *Tibet Is My Country,* 233–234.

8. See also Isabel Hilton, *The Search for the Panchen Lama* (New York: W. W. Norton, 1999), 73–75.

9. Quoted in Goldstein, *History of Modern Tibet, 1931–1951,* 684.

10. Shakya, *Dragon in the Land,* 36.

11. See Hilton, *Search for Panchen Lama,* 119; and Shakya, *Dragon in the Land,* 68–69.

12. Shakya, *Dragon in the Land,* 113.

13. This story was told to Gyalo Thondup by Sandu Lobsang Rinchen, one of the interpreters.

14. Dalai Lama, *My Land,* 88.

15. See Shakya, *Dragon in the Land,* 90, quoting Dai Yannian, Edna Driscoll, Yan Qinghong, and Zhu Yuan, eds., *Tibet: Myth vs. Reality* (Beijing: Beijing Review, 1988), 134.

CHAPTER 13

1. See also Shakya, *Dragon in the Land,* 110.

CHAPTER 14

1. The trip had lasted from May 28, 1952, when they left Lhasa, until June 19, 1952, when they arrived in Darjeeling.

CHAPTER 15

1. See Dalai Lama, *Freedom in Exile,* 147.

CHAPTER 16

1. See Dalai Lama, *Freedom in Exile,* 98–99.
2. *Ibid.,* 98.

CHAPTER 17

1. See Shakya, *Dragon in the Land,* 140–141.
2. In addition to the letter of invitation from the Maha Bodhi Society, Prime Minister Nehru sent an official invitation, written on October 1, 1956, the seventh anniversary of the establishment of the People's Republic of China, hinting at possible problems with China if the Dalai Lama was not allowed to come.
3. Dalai Lama, *My Land,* 147–148.
4. See Dalai Lama *Freedom in Exile,* 117, for a description of this conversation. When the Dalai Lama told Nehru that he was considering seeking political asylum, Nehru said, "You must go back to your country and try to work with the Chinese on the basis of the Seventeen Point Agreement."
5. Gyalo Thondup learned this from Kazi Sonam Topgal, who was the interpreter for the Dalai Lama and Nehru.
6. The Dalai Lama's visit to Kalimpong began on January 22, 1957.
7. Mao Zedong also described Kalimpong as a center of espionage. In his original February 27, 1957, speech "On the Correct Handling of Contradictions Among the People," he said "There is this place in India called Kalimpong where they specialise in sabotaging Tibet. Nehru himself told the premier that this place is a centre of espionage, primarily American and British." The full version of the

speech, which includes the Kalimpong remarks, did not become available in the West until in 1985. See Shakya, *Dragon in the Land*, 158–159.

8. Regarding Zhou Enlai advising the Dalai Lama not to go to Kalimpong, the Dalai Lama wrote: Mr. Nehru "seemed to agree that the people up there might be troublesome and might try to persuade me not to go back to Tibet. India was a free country, he said, and nobody could stop the people of Kalimpong expressing their own opinions. But he added that if I really wanted to go, his government would make all the arrangements and look after me." Dalai Lama, *My Land*, 153.

CHAPTER 18

1. The Hongunji monastery has branches in both Tokyo and Kyoto. Norbu stayed in both places.

2. Hisao Kimura, *Japanese Agent in Tibet* (London: Serindia Publications, 1990).

3. See Marco Pallis, *Peaks and Lamas* (Delhi: Book Faith India, 1946).

4. Kenneth Conboy and James Morrison. *The CIA's Secret War in Tibet* (Lawrence, KS: University Press of Kansas, 2002).

5. The Dalai Lama in *Freedom in Exile*, 121–122, wrote: "Although there was no talk at this time of an armed struggle against the Chinese, my brothers, unbeknown to me, had already made contact with the American Central Intelligence Agency. Apparently the Americans felt that it was worthwhile to provide limited assistance to the Tibetan freedom fighters, not because they cared about Tibetan independence but as part of their worldwide efforts to destabilise all Communist governments. To this end they undertook to supply a limited amount of simple weaponry to the freedom fighters by airdrop. They also made plans for the CIA to train some of them in techniques of guerrilla warfare and then parachute them back into Tibet. Naturally, my brothers judged it wise to keep this information from me. They knew what my reaction would have been."

6. See Geshe Wangyal, *The Jeweled Staircase* (Ithaca, NY: Snow Lion Publications, 1986).

7. John Kenneth Knaus. *Orphans of the Cold War: America and the Tibetan Struggle for Survival* (New York: Public Affairs, 1999), 144.

8. See Shakya, *Dragon in the Land*, 165–166

9. Lhamo Tsering. *Resistance, Volume 1, The Early Political Activities of Gyalo Thondup, Older Brother of H. H. the Dalai Lama, and the Beginning of My Political Involvement (1945–1959)* (Dharamsala, India: Amnye Machen Institute, 1992), 65.

10. Good figures on the number of Chinese soldiers and Tibetan resistance fighters are hard to come by. Many estimates of the number of Chinese troops are much too high, including those of Gyalo Thondup's deputy, Lhamo Tsering, who put the number of Chinese infantrymen at eighty thousand, with another eighty

thousand cavalry. There may have been thirty-five to forty thousand freedom fighters in all of Tibet and maybe ten thousand Chinese infantrymen and another fifteen to twenty thousand cavalry in Lithang.

11. Lhamo Tsering, *Early Political Activities*, 68.

12. As Tsering Shakya points out, "from the middle of 1958 until the Lhasa uprising in March 1959, there existed a peculiar situation in which neither the traditional Tibetan Government nor the Chinese had much control of the course of events in Tibet. . . . The Khampa resistance fighters were now able to cover territory stretching from the eastern and south-eastern routes leading into India. The Chinese were desperate to eliminate the Khampas." Shakya, *Dragon in the Land*, 181.

13. Athar returned to Tibet in July 1958 through Bhutan. The first arms drop took place that month. For list of what was dropped, see Lhamo Tsering, *Early Political Activities*, 53.

14. See Dalai Lama, *Freedom in Exile*, 127: "When I went into exile, I heard stories of how weapons and money were dropped into Tibet by aircraft. However, these missions caused almost more harm to the Tibetans than to the Chinese forces. Because the Americans did not want their assistance to be attributable, they took care not to supply US-manufactured equipment. Instead, they dropped only a few badly made bazookas and some ancient British rifles which had once been in general service throughout India and Pakistan and thus could not be traced to their source in the event of capture. But the mishandling they received whilst being air-dropped rendered them almost useless."

15. Dalai Lama, *Freedom in Exile*, 130.

CHAPTER 19

1. Both Generals Zhang Jingwu and Zhang Guohua were in Beijing at the time.

2. See Dalai Lama, *Freedom in Exile*, 127.

3. Some estimated that up to thirty thousand people were outside the Norbulingka. See Dalai Lama, *My Land*, 170; and Dalai Lama, *Freedom in Exile*, 132.

4. Dalai Lama, *Freedom in Exile*, 133.

5. Dalai Lama, *My Land*, 175.

6. Ibid., 189.

7. The Dalai Lama wrote that the only way to get the crowd to disperse was for him to leave. Then the crowd would have no reason to surround the Norbulingka. See Dalai Lama, *Freedom in Exile*, 135–136.

8. Dalai Lama, *My Land*, 198–199.

9. The Dalai Lama, *Freedom in Exile*, 139, says a party of freedom fighters with ponies was also waiting.

10. These are the Dalai Lama's figures. Dalai Lama, *Freedom in Exile*, 140.

11. According to the Dalai Lama, his cook was one of the young men trained by the CIA. He also wrote that there was another CIA operative in the party, a radio operator who "was apparently in touch with his headquarters throughout the journey. Exactly whom he was in contact with, I do not know to this day. I only know that he was equipped with a Morse-key transmitter." Dalai Lama, *Freedom in Exile*, 140.

12. 300,000 rupees at the exchange rate in 1959–1960 equaled US$63,000. However, Gyalo Thondup says it was 700,000 rupees.

13. Dalai Lama, *My Land*, 209. The Dalai Lama remembers this meeting as being at Chongay.

CHAPTER 20

1. This announcement was made on March 28, 1959. See Shakya, *Dragon in the Land*, 207.

2. See Dalai Lama, *My Land*, 218, for his description of how the statement was prepared.

3. Dalai Lama, *My Land*, 219.

4. Gyalo Thondup had known Trikamdas and D. K. Sen since 1957. They served as his legal advisors. One was based in Darjeeling and Delhi, the other was permanently in Delhi.

CHAPTER 21

1. Most of this section describing the CIA recruits and their activities in Tibet and Mustang comes from the memoirs of Gyalo Thondup's deputy, Lhamo Tsering, who oversaw day-to-day operations of the program and kept copious notes.

2. These figures come from the documentary film by Ritu Sarin and Tenzing Sonam, *The Shadow Circus: The CIA in Tibet* (BBC Television: White Crane Films, 1998). Tenzing Sonam is Lhamo Tsering's son.

3. See Lhamo Tsering, *Early Political Activities*, 148.

4. Lhamo Tsering, *Early Political Activities*, 153–154.

5. *Ibid.*, 202.

6. *Ibid.*, 155.

7. *Ibid.*, 160.

8. *Ibid.*, 58.

9. *Ibid.*, 74.

10. See Knaus, *Orphans*, 238, for a description of Mustang.

CHAPTER 22

1. Lukhangwa told this story to Gyalo Thondup, when he was accompanying the Dalai Lama during his visit to India in 1956.

CHAPTER 23

1. NEFA became the state of Arunachal Pradesh in 1972.

CHAPTER 24

1. Nixon assumed the presidency on January 20, 1969.
2. His father, King Mahendra, had died in in 1972.
3. See Sarin and Sonam, *The Shadow Circus*.

CHAPTER 25

1. Gyalo Thondup bought the Hong Kong flat for around USD $35,000, leaving about USD $15,000 plus earnings from his business in India to live on. He sold the flat in 1982 for approximately half a million US dollars. Now it is worth 4 or 5 million US dollars. Later he bought a small flat in Kowloon.

CHAPTER 27

1. See *A Poisoned Arrow: The Secret Report of the 10th Panchen Lama* (London: Tibet Information Network, 1997).

CHAPTER 28

1. In Chinese, *chule duli yiwai shenme dou keyi tan* (除了独立意外什么都可以谈).

CHAPTER 29

1. John Avedon, *In Exile from the Land of Snows* (New York: Vintage, 1986), 330–351, has an excellent description of these delegations.
2. The itinerary began in Hong Kong and went through Guangzhou to Beijing then Lanzhou, Xining, Rebgong, Golok, Labrang, Jyekundo, Kokonor, Golmud, Chengdu, and Lhasa.
3. I tried repeatedly through several channels to obtain copies of at least some of these letters and petitions but never succeeded. At various times I was told

they were lost, that they were in the Kashag's archives but not available to foreign scholars, and that since many were addressed to the Dalai Lama, they were in his archives. These petitions would be an anthropological treasure trove if anyone were given access to them.

4. See *Tibet Information Network*, News Update, April 12, 1999, for full text, http://www.tibetinfo.net/news-updates/nu120499.htm.

5. Gyalo Thondup is recording these five points from memory. The original five-point document is in the Kashag's office. There are several versions of Hu Yaobang's five points. Tsering Shakya lists them as follows: (1) The Dalai Lama should recognize that China has now entered a new period of stability and economic change. If he doubts the reforms, he should observe the changes for the next few years. (2) The Dalai Lama should not raise the history of repression that followed the suppression of the 1959 rebellion. (3) The Chinese Government sincerely welcomes the Dalai Lama and his followers to return to the motherland. China hopes that the Dalai Lama will contribute to uphold China's unity and promote solidarity between Han and Tibetan nationalities. (4) The Dalai Lama will have the same status as he had enjoyed in 1959. He may be appointed vice-chairman of the NPC. But it will be necessary that he not live in Tibet or hold any position in Tibet, as there are younger Tibetans who have taken office and are doing their jobs well. He may visit Tibet as often as he likes. (5) When the Dalai Lama returns, he may make press statements, and arrangements will be made to receive him by a suitable minister. These are quoted from Xinhua, November 12, 1984. See Shakya, *Dragon in the Land*, 384–385.

6. Yan Mingfu had been appointed in 1985.

CHAPTER 30

1. See Robert Barnett, "Report from Lhasa," November 3, 1987, telex from Kathmandu, Nepal, November 19, 1987; Eliot Sperling, "Testimony of Elliot Sperling before the House Subcommittee on Asian and Pacific Affairs and Human Rights an International Organizations on the Situation in Tibet," Washington, DC: Asia Watch, October 14, 1987.

CHAPTER 31

1. See "The Panchen Lama Speaks: Text of the Panchen Lama's Address to the TAR Standing Committee Meeting of the National People's Congress Held in Peking on 28 March 1987" (Dharamsala, India: Department of Information and International Relations, Central Tibetan Administration of His Holiness the Dalai Lama, 1991).

AFTERWORD

1. During a March 7, 2014 meeting with His Holiness the Dalai Lama, we discussed three instances of possible murder in Tibet. Both the Dalai Lama and Gyalo Thondup agree that Reting Regent was murdered. Gyalo Thondup believes that his father was murdered but the Dalai Lama does not. The Dalai Lama suspects that the Panchen Lama was murdered, though notes that only an autopsy would tell, while Gyalo Thondup believes he died of natural causes.

2. See "Statement by NPC Committees in Protest Against U.S. Congress Amendment Press Release" (Washington, DC: Embassy of the People's Republic of China, December 28, 1987).

3. See *The Truth About the Beijing Turmoil 1989* (Beijing: Beijing Publishing House, 1992), 3.

4. Steve Lehman, *The Tibetans: A Struggle to Survive. New York* (New York: Umbrage,) 1998.

5. Ibid., 16–26.

6. Ibid., 10–11.

7. Ibid., 178–196.

8. See the Kerner Commission, *Report of the National Advisory Commission on Civil Disorders* (New York: Bantam Books, 1968); the Walker Report, *Rights in Conflict: The Violent Confrontation of Demonstrators and Police in the Parks and Streets of Chicago during the Week of the Democratic National Convention* (New York: Bantam Books, 1968); and Hugh Davis Graham and Ted Robert Gurr, eds., *Violence in America: Historical and Comparative Perspectives* (New York: Signet Books, 1969).

9. Lhamo Tsering, *Early Political Activities*, 68–69, 86, 105.

10. Ibid.

11. Ibid.

12. Dalai Lama, *My Land*, 209.

SELECTED
BIBLIOGRAPHY

A Poisoned Arrow: The Secret Report of the 10th Panchen Lama. London: Tibet Information Network, 1997.

Arjia Rinpoche. *Surviving the Dragon: A Tibetan Lama's Account of 40 Years under Chinese Rule.* New York: Rodale, 2010.

Armstrong, Karen. *Buddha.* New York: Penguin, 2001.

Arpi, Claude. *Dharamsala and Beijing: The Negotiations That Never Were.* Atlanta: Lancer, 2013.

Avedon, John F. *In Exile from the Land of Snows.* New York: Random House, 1979, 1986.

Bagdro, Ven. *Tibetan Spirit Cannot Be Crushed.* New Delhi: Norbu Graphics, 2013.

Barnett, Robert. "Report from Lhasa, November 3, 1987," sent by telex from Kathmandu, Nepal, November 19, 1987.

Barnett, Robert, and Shirin Akiner, eds. *Resistance and Reform in Tibet.* Bloomington: Indiana University Press, 1994.

Bell, Charles. *Portrait of a Dalai Lama: The Life and Times of the Great Thirteenth.* London: Wisdom Publications, 1946, 1987.

Bernstein, Jeremy. "A Journey to Lhasa." *The New Yorker,* December 14, 1987, 47–105.

Carlson, Allen. *Beijing's Tibet Policy: Securing Sovereignty and Legitimacy.* Washington, DC: East-West Center, 2004.

Central Tibetan Administration in Exile. *The Panchen Lama: Politics Intruding on a Religious Discovery.* Dharamsala, India: Department of Information and International Relations, Central Tibetan Administration of His Holiness the Dalai Lama, 1995.

China Reconstructs Press. *Tibetans on Tibet.* Beijing: China Reconstructs Press, 1988.

Choedon, Dhondub. *Life in the Red Flag People's Commune.* Dharamsala, India: The Information Office of His Holiness the Dalai Lama, 1978.

Conboy, Kenneth, and James Morrison. *The CIA's Secret War in Tibet.* Lawrence, KS: University Press of Kansas, 2002.

Dalai Lama. *Freedom in Exile: The Autobiography of the Dalai Lama.* San Francisco: Harper, 1990.

Dalai Lama. *My Land and My People: Memoirs of the Dalai Lama.* New York: Potala Corporation, 1983.

Desai, Kiran. *The Inheritance of Loss.* New York: Grove Press, 2006.

Dikotter, Frank. *The Tragedy of Liberation: A History of the Chinese Revolution 1945–1957* (New York: Bloomsbury Press, 2013).

Dunham, Mikel. *Buddha's Warriors: The Story of the CIA-Backed Tibetan Freedom Fighters, the Chinese Invasion, and the Ultimate Fall of Tibet.* New York: Penguin, 2004.

Fleming, Peter. *Bayonets to Lhasa: The First Full Account of the British Invasion of Tibet in 1904.* London: Rubert Hart-Davis, 1961.

Ford, Robert. *Wind between the Worlds.* Berkeley: Snow Lion Graphics, 1987; also published as *Captured in Tibet* (Hong Kong: Oxford University Press, 1990).

French, Patrick. *Younghusband: The Last Great Imperial Adventurer.* London: Flamingo, 1995.

Goldstein, Melvyn C. *A History of Modern Tibet, 1913–1951: The Demise of the Lamaist State.* Berkeley: University of California Press, 1989.

Goldstein, Melvyn C. *A History of Modern Tibet, Volume 2: The Calm before the Storm, 1951–1955.* Berkeley: University of California Press, 2007.

Goldstein, Melvyn C. *A History of Modern Tibet, Volume 3: The Storm Clouds Descend, 1955–1957.* Berkeley: University of California Press, 2014.

Goldstein, Melvyn C. *The Snow Lion and the Dragon: China, Tibet and the Dalai Lama.* Berkeley: University of California Press, 1997.

Goldstein, Melvyn C., Dawei Sherap, and William R. Siebenschuh. *A Tibetan Revolutionary: The Political Life and Times of Bapa Phuntso Wangye.* Berkeley: University of California Press, 2004.

Goldstein, Melvyn C., and Matthew T. Kapstein, eds. *Buddhism in Contemporary Tibet: Religious Revival and Cultural Identity.* Berkeley: University of California Press, 1998.

Goldstein, Melvyn, William Siebenschuh, and Tashi Tsering. *The Struggle for Modern Tibet: The Autobiography of Tashi Tsering.* Armonk: M.E. Sharpe, 1997.

Grunfeld, A. Tom. *The Making of Modern Tibet.* Armonk, NY: M. E. Sharpe, 1987.

Halper, Lezlee Brown, and Stefan Halper. *Tibet: An Unfinished Story.* New York: Oxford University Press, 2014.

Hilton, Isabel. *The Search for the Panchen Lama.* New York: W. W. Norton, 1999.

Hopkirk, Peter. *Trespassers on the Roof of the World: The Secret Exploration of Tibet.* Boston: Houghton Mifflin Company, 1982.

Information Office of the State Council of the People's Republic of China, *Tibet: Its Ownership and Human Rights Situation.* Beijing: Information Office of the State Council of the People's Republic of China, 1992.

International Campaign for Tibet. *60 Years of Chinese Misrule/Arguing Cultural Genocide in Tibet.* Washington, DC: International Campaign for Tibet, 2012.

International Campaign for Tibet and Human Rights Law Group. *The Myth of Tibetan Autonomy: A Legal Analysis of the Status of Tibet.* Washington, DC: International Campaign for Tibet and the Human Rights Law Group, 1994.

Iyer, Pico. *The Open Road: The Global Journey of the Fourteenth Dalai Lama.* New York: Knopf, 2008.

Johnson, Tim. *Tragedy in Crimson: How the Dalai Lama Conquered the World but Lost the Battle with China.* New York: Nation Books, 2011.

Kimura, Hisao as told to Scott Berry. *Japanese Agent in Tibet.* London: Serindia Publications, 1990.

Knaus, John Kenneth. *Beyond Shangri-La: America and Tibet's Move into the Twenty-First Century.* Durham, NC: Duke University Press, 2012.

Knaus, John Kenneth. *Orphans of the Cold War: America and the Tibetan Struggle for Survival.* New York: Public Affairs, 1999.

Kurosawa, Akira. *Rashomon.* New York: Grove Press, 1969.

Laird, Thomas. *The Story of Tibet: Conversations with the Dalai Lama.* New York: Grove Press, 2006.

Laird, Thomas. *Into Tibet: The CIA's First Atomic Spy and His Secret Expedition to Lhasa.* New York: Grove Press, 2002.

Lehman, Steve. *The Tibetans: A Struggle to Survive* (New York: Umbrage, 1998).

Liu Xiaoyuan. *Recast All Under Heaven: Revolution, War, Diplomacy, and Frontier China in the 20th Century.* New York: Continuum International Publishing Group, 2010.

Lo Kuan-chung. *Three Kingdoms: China's Epic Drama.* Translated and edited by Moss Roberts. New York: Pantheon, 1976.

Lopez, Donald S. Jr. *Prisoners of Shangri-La: Tibetan Buddhism and the West.* Chicago: University of Chicago Press, 1998.

Macdonald, David. *Twenty Years in Tibet.* New Delhi: Gyan Publishing House, 2008.

McCorquodale, Robert, and Nicholas Orosz, eds. *Tibet: The Position in International Law.* London: Edition Hansjörg Mayer and Serindia, 1994.

McGranahan, Carole. *Arrested Histories: Tibet, the CIA, and Memories of a Forgotten War.* Durham, NC: Duke University Press, 2010.

Michael, Franz. *Rule by Incarnation: Tibetan Buddhism and Its Role in Society and State.* Boulder, CO: Westview Press, 1982.

Mirsky, Jonathan. "Tibet Since the Invasion," a review of John Avedon's *In Exile from the Land of Snow.* New York: *New York Times Book Review,* June 24, 1984, 11–12.

Mullik, B. N. *The Chinese Betrayal: My Years with Nehru.* New Delhi: Allied Publishers, 1971.

Neterowicz, Eva M. *The Tragedy of Tibet.* Washington, DC: Council for Economic and Social Studies, 1989.

Norbu, Jamyang. *Warriors of Tibet: The Story of Aten and the Khampas' Fight for the Freedom of their Country.* London: Wisdom Publication, 1979, 1986.

Norbu, Thubten Jigme. *Tibet Is My Country: Autobiography of Thubten Jigme Norbu, Brother of the Dalai Lama as Told to Henrich Harrer.* London: Wisdom Publications, 1987.

Norbu, Thubten Jigme, and Colin Turnbull. *Tibet: Its History, Religion and People.* Middlesex, England: Penguin Books: 1968.

Norman, Alexander. *Secret Lives of the Dalai Lama: The Untold Story of the Holy Men Who Shaped Tibet, from Pre-History to the Present Day.* New York: Doubleday Religion, 2008.

Nulo, Naktsang. *My Tibetan Childhood: When Ice Shattered Stone.* Durham, NC: Duke University Press, 2014.

Office of His Holiness the Dalai Lama. *From Liberation to Liberalisation: Views on "Liberated" ibet.* Dharamsala, India: Information Office of His Holiness the Dalai Lama, 1982.

Paljor, Kunsang. *Tibet: The Undying Flame.* New Delhi: Information and Publicity Office of His Holiness the Dalai Lama, 1977.

Pallis, Marco. *Peaks and Lamas: A Classic Book on Mountaineering, Buddhism and Tibet.* Washington, DC: Shoemaker & Hoard, 1949.

Panchen Lama. Dharmasala, India. "The Panchen Lama Speaks: Address to the TAR Standing Committee Meeting of the National People's Congress held in Peking on 28 March 1987." Department of Information and International Relations, Central Tibetan Administration of His Holiness the Dalai Lama, 1991.

Pema, Jetsun. *Tibet: My Story.* Boston, MA: Element Books, 1997.

Rabgey, Tashi, and Tseten Wangchuk Sharlho, *Sino-Tibetan Dialogue in the Post-Mao Era: Lessons and Prospects.* Washington, DC: East-West Center, 2004.

Richardson, Hugh E. *Tibet and Its History.* Boston, MA: Shambhala, 1984.

Sarin, Ritu, and Tenzing Sonam, *The Shadow Circus: The CIA in Tibet.* BBC Television: White Crane Films, 1998.

Saunders, Harold H., Melvyn C. Goldstein, Richard Holbrooke, Sidney R. Jones, David M. Lampton, and Dwight Perkins. *Tibet: Issues for Americans.* New York: National Committee on U.S. China Relations, 1992.

Shakabpa, W. D. *Tibet: A Political History.* New York: Potala Publications, 1988.

Shakya, Tsering. *The Dragon in the Land of Snows.* New York: Penguin, 1999.

Shoumatoff, Alex. "Sun without a Moon." *Vanity Fair,* August 1996, 98–143.

Smith, Warren W. Jr. *Tibetan Nation: A History of Tibetan Nationalism and Sino-Tibetan Relations.* Boulder, CO: Westview Press, 1996.

Sperling, Elliot. "Testimony of Elliot Sperling before the House Subcommittee on Asian and Pacific Affairs and Human Rights and International Organizations on the Situation in Tibet." Washington, DC: Asia Watch, October 14, 1987.

Talty, Stephan. *Escape from the Land of Snows: The Young Dalai Lama's Harrowing Flight to Freedom and the Making of a Spiritual Hero.* New York: Crown Publishers, 2011.

Taring, Rinchen Dolma. *Daughter of Tibet.* London: Wisdom Publications, 1970, 1986.

Taylor, Jay. *The Generalissimo: Chiang Kai-shek and the Struggle for Modern China.* Cambridge, MA: Harvard University Press, 2009, 2011.

Thurston, Anne F. *Enemies of the People: The Ordeal of China's Intellectuals during China's Great Cultural Revolution* (New York: Knopf, 1986).

"Tibet: Part of China for 700 Years." New York: People's Republic of China Mission to the United Nations, December 1987.

Tsering, Diki. *Dalai Lama, My Son: A Mother's Story.* Edited by her grandson Khedroob Thondup. New York, Compass Books: 2000.

Tsering, Lhamo. *Resistance, Volume I, The Early Political Activities of Gyalo Thondup, Older Brother of H.H. the Dalai Lama, and the Beginnings of My Political Involvement (1945–1959).* Dharamsala, India: Amnye Machen Institute, 1992.

Tsering, Lhamo. *Resistance, Volume II, The Secret Operation into Tibet (1957–1962).* Dharamsala, India: Amnye Machen Institute, 1992.

Tsering, Lhamo. *Resistance, Volume III, An Account of the Establishment of the Tibetan National Volunteer Defence Force in Mustang and Operation against the Communist Chinese Inside Tibet: Part I.* Dharamsala, India: Amnye Machen Institute, 1992.

Wangyal, Geshe. *The Jeweled Staircase.* Ithaca, NY: Snow Lion Publications, 1986.

Wangyal, Geshe. *The Door of Liberation.* Boston, MA: Wisdom Publications, 1995.

Woeser, Tsering, and Lixiong Wang. *Voices from Tibet: Selected Essays and Reportage.* Translated by Violet Law. Hong Kong: Hong Kong University Press, 2013.

Yeh, Emily T. *Taming Tibet: Landscape Transformation and the Gift of Chinese Development.* Ithaca, NY: Cornell University Press, 2013.

Yuthok, Dorje Yudon. *House of the Turquoise Roof.* Translated and edited by Michael Harlin. Ithaca, NY: Snow Lion Publications, 1990.

GLOSSARY

Gompo Tashi Andrugtsang: Founder and leader of the *Chushi Gangdruk* (Four Rivers and Six Ranges) which became the main fighting force in the Tibetan resistance and recipient of CIA training and assistance

Athar: resistance fighter from Lithang, member of the first group to be trained by the CIA

Chadrel Rinpoche: A high lama in Tashilunpo Monastery responsible for leading the search for the Eleventh Panchen Lama, later imprisoned

Chiang Kai-shek: President of the Republic of China from 1928 until his death in 1975, first (until 1949) in China and thereafter on the island of Taiwan

Tenzin Choegyal (Ngari Rinpoche): Youngest brother of Gyalo Thondup and the Dalai Lama

Diki Dolkar (1925–1986): also known by her Chinese name of Zhu Dan: wife of Gyalo Thondup, married in 1948

Tsering Dolma (1920–1964): Gyalo Thondup's older sister

William Grimsley: Head of the CIA office in Delhi in 1969 when he delivered the message that the CIA was stopping its support for the Tibetan resistance

Wangdu Gyatotsang: former monk and nephew of resistance leader Andrug Gompo Tashi, joined the resistance himself and was one of the first to receive training from the CIA

Kewtsang Rinpoche: The leader of the search team that discovered Lhamo Thondup in Taktser village in Amdo and concluded that the child was the reincarnation of the Thirteenth Dalai Lama

Palden Lhamo: The protective deity of Tibet

Lhotse: Member of the first group of resistance fighters to be trained by the CIA

Li Jusheng: Deputy Director of Xinhua news agency in Hong Kong in 1979 and Gyalo Thondup's escort during his visit to China that year

Li Weihan: Head of the United Front Work Department in 1950 and lead Chinese negotiator during negotiations over the Seventeen Point Agreement

Lukhangwa: Appointed one of two acting prime ministers of Tibet following the Chinese attack on Chamdo in 1950

Ma Bufang: Governor General of Qinghai (Amdo) from 1928–1949

B. N. Mullik: Director of Indian intelligence from 1950–1965

Jawaharlal Nehru: Prime Minister of India from 1947–1964

Ngabo Ngawang Jigme: Governor of Chamdo in 1950 at the time of the Chinese attack, lead Tibetan negotiator during the negotiations over the Seventeen Point Agreement, and later one of the highest ranking Tibetans in the Chinese government

Thubten Jigme Norbu (1922–2008): Older brother of Gyalo Thondup, became Taktser Rinpoche at Kumbum Monastery, later moved to the United States

Phala: The Dalai Lama's lord chamberlain for much of the period covered here

Reting Regent (Rinpoche): Incarnated lama from Reting Monastery, made regent following the death of the Thirteenth Dalai Lama, responsible for finding the next Dalai Lama, resigned in early 1941, arrested and killed in April 1947

Lobsang Samten (1932–1985): Younger brother of Gyalo Thondup, elder brother of Fourteenth Dalai Lama (childhood name: Rinzen Thondup)

W. D. Shakabpa (1907–1989): Tibetan nobleman, Finance Minister, and leading Tibetan political figure for much of the twentieth century

S. N. Sinha: Indian representative in Lhasa in 1950 at the time of the Chinese attack on Chamdo

Phuntsog Tashi Takla: Gyalo Thondup's brother-in-law (married to Tsering Dolma), frequent Chinese interpreter for the Tibetan leadership and head of the Dalai Lama's bodyguards

Taktra Rinpoche: Assumed the position of regent following Reting's resignation in 1941, resigned his position in 1950

Tan Guansan: Political commissar and deputy party secretary of Tibet throughout the 1950s. His invitation to the Dalai Lama to attend a cultural performance sparked the 1959 revolt

Lobsang Tashi: monk official who became one of the two prime ministers at the time of the Chinese attack on Chamdo

Lhamo Thondup: Younger brother of Gyalo Thondup who became Tenzin Gyatso the Fourteenth Dalai Lama in 1939

Dasang Damdul Tsarong (Tsarong the elder): Leading figure during the reign of the Thirteenth Dalai Lama, responsible for running the Tibetan mint

George Tsarong: Son of Dasang Damdul Tsarong, wealthy Tibetan businessman

Chokyang Tsewang: (also spelled Choegren Tsering) (1899?–1947?): The father of Gyalo Thondup and the Fourteenth Dalai Lama, given the title of Yabshi Kung after his son became the Dalai Lama

Surkhang: Leading member of the Tibetan cabinet, escaped to India with the Dalai Lama and later moved to Taiwan

Diki Tsering (1900–81): mother of the Thirteenth Dalai Lama and Gyalo Thondup, given the name Lhamotso and title of Gyayum Chemo (the Great Mother) after son became the Thirteenth Dalai Lama

Lhamo Tsering: longtime deputy to Gyalo Thondup, serving as an interlocutor between the CIA and the Tibetan resistance fighters, later jailed in Nepal

Geshe Wangyal: A Kalmyk Mongolian monk who spent nine years at the Drepung Monastery in Lhasa, passing the *geshe* exam, later moving to the United States where he served as the interpreter for the CIA of messages sent by the Tibetan resistance

Wulanfu (also spelled Ulanfu): Onetime first party secretary of Inner Mongolia and a Mongolian himself, was director of the Communist Party's United Front Work Department in 1979 when Gyalo Thondup returned to China

Xi Zhongxun (1913–2002): Member of China's first generation of Communist Party leaders, responsible for Dalai Lama's 1954 trip to China, purged several times, but responsible for United Front work beginning in the early 1980s, took over from Yan Mingfu in the United Front Work department in 1989, father of China's current Party General Secretary and President, Xi Jinping

Yan Mingfu: Mao Zedong's Russian translator in the 1950s, became head of the United Front Work Department in 1985 and was removed in 1989 for his role during the popular protests in Beijing in the spring of 1989, later returned as deputy director of China's Ministry of Civil Affairs

Yuan Zhongxian: First Chinese ambassador to India following the founding of the People's Republic of China in October 1949

Zhang Guohua: Commander of the Eighteenth Army Corps of the People's Liberation Army that attacked Chamdo in October 1950, and later commanded the Chinese forces in the 1962 border war with India

Zhang Jingwu: As Mao Zedong's representative in Tibet in 1950 was the highest ranking Chinese official in Tibet and a participant in the Seventeen Point Agreement discussions, delivered the agreement to the Fourteenth Dalai Lama

Zhou Enlai: Premier of the People's Republic of China from 1949 until his death in 1976

Zhu Shigui (Chu Shih-kuei): Guomindang general and father-in-law of Gyalo Thondup

Zhu Xiaoming: Senior official in the Communist Party's United Front Work Department beginning in the 1990s

INDEX

as governor general of Kham,
99–101
Gyalo Thondup's father and, 54–55
in hiding, 182
Khampas and, 101–2
as rubber stamp, 116
Seventeen Point Agreement and,
110–12, 111 (photo), 114
speech draft for Dalai Lama, 161–62
Tenth Panchen Lama and, 110
as Tibetan patriot, 116
as traitor, 115
as vice-chairman of National People's
Congress, 115–16
Ninth Panchen Lama, 24–25, 108
Nixon, Richard, 232
Nobel Peace Prize, 283
Nonalignment policy, 173, 223
Nonviolent resistance, 76, 148
Noodle factory
role of, 221
start of, 294
troubles at, 294
Norbu (Thubten Jigme Norbu, brother
of Dalai Lama)
as abbot of Kumbum monastery, 105
birth, 9, 16
criticism of Chinese presence in
Tibet, 163–64
encounters with Chinese
Communists, 105–6
in Fairfax, Virginia, 123, 124
at Hongunji monastery, 167
log cabin of, 123, 124 (photo)
as reincarnation of Taktser Rinpoche,
10, 17, 24
temper of, 54
trip to Lhasa (1950), 104–6
Norbulingka Palace
Dalai Lama at, 45–46, 175–76, 182
Dalai Lama's escape from, 183–85

demonstrators around, 182–83,
185–86, 191, 192
"Jewel Park," 45
killings near, 186
shelling of, 183, 185–86
North Point, St. Joseph's, 59, 126, 215,
220, 294
Nyethang, 127

Office of Tibet, 62, 70, 83, 85, 91,
218–19, 225–26, 262
Office of Tibetan and Mongolian
Affairs, 62, 83, 108–9, 118
Om Mani Padme Hum, 180
Oracle, Nechung, 17–18

Pakpala Kunchung, 182
Palden Lhamo (goddess), 16, 17, 38,
150
Pallis, Marco, 174
Pan Desheng, 243
Panchen Lamas
Choekyi Nyima, 287
damage to tombs, 280, 290
Eleventh Panchen Lama controversy,
285–87, 290–91
Ninth Panchen Lama, 24–25, 108
Panchsheel Treaty, 151, 193, 233
Pandatsang, 150, 215, 217
Panikkar, Sardar K. M., 89, 91, 92,
94
Pant, Apa, 148, 157, 160
Parker, Ronald, 58
Peng Dehuai, 186, 244–45, 289
People's communes, 208, 238, 250
People's Daily, 238
People's Liberation Army, 69, 94, 99,
103, 114, 159, 186–87, 207
People's Republic of China, 96, 109,
268, 274, 276, 289
Peter, Prince, 168